John Donne: Preacher

John Donne: Preacher

by William R. Mueller

OCTAGON BOOKS

A DIVISION OF FARRAR, STRAUS AND GIROUX

New York   1977

Copyright © 1962 by Princeton University Press

Reprinted 1977
by special arrangement with Princeton University Press

OCTAGON BOOKS
A DIVISION OF FARRAR, STRAUS & GIROUX, INC.
19 Union Square West
New York, N.Y. 10003

Library of Congress Cataloging in Publication Data

Mueller, William Randolph, 1916-
    John Donne, preacher.

    Reprint of the ed. published by the Princeton University Press,
Princeton, N.J.
    Includes bibliographical references and index.
    1. Donne, John, 1572-1631—Religion and ethics. 2. Donne,
John, 1572-1631—Prose.
[PR2248.M8   1977]   821'.3   77-11903
ISBN 0-374-95988-9

Manufactured by Braun-Brumfield, Inc.
Ann Arbor, Michigan
Printed in the United States of America

THIS BOOK IS GRATEFULLY DEDICATED TO

MRS. SIMON GUGGENHEIM

TO WHOM AND TO WHOSE FAMILY

AMERICAN SCHOLARSHIP AND LETTERS

ARE IMMENSELY INDEBTED

Preface

FOR the completion of this study of John Donne as preacher my indebtedness is manifold. The Woman's College of the University of North Carolina and Goucher College contributed research grants for the gathering of material and the preparation of the manuscript. The Princeton University Press subsidized the publication of the study through funds made available by the Ford Foundation. A John Simon Guggenheim Foundation Fellowship during the 1958-1959 academic year enabled me to complete the bulk of the work.

Certain studies have been of immense help. Isaak Walton's *Life of Dr. John Donne* and Edmund Gosse's *The Life and Letters of John Donne* were my constant references in the writing of the first chapter. Geoffrey Keynes's *A Bibliography of John Donne* was of great assistance in all bibliographical matters. The libraries on whose resources I have primarily depended are those of the Johns Hopkins University and Goucher College.

It is impossible to express the fullness of my gratitude to Mrs. Evelyn M. Simpson and the late Professor George R. Potter for their edition of *The Sermons of John Donne*, one of the truly fine editorial achievements of the twentieth century. My own book would hardly have been written without their editorial gift. And Mrs. Simpson's encouraging letters to me in 1958 and 1959, when I was working intensively with the sermons, were deeply appreciated.

Mr. Harold A. Small of the University of California Press, the person responsible for seeing the Potter-Simpson edition through to publication, has been unfailingly generous to me from the time I began my study; his latest courtesy was sending me the galley proof of Volume x so that I might make use of the contents of that volume before it was published. Mrs. Dorothy C. Wheeler has been a faithful and an able typist; Mrs. Donna Bishop, a careful proofreader of most of the quotations from the sermons; Mrs. Gail M. Filion of the Princeton University Press, a helpful copy editor. Professor Horton Davies of Princeton University has made a number of suggestions which I have profitably followed. And my wife, even more accessible to me than the aforementioned persons, has assisted in many ways.

To all these institutions, foundations, and persons I am very grateful.

WILLIAM R. MUELLER

Goucher College
May 29, 1962

REFERENCES AND ABBREVIATIONS

Quotations from Donne's poems are taken from H. J. C. Grierson's one-volume edition of *The Poems of John Donne* (London: Oxford University Press, 1933). The following forms of reference to frequently quoted works are used:

A   (followed by volume and page): Lancelot Andrewes, *Ninety-Six Sermons*, 5 vols. (Oxford: John Henry Parker, 1841-1843).

D   (followed by volume and page): *The Sermons of John Donne*, 10 vols., edd. George R. Potter and Evelyn M. Simpson (University of California Press: Berkeley and Los Angeles, 1953-1962).

G.   (followed by volume and page): Edmund Gosse, *The Life and Letters of John Donne*, 2 vols. (London: William Heinemann, 1899).

W.   (followed by page): Isaak Walton, *The Lives of John Donne, Sir Henry Wotton, Richard Hooker, George Herbert, and Robert Sanderson* (The World's Classics, London: Oxford University Press, 1927).

Contents

John Donne: Preacher

CHAPTER ONE

The Life and Death of
Dr Donne

W HEN John Donne, on February 25, 1631, as-
cended into the pulpit of Whitehall Palace,
where both he and the illustrious Lancelot Andrewes before him had delivered many sermons, he was to
preach for the last time, climaxing a priesthood of sixteen
years and a deanship of nine. He had arrived in London only
a few days before, having spent the winter in Essex with
an illness so serious and confining that the rumor of his
own death had reached him. If that rumor, accompanied as
it was by high tributes to the goodness of his life, had not
disturbed him, another rumor, this one marked by uncharitable asperity, vexed him considerably. He was reputed
to have magnified the seriousness of his condition so that
he might live at his ease, free from the preaching duties
which fell upon the Dean of St. Paul's. Stung by an accusa-
tion certainly refuted by the many evidences of responsibility which he had always borne to his charge, he took occasion
to deny it in a letter to George Gerrard, written on January
7, 1631: "It hath been my desire (and God may be pleased
to grant it me) that I might die in the pulpit; if not that,
yet that I might take my death in the pulpit, that is, die the
sooner by occasion of my former labours." The letter goes
on to express Donne's hope that he will soon be in London
to preach his customary Lent sermon—unless, Donne goes
on wittily, the Lord Chamberlain has given him up for
dead and removed his name from the rolls. (G ɪɪ:268-269)
   The expressed desire of Donne's letter—that he might
die the sooner by virtue of his preaching labors—was, it

[3]

appears, to be granted. When he arrived, sick and emaci-
ated, in London, his friends sought to dissuade him from
undertaking the extremely arduous task of preaching for
an hour on that momentous occasion and before that distinguished congregation. And when the persistent Dr.
Donne nevertheless appeared in the pulpit, poised in that
delicate balance between life and death, his hearers must
have remarked on the aptness of his text, drawn from his
favorite Book of Psalms: "And unto God the Lord belong
the issues of death. i.e. from death." Within five weeks
Donne was dead, and when the sermon was published the
next year its title page included the following appropriate
words: "Deaths Duell, Or, A Consolation to the Soule
against the dying Life, and liuing Death of the Body. . . .
Being his last Sermon, and called by his Maiesties houshold
The Doctors owne Funerall Sermon."

Donne's last sermon—"Death's Duel," as it has come
to be called—is his own funeral sermon and more. It is a
distillation of his preaching of sixteen years, a summation
of the pulpit oratory of England's most famous preacher.
In essence it speaks of the vanity of human life, of the
mightiness of God's redemptive power, and of the avenue
to salvation through meditation upon the action and passion
of the last day of the Lord. The sermon begins with the
customary disquisition upon the text, in which Donne sees a
threefold meaning in proper accordance with a three-per-
soned God. First, it is the power of God the Father which
gives us an issue, a deliverance, from death even when we
are on the very threshold of the grave; secondly, it is the
comfort of the Holy Ghost which, when our death is im-
minent, enables us to face it in peace by means of his promise that death is but the entrance to everlasting life; thirdly,
it is the mercy of the Son which assures us that he has taken
the issue of death upon himself for the purpose of our salvation, and that the only road from earthly misery to heav-

enly glorification is the way of death by the Cross. (D x: 230-231)

Our entire life is but a series of deaths, and even our entrance into this life through our mother's womb partakes as much of the nature of death as of life. It is with a grandiloquent and horrible prose, a prose which had stunned his hearers for many years, that Donne reflects on the vanity and decay of every act that falls within the limits of, and is destroyed by the specters of, time and space:

"Wee have a winding sheete in our Mothers wombe, which growes with us from our conception, and wee come into the world, wound up in that *winding sheet*, for wee come to *seeke a grave;* And as prisoners discharg'd of actions may lye for fees; so when the *wombe* hath discharg'd us, yet we are bound to it by *cordes* of flesh, by such a *string*, as that wee cannot goe thence, nor stay there. We celebrate our owne funeralls with cryes, even at our birth; as though our *threescore and ten years of life* were spent in our mothers labour, and our circle made up in the first point thereof. . . . this whole *world* is but an *universall church-yard*, but our *common grave;* and the life and motion that the greatest persons have in it, is but as the shaking of buried bodies in their graves by an *earth-quake*. That which we call life, is but *Hebdomada mortium, a week of deaths*, seaven dayes, seaven periods of our life spent in dying, *a dying seaven times over;* and there is an end. *Our birth dyes* in *infancy*, and our *infancy* dyes in *youth*, and *youth* and the rest dye in *age*, and *age* also dyes, and *determines all*. Nor doe all these, youth out of infancy, or age out of youth arise so, as a *Phœnix* out of the *ashes* of another *Phœnix* formerly *dead*, but as a *waspe* or a *serpent* out of a *caryon*, or as a *Snake* out of *dung*. Our *youth* is *worse* then our *infancy*, and our *age worse* then our *youth*. Our *youth* is *hungry and thirsty*, after those *sinnes*, which our *infancy knew not;* And our *age* is *sory* and *angry*, that it *cannot pursue* those *sinnes* which our *youth* did. And besides, al the way, so many deaths, that is, so many deadly calamities accompany every condition, and every period of this life, as that death it selfe would bee an ease to them that suffer them." D x:233-234)

But if Donne would play such a prolonged and somber tune upon the dreariness of mortality taken by itself, he would also turn to the silver trumpet which sounds the resurrection into immortality. "Death's Duel" proclaims the victory of the redeeming Christ over all those forces which seek to make mortality an end in itself; it is a duel in which death must die. The very lengthy closing paragraph of the discourse properly makes the sermon Donne's own funeral sermon or the funeral sermon of any devout Christian, for the last thousand words constitute a meditation, graphically delivered, on the last day of the life of Christ, from the hour of the Passover Feast to the hour of his death. Donne urges his congregation—and himself—to trace back over the last day in their own lives and ask themselves if they have followed the perfect pattern set by Christ on his own last day. Have they humbly sought a reconciliation with all people, even with those who have resisted their love? Have they spent hours of their time, as Christ did, in prayer, and was their prayer, like his, accompanied by a shedding of tears and a readiness to shed their own blood? Did they willingly meet with the violences and humiliations attendant upon their standing fast in their faith? Step by step, Donne takes his congregation through his Saviour's last hours, asking them to what extent their lives have conformed to his. And in conclusion he draws a vivid picture of the crucifixion. It is in this picture, at once ghastly and joyful, that Donne sees his own salvation, wrought by tears and sweat and blood; this is the climax of his own funeral sermon in which he sees his redemption sealed:

"There now hangs that *sacred Body* upon the *Crosse*, re-*baptized* in his owne *teares* and *sweat*, and *embalmed* in his *owne blood alive*. There are those *bowells of compassion*, which are so conspicuous, so manifested, as that you may *see them through his wounds*. There those *glorious eyes* grew faint in their light: so as the *Sun ashamed* to survive them, *departed with his light too*. And then that *Sonne of God*, who was *never from us*, and yet had now come a *new way unto* us in *assuming our nature*, delivers that *soule* (which was *never out* of his *Fathers hands*) by a *new way*, a *voluntary emission* of it into his Fathers hands; For though to this *God our Lord, belong'd these issues of death*, so that considered in his owne contract, he *must* necessarily *dye*, yet at *no breach* or *battery*, which they had made upon his *sacred Body*, issued his soule, but *emisit*, hee *gave up the Ghost*, and as *God breathed a soule into* the *first Adam*, so this *second Adam breathed his soule into God, into the hands of God*. There wee leave you in that *blessed depend-ancy*, to *hang* upon *him* that *hangs* upon the *Crosse*, there *bath* in his *teares*, there *suck* at his *woundes*, and *lye downe in peace* in his *grave*, till hee vouchsafe you a *resurrection*, and an *ascension* into that *Kingdome*, which hee *hath pur-chas'd for you*, with the *inestimable price* of his *incorruptible blood*. AMEN." D x:247-248)

A study of Donne's sermons may begin with a reading of his last, so fine and representative an example of the hundreds which went before it. From its initial, careful attention to the various possible interpretations of the text; through the more detailed development of each possibility, all presented in a vivid imagery which convinces one of the lifelessness of this life; on down to the arresting picture of Christ on the Cross, shedding his tears and blood so that the congregations at Whitehall and at all the four corners of the earth might live—all of this is typically Donne, a bit more macabre than usual, perhaps, but nevertheless in a style and content that are unmistakably his. What manner of man was he, who, descending from the pulpit on this day in the King's presence, was to die but a little over a month later, on March 31, 1631?

Little is known of Donne's early life.[1] He was born in 1572,[2] two years after Pope Pius V had excommunicated Queen Elizabeth I from the Roman Communion and proclaimed to Englishmen their freedom from the oath attesting to their Queen's sovereignty; one year after the Thirty-nine Articles of the Church of England were recorded in their present form; the same year which saw publication of that first strong Puritan blast at Anglicanism, a manifesto entitled *An Admonition to the Parliament*. He was born in a time when the course of a man's life—and the proximity of his death—could be crucially shaped by his religious convictions, particularly if he was willing to speak them forth.

The two most distinguishing characteristics of Donne's ancestors are their eminent achievements and their Roman Catholicism. Such a statement refers not so much to Donne's paternal ancestry, for the family tree cannot be traced back on that side beyond his father, John, a Roman Catholic and a well-to-do London merchant who died on January 16, 1576. But through his mother, born Elizabeth Heywood, Donne was descended from a stock as illustrious as it was Roman Catholic. Its line went back to the family of

---

[1] I have attempted, in the following brief biographical sketch, to include only those matters which seem to me to bear most directly on Donne's ministry.

[2] See F. P. Wilson, "Notes on the Early Life of John Donne," *The Review of English Studies*, III (July 1927), 276-278; *Notes and Queries*, CLIII (July 23, 1927), 56; H. W. Garrod, "The Date of Donne's Birth," *The Times Literary Supplement*, December 30, 1944, p. 636; W. Milgate, "The Date of Donne's Birth," *Notes and Queries*, CXCI (November 16, 1946), 206-208; I. A. Shapiro, "Donne's Birthdate," *Notes and Queries*, CXCVII (July 19, 1952), 310-313.

one of the saints of the Church, Sir Thomas More. It numbered a lawyer, John Rastell; a physician, John Clement; a judge, William Rastell; and a man of letters, John Heywood.[3] Virtually all of its prominent members had been forced, during the reign of Edward VI or Elizabeth I (or both), to flee their native land because of their religious convictions. In the summer of 1581, when Donne was nine years old, his Uncle Jasper Heywood, poet and translator of three of Seneca's tragedies, succeeded England's most distinguished Jesuit, Father Robert Parsons, in the very important position of Superior of the English Jesuit Mission, only to be shortly thereafter banished from his country. When we add to all this the fact that John Donne's brother, Henry, was arrested in May 1573 for harboring a prescribed Roman Catholic Seminarist in his dwelling, was placed in the Clink Prison for his pains, and there died of a fever a few weeks later, we can assent to the truth of Donne's statement in "An Advertisement to the Reader," preface to *Pseudo-Martyr*, published in 1610: ". . . I haue beene euer kept awake in a meditation of Martyrdome, by being deriued from such a stocke and race, as, I beleeue, no family, (which is not of farre larger extent, and greater branches,) hath endured and suffered more in their persons and fortunes, for obeying the Teachers of Romane Doctrine, then it hath done."[4]

It is impossible to measure the extent to which John Donne's lineage affected the man who was to become one of the most influential voices in the Church of England during the second and third decades of the seventeenth century. His mother must certainly have entrusted his early

---

[3] For more detailed information on these figures, see the *Dictionary of National Biography*.

[4] *Pseudo-Martyr. Wherein Ovt Of Certaine Propositions and Gradations, This Conclusion is euicted. That Those Which Are of the Romane Religion in this Kingdome, may and ought to take the Oath of Allegeance* (London, 1610), p. 1.

schooling to a Roman Catholic—Walton tells us that Donne had the benefit of a private tutor until his tenth year (W:23)—and Donne's early years must certainly have absorbed the story of Rome's epic struggle to maintain power and to guide all sinners to God's Kingdom. And he may well, in the early 1580's, have felt with his mother an outraged sense of indignation that Uncle Jasper Heywood was being so badly treated by his native country. Had it been then surmised that John Donne would one day speak out against the Roman Catholics, particularly the Jesuits, from the pulpit of St. Paul's Cathedral, Donne himself would doubtless have been bewildered and his mother grievously shocked. At the same time, his early indoctrination into the ways and activities of the Roman Church was a fine training for one who was some day to inveigh against it.

In October 1584 Donne entered Hart Hall at Oxford, then a refuge for those of Roman Catholic persuasions.[5] He remained at Oxford for about three years, acquitting himself well but forbearing to take a degree since that would have entailed subscription to the Oath of Allegiance, something to be avoided by anyone of Papist inclinations. His transfer to Trinity College, Cambridge, in 1587, is of particular interest in that the principal religious tension at Cambridge was between Canterbury and Geneva, not between Rome and Canterbury as it was at Oxford.[6] Donne's three years at Cambridge must have given him good opportunity to come into close conversation and relationship with intelligent Anglican apologists, and when he left Trinity College in his late teens he may well have asked himself how loyal he was and was to remain to his distinguished ancestors who had suffered so much for the Papist cause.

For the most accurate chronological account of Donne's

[5] Charles Monroe Coffin, *John Donne and the New Philosophy* (New York: Columbia University Press, 1937), p. 29.
[6] *Ibid.*, p. 33.

activities during the 1590's we are indebted to John Sparrow.[7] Donne studied law at Thavies Inn and at Lincoln's Inn, made the continental tour, and saw naval service against the Spaniards. Early in 1598 he accepted the position, destined to last four years, of principal secretary to Sir Thomas Egerton, one of England's most respected citizens. Before entering the service of Sir Thomas he probably wrote the large bulk of his songs and sonnets, elegies, and satires.

There has been controversy about the possible autobiographical implications of Donne's most cynical and sensual love poems, which, fascinating in themselves, gain an additional interest from the fact that they were written by a future Dean of St. Paul's Cathedral. Edmund Gosse's attempts to draw various autobiographical conclusions (see, for example, G 1:60ff.) are to me unconvincing. Donne's erotic love poems, I believe, bear more the mark of the artist than of the man, and are primarily the pieces of a poet surfeited by the Petrarchan excesses of his day. Of Donne's youthful behavior we know virtually nothing; his own occasional later remarks about certain irregularities of conduct may have been no more than oversensitive reflections about a normal young manhood. We can perhaps do no better than accept Sir Richard Baker's brief comment about the young Donne: ". . . Mr. *John Dunne* . . . lived at the *Innes of Court*, not dissolute, but very neat; a great Visitor of Ladies, a great frequenter of Playes, a great writer of conceited Verses . . . ."[8]

It was probably early in 1598 when Sir Thomas Egerton,

---

[7] "The Date of Donne's Travels," *A Garland for John Donne: 1631-1931*, ed. Theodore Spencer (Cambridge, Massachusetts: Harvard University Press, 1931), pp. 121-151. See also two brief notices by I. A. Shapiro, "John Donne and Lincoln's Inn, 1591-1594," *The Times Literary Supplement*, October 16, 1930, p. 833, and October 23, 1930, p. 861.

[8] *A Chronicle of the Kings of England*, 4th edition (London, 1665), p. 450.

one of the most influential men in the realm, invited Donne to become his chief secretary, a post apparently accepted with alacrity. Donne, at the age of about twenty-six, was thus honored by an appointment which would seem to have boded well for any ambitions he may have had for a court or civil post in his native England. A brilliant lawyer, Egerton had been trained at Donne's own Lincoln's Inn, had served as Solicitor-General and then Attorney-General, and had been appointed Master of the Rolls in 1594 and Lord Keeper of England in 1596. That a man of such stature should have chosen Donne to assist him was a distinct, though due, tribute to the young man who had done well at Oxford, Cambridge, Thavies Inn, and Lincoln's Inn, and who had shown a decidedly nimble mind in his manuscript poetry. It is, of course, interesting to speculate on what Donne's religious affections were at this time. That he was not following in the tradition of his ancestors must have been evident as early as 1593, the generally assigned date of "Satire III," a poem expressing a religious faith searching anxiously for an institution embodying "true religion." The speaker, whom I think we may properly identify with Donne himself, states that some seek religion at ancient and gaily appareled Rome, others at young and homespun Geneva, still others at Canterbury; some eschew all three, while others embrace them all with equal affection. The road to Truth, continues Donne, is circuitous: ". . . On a huge hill,/Cragged, and steep, Truth stands, and hee that will/Reach her, about must, and about must goe." One must not give unthinking acceptance to a King Philip or a Henry VIII, to a Pope Gregory or a Martin Luther, but must find his Truth through God's revelation. Whatever Donne's religion may have been five years later when Sir Thomas Egerton went in search of a secretary, it was not the faith of his fathers; had it been so, Egerton would most certainly have continued his search.

Walton tells us that Donne was well received in the Egerton household and that his company and conversation were treasured by Sir Thomas (W:27). The attractiveness of the young secretary was also noted by Lady Egerton's niece, Anne More, who seems to have been adopted into the Egerton family, though her father, a long-time Parliamentarian, Sir George More, still lived in the More family mansion at Loseley. It is difficult to overestimate the effect which Donne's love for Anne, twelve years his junior, had on his career. It seems highly probable that, but for his marriage to Anne, Donne would have become one of England's leading legal statesmen: he had the ability to do so, he was under the expert guidance of one of Queen Elizabeth's favorites, and he coveted a high place in his nation's political life. Had Donne been able to satisfy his secular ambitions, it is unlikely that he would have considered ordination; England would probably have gained a great statesman and lost a great preacher. All of this is, of course, speculative. But what is not speculative is the fact that, in December 1601, John Donne and Anne More were secretly married. When, some two months later, Sir George More learned the news, the results were explosive, for to marry a young lady without her father's permission was a legal as well as a personal offense. Sir George, hardly a man to take such an event in his stride, occasioned Donne's dismissal from his secretarial post and his imprisonment. Donne's comment on his marriage was more than a wry pun: "John Donne, Anne Donne, Un-done."

Donne's worldly miseries, to pursue him for a number of years, were off to a flying start. Though his life was never for any extended length of time bathed by the noonday sun of earthly felicity, the first decade of the seventeenth century, when Donne was in his late twenties and his thirties, was the most abysmal time of all. It is true that he was released from prison soon after his commitment and that Sir George was unsuccessful in his attempts to annul the marriage, which was legally ratified on April 27, 1602. But Donne was not to be received back into the employment of Egerton, despite his own pleas and even those of his father-in-law. Unfortunately, a well-educated young man of three and a half centuries ago did not find available the variety of possible livelihoods which he would find today, and Donne, having by 1602 run through the substantial inheritance from his father, found himself married, low in funds, and at least temporarily cut off from legal or secretarial work which he could do so well. His bleak situation was alleviated by the kindness of his wife's cousin, Sir Francis Wooley, who offered Donne a home on his estate at Pyrford. Here the Donnes remained for two or three years, Anne bearing the first two of her twelve children, John studying civil and canon law. (W:35)

A task for which Donne was exceptionally well suited fell to his lot in 1605, occasioning a change of residence to Mitcham, where the Donnes remained until 1609. Donne was invited to assist the gentle, tactful, and studious Thomas Morton (later to become Dean of Gloucester and then Bishop of Durham), who had been assigned the delicate responsibility of persuading the English Papists who refused, illegally, to attend Anglican services of the error of their ways. Morton's task was to present the position of the English State and the Anglican Church, with the hope that the recusancy—failure to attend the Anglican services —of those sympathetic to Rome might be decreased. His choice of Donne as his assistant showed good judgment, for there was probably no Englishman with so detailed a knowledge of the issues between Rome and Canterbury, with so impressive a legal background, and with so thorough a command of language. Donne remained at this work at least through 1607; precisely what the division of labor between Donne and Morton was, we do not know.

[14]

It seems highly probable that this stage of Donne's career was a step toward his eventually taking orders in the Anglican Church. His acceptance of Morton's invitation indicates that he had at the least moved well toward Anglicanism, since he could hardly have been induced, regardless of his hapless circumstances, to assume a position in which he did not believe. And it is probable that his research and writing for Morton inclined him further toward whole-hearted acceptance of the position of the English Church. Whatever was taking place in his heart and mind, his work with Morton must certainly have attracted the gratified attention of King James and have been one of the factors which later led him to insist that, if Donne was to expect any favor at his hands, it was to be in the priesthood of the Established Church. Donne also greatly impressed Morton with his ability and his sanctity, and we owe to Walton an account of what must have been Donne's first serious consideration of taking orders, at the behest of Morton himself (W:32-35). The day after Morton was made Dean of Gloucester on June 22, 1607, he besought his assistant to accept a benefice in his possession, but Donne, after consideration, became convinced that, for the time being at least, he felt no call to the priesthood.

The next year or so of Donne's life was marked by its misery. His health and fortunes were both at an ebb as he sought gainful employment now that his work with Morton was at an end. He sought, successively and vainly, a position in Queen Anne's household (G 1:156), a secretaryship in Ireland (G 1:199), and a similar post in Virginia (G 1:209). Meanwhile he remained at Mitcham in depressed spirits and ill health, as his letters to Sir Henry Goodyer, his most frequent correspondent, so fully attest. A letter of August 10, 1608, sent "From my Hospital at Mitcham," as Donne phrases it, shows the general tenor of his correspondence:

"And the reason why I did not send an answer to your last week's letter was because it then found me under too great a sadness, and at present it is thus with me. There is no one person but myself well of my family; I have already lost half a child, and with that mischance of hers, my wife is fallen into such a discomposure as would afflict her too extremely, but that the sickness of all her other children stupefies her; of one of which, in good faith, I have not much hope; and these meet with a fortune so ill provided for physic and such relief, that if God should ease us with burials, I know not how to perform even that: but I flatter myself with this hope that I am dying too; for I cannot waste faster than by such griefs." (G 1:189)

Also composed in 1608, though not published until almost forty years later, was the treatise entitled *Biathanatos*, the nature of which is carefully described on its title page: "A Declaration Of That Paradoxe, Or Thesis, that Selfe-homicide is not so Naturally Sinne, that it may never be otherwise. Wherein The Nature, and the extent of all those Lawes, which seeme to be violated by this Act, are diligently surveyed." The work is a probable reflection of its author's melancholy meditations during his lean years.

But if the years 1607 and 1608 were in many ways a barren winter in the life of Donne, there were signs of an approaching spring. It was in 1607 that he began his correspondence with a lady who was destined to be his devoted friend for the next twenty years, Mrs. Magdalen Herbert, mother of two distinguished sons: Edward, the future philosopher and Lord Herbert of Cherbury, and George, perhaps the most dedicated religious poet of the seventeenth century. In the following year he began his friendship with the other woman who, excepting his wife, was with Mrs. Herbert to engage his deepest affection. This was the charming and wealthy Lucy Russell, Countess of Bedford, from whom Donne received the patronage deemed so necessary to a man of his limited means. Also in 1608, approximately seven years after Donne's marriage, Sir George More agreed to a dowry which alleviated considerably the impoverishment of the Donne family.

According to the careful study of Miss Helen Gardner, a good portion of Donne's religious poetry was written during the difficult Mitcham years. There is now rather general agreement that the seven interlocking sonnets which constitute *La Corona* were written before 1610, and quite possibly in 1607. *A Litanie* was probably composed in 1608. Miss Gardner argues also that six of the *Holy Sonnets*, those six on eschatological themes—death, judgment, hell, and heaven—were written between February and August of 1609, and that ten of the other ones were probably written before the composition of *The Second Anniversary* in 1612.[9]

Donne's poetic composition during the two years following Morton's urgent entreaty, in June 1607, that he take orders is of considerable relevance in any effort to trace his gradual progress toward entrance into the priesthood in 1615. For it is to his poetry that we should turn for the most intimate disclosure of his religious temper. That he worked with Morton on treatises designed to convince recusants of their obligation to follow the civil and religious laws of their native country, or that he later wrote *Pseudo-Martyr* in an attempt to persuade English Roman Catholics that the taking of the Oath of Allegiance was not incompatible with their deepest religious loyalties—these activities could prove no more than that he had broken away from his Roman Catholic ancestry, that he saw some merit

[9] *John Donne: The Divine Poems*, edited with introduction and commentary by Helen Gardner (Oxford at the Clarendon Press, 1952), pp. xxi-lv. In the Grierson edition of Donne's poems, the six eschatological sonnets are numbered II, IV, VI, VII, IX, and X.

in the temporal claims of English Church and State, perhaps that he saw his employment as an immediate means to feed his family and as a possible prelude to civil preferment. But such scholarly and apologetic activity was no certain evidence in itself of any spiritual fervor. It is highly doubtful, on the other hand, that his poetry was motivated by any such extraneous considerations. Even if, as critics have argued, *La Corona* and *A Litanie* are lacking in emotional intensity, they do show the center of Donne's thought. At the time of his deepest personal miseries, we find no longer the cynicism and skepticism which characterized the poetry of the 1590's, but rather a turning to the events and results of his Lord's life, passion, and triumph. And in the *Holy Sonnets*, more personal and subjective, Donne reflects on the vastness of his sins and on the incomparable mercy of the redeeming God. In these sonnets are found themes which were to appear again and again throughout the sermons written later and over a period of sixteen years.

Pseudo-Martyr, written in 1609 and published in the next year, looks back to Donne's work with Morton and forward to various statements on Church and State which were to run through many of the sermons. Its title page asserts the work's conclusion, "That Those Which Are of the Romane Religion in this Kingdome, may and ought to take the Oath of Allegeance." In the book's "Preface to The Priestes, and Iesuites, and to their Disciples in this Kingdome" is the very interesting apologetic statement of a man who seems to fear some base imputation upon his motives for writing such a work:

"They who haue descended so lowe, as to take knowledge of me, and to admit me into their consideration, know well that I vsed no inordinate hast, nor precipitation in binding my conscience to any locall Religion. I had a longer worke to doe then many other men; for I was first to blot out, cer-

taine impressions of the Romane religion, and to wrastle both against the examples and against the reasons, by which some hold was taken; and some anticipations early layde vpon my conscience, both by Persons who by nature had a power and superiority ouer my will, and others who by their learning and good life, seem'd to me iustly to claime an interest for the guiding, and rectifying of mine vnderstanding in these matters. And although I apprehended well enough, that this irresolution not onely retarded my fortune, but also bred some scandall, and endangered my spirituall reputation, by laying me open to many mis-interpretations; yet all these respects did not transport me to any violent and sudden determination, till I had, to the measure of my poore wit and iudgement, suruayed and digested the whole body of Diuinity, controuerted betweene ours and the Romane Church."[10]

As the quotation suggests, there were doubtless people of Donne's own time, as there have been people since, who questioned the integrity of his move toward and into the Church of England. A Roman Catholic Englishman in his day was a man almost without a country, certainly one who was denied many of the privileges of his nation and who would find it difficult to find an employment in which he could prosper. The charges of expediency and time-serving could have been, and probably were, hurled his way. In any case, one could hardly deny the truth of his claim that he had "digested the whole body of Diuinity" of Rome and Canterbury. Walton tells us that Donne's omnivorous reading of religious literature began in his nineteenth year (W:25); certainly by 1609, after his work with Morton, Donne needed bow to no one in the knowledge of contemporary religious controversy. Though some may have charged Donne with expediency, no one in his right mind

[10] *Pseudo-Martyr*, B2^v-B3^r.

[19]

could have accused him of ignorance or of blindness in what he was doing.

To the student of Donne's sermons, interest in *Pseudo-Martyr* goes well beyond those passages in which Donne seeks to clarify his personal position. For this treatise contains arguments, of both political and theological nature, which were to be voiced in his pulpit years. Many times in his sermons he returns to what he states in *Pseudo-Martyr* to be the basic corruptness of the Church of Rome, as manifested primarily in three "errors": 1) the debasing of secular magistrates and the exalting of ecclesiastics; 2) the misconception of their doctrine of good works, with its view that a man can in the eyes of God go beyond the call of duty; 3) the belief that there is a purgatorial state, the torments of which may be escaped through the superabundant merits and sufferings of the martyrs.[11] On April 17, 1610, Donne was rewarded for his work with Morton and his publication of *Pseudo-Martyr:* Oxford University conferred upon him the honorary degree of Master of Arts (G 1:252).

Donne's fortunes during the four years preceding his ordination in early 1615 were to an extent governed by his response to the death of Elizabeth Drury in December 1610 at the age of fifteen.[12] Donne marked her death by the composition of *A Funerall Elegie,* which he sent to her wealthy father, Sir Robert Drury, whose grief, according to reports, was extravagant (G 1:273). Elizabeth had been, in her father's eyes at least, a young lady of considerable distinction, and there were rumors that he had hopes of her eventual marriage to Prince Henry. A few months later Donne followed up the elegy with the writing of a longer memorial entitled *An Anatomy of the World,* and at some

[11] *Ibid.,* p. 15.
[12] For the date of Elizabeth's death see John Sparrow, "Two Epitaphs by John Donne," *The Times Literary Supplement,* March 26, 1949, p. 208.

time in 1611 both pieces were published under the title of *An anatomy of the World. Wherein, by occasion of the vntimely death of Mistris Elizabeth Drury the frailty and the decay of this whole world is represented.* So grateful was Sir Robert that at some time in 1611—whether before or after the writing of the *Anatomy* is not known—he invited the Donnes and their seven children to move rent-free into a house beside his own residence, Drury House, located in Drury Lane.[13] Donne then wrote another memorial to Elizabeth, and in the early months of 1612 the *Anatomy* and the later piece were published together under the general title of *First and Second Anniversaries.* The later composition bore the full title of *The Second Anniuersarie. Of the progres of the Soule. Wherein: By Occasion Of The Religious Death of Mistris Elizabeth Drury, the incommodities of the Soule in this life and her exaltation in the next, are Contemplated.*

It is doubtful that any of Donne's other poetry was subjected to such unsympathetic and misleading criticism as were the *Anniversaries* until they received the discriminating attention of Professor Louis Martz.[14] The charge had been that the eulogies on Elizabeth Drury were distastefully extravagant and overdrawn, bent primarily on winning Sir Robert's patronage. Though it is true that Elizabeth's death did furnish Donne opportunity to gain patronage, it also provided him occasion to reflect on the nature of this world and the next and to try to determine his own proper relationship to both. In the *Anniversaries* he takes stock of himself—much as Milton does in *Lycidas*—and thus the me-

[13] R. C. Bald, *Donne & the Drurys* (Cambridge at the University Press, 1959), pp. 113-114.

[14] See Louis L. Martz, "John Donne in Meditation: 'The Anniversaries,' " *ELH: A Journal of English Literary History*, XIV (December 1947), 247-273; and his excellent *The Poetry of Meditation* (New Haven: Yale University Press, 1954).

morials are important documents in tracing Donne's pilgrimage toward the ministry.

As Donne remarked to Ben Jonson, Elizabeth is symbolic of the "Idea of a Woman." The subject of the *Anniversaries* is thus both the deceased fifteen-year-old daughter of the wealthy Sir Robert Drury and a symbol of the departure of virtue from this world. In *The First Anniversary*, a lamentation on the corruptness and mortality of the whole of creation, Elizabeth's death furnishes the microcosmic reflection of our unhappy condition. *The Second Anniversary*, for the most part a series of meditations leading to a triumphant conclusion, might well serve as a prelude to the mighty music of Donne's pulpit years. His bidding his soul to meditate on death, his reflections on original sin and on the vanity and transitoriness of this world, his finding a resolution to these melancholy thoughts in the soul's contemplations upon the joys of heaven (Elizabeth Drury's present abode)—these poetic meditations are motifs later to be developed and to run with manifold variations throughout the sermons.

Professor Martz, to whom Donne scholars are considerably indebted for his study of the *Anniversaries*, relates the two poems to Donne's "other meditations of this period— including, perhaps, many of the 'Holy Sonnets,' " and to the *Essays in Divinity*, written a year or two later; and he argues that all of them show Donne in the process of seeking or determining his calling.[15] It is highly doubtful, however, that Sir Robert Drury placed such an interpretation upon the *Anniversaries*. He saw in them a fitting tribute to the daughter for whom he had enjoyed such high hopes, and he evidenced the measure of his gratitude by inviting Donne and his family to live on his estate at his expense.

After spending almost a full year on the Continent with the Drurys, Donne returned to Anne, their seven children,

[15] *The Poetry of Meditation*, pp. 216-221.

and Drury Lane in the autumn of 1612. Almost immediately upon his return he wrote to Lord Rochester, a great favorite of King James at this time, saying that he had "obeyed at last, after much debatement within me, the inspirations (as I hope) of the Spirit of God, and resolved to make my profession Divinity," and he asked Rochester's assistance (G II:20-21). The letter is a puzzling one. For one thing Donne hardly needed the help of a king's favorite to be ordained into the Anglican Church, though he may have felt that the intercession of Rochester would gain for him some particularly favorable ecclesiastical preferment. For another, if Gosse is correct in assigning the letter to October 1612, then there is a period of two years before we have any further word from Donne about his feeling of a call to the ministry.

The next two years were filled with illness, grief, and a continuing search for a livelihood which would give Donne some measure of independence. His letters once again take on the melancholy tone of much of his correspondence from Mitcham: he writes, for example, of serious difficulty with his eyes (G II:30), and of the illnesses plaguing his wife and children (G II:36). That he had turned at least a partially deaf ear to the call of the Holy Ghost which had come to him in 1612 is evidenced by the fact that, at some time in 1614, he wrote to Rochester, then the Earl of Somerset, begging his favor again, this time that he might recommend Donne for the post of Ambassador to Venice, shortly to be vacated (G II:40-41). Again he was to be disappointed, as the ambassadorship was bestowed on Sir Henry Wotton. Grief followed upon grief, as Donne's daughter Mary died in May 1614 and his son Francis in November of the same year. And between the two deaths we find evidence of Donne's continuing frustration as he writes his brother-in-law Sir Robert More that "no man attends court fortunes with more impatience than I do" (G II:46). Six months after this letter of July 28, 1614, Donne was an ordained minister of the Church of England.

But at some time before his entrance into the priesthood, probably "at the end of 1614 or the beginning of 1615,"[16] Donne wrote his *Essays in Divinity*. Donne's son John, who edited this work and published it in 1651, wrote in the prefatory "To the Reader" that ". . . these *Essayes . . .* were the voluntary sacrifices of severall hours, when he [Donne, Sr.] had many debates betwixt God and himself, whether he were worthy, and competently learned to enter into Holy Orders." As is true of so many of Donne's writings, poetry and prose, in the decade before his ordination, *Essays in Divinity* touches upon many of those themes which were later to take their place in the sermons. He distinguishes between natural theology (the evidences of God in the created world) and revealed theology (God's revelation of himself through the written Word of Scripture); he speaks of the foolishness of being so curious as to question unrevealed mysteries; he considers the place of reason and of faith in one's pilgrimage to God; he calls for unity among the various churches which worship Jesus Christ.

Gosse assigns to November 1614 an episode which would seem to be Donne's final effort to secure some suitable secular position (G II:57-60). We are indebted to Walton for our knowledge of the episode, though he gives it an earlier date (W:45-46). The story goes that the Earl of Somerset, upon the death of one of the clerks of the Council, summoned Donne and told him that he was going directly to the King to secure for Donne the recently vacated post. But the King's response to Somerset's petition must have convinced Donne once and for all of the futility of pressing further for any kind of secular preferment; according to Walton, James replied: " 'I know Mr. *Donne* is a

---

[16] John Donne, *Essays in Divinity*, ed. Evelyn M. Simpson (Oxford at the Clarendon Press, 1952), p. ix.

learned man, has the abilities of a learned Divine; and
will prove a powerful Preacher, and my desire is to pre-
fer him that way, and in that way, I will deny you
nothing for him.' " Late in January 1615, Dr. John King,
Bishop of London, ordained Donne, first as deacon, then
as priest (G 11:70-71). Morton's hope, expressed about eight
years earlier, was at last fulfilled.

There has been much idle, if interesting, speculation
about Donne's innermost motives for turning to the priesthood. Certainly the most favorable interpretation was
placed on Donne's decision by Walton, who, after describing the ways in which God had worked upon St. Paul,
Moses, Jacob, and St. Augustine, declared that, with
Donne's ordination, "the *English Church* had gain'd a
second St. *Austine,* for, I think, none was so like him before
his Conversion: none so like St. *Ambrose* after it: and if
his youth had the infirmities of the one, his age had the
excellencies of the other; the learning and holiness of both."
He goes on to quote Donne's post-ordination statement that
"he was now gladder to be a door-keeper in the house of
God, then he could be to injoy the noblest of all temporal
imployments" (W:47-48). The least charitable interpretation, on the other hand, would be to say that Donne, finally
convinced that all ways to temporal preferment were
blocked, had accepted the only opportunity left open to him.
Whatever Donne's motivation may have been, we can be
sure that his subtle, introspective mind reflected carefully
before making the decision, and we have no evidence to
suggest that he ever questioned his decision, once it was
made. Perhaps he was convinced of God's direct call to
him; perhaps he felt that the petitions of persons like Morton and King James were sufficient indication that he had
been called to the Lord's work; perhaps he felt by 1615
that he could best serve both Church and State by accepting

[25]

the one profession within his reach.[17] In any case his sixteen years of preaching would seem to indicate the wisdom of his decision.

Not a great deal is known about Donne's ministerial activity between the time of his ordination and his election as Divinity Reader to Lincoln's Inn on October 24, 1616. Walton informs us that Donne's first sermon was preached at the rural parish of Paddington and that King James soon invited him to preach at Whitehall (W:48-49). Walton's retrospective comment on Donne's first sermon before the King may well have been more dependent on Walton's sitting at the feet of the later Donne than upon the actual event at some time in 1615; we are told that Donne exceeded the expectations of those who heard him,

"preaching the Word so, as shewed his own heart was possest with those very thoughts and joys that he laboured to distill into others: A Preacher in earnest; weeping sometimes for his Auditory, sometimes with them: always preaching to himself, like an Angel from a cloud, but in none; carrying some, as St. *Paul* was, to Heaven in holy raptures, and inticing others by a sacred Art and Courtship to amend their lives; here picturing a vice so as to make it ugly to those that practised it; and a vertue so, as to make it be beloved even by those that lov'd it not; and all this with a most particular grace and an unexpressible addition of comeliness" (W:49).

Walton also records that Donne was made the King's chaplain in the summer of 1615, at which time he was granted the honorary degree of Doctor of Divinity by Cambridge University (W:50). In the spring of 1616 he received the benefice of Keyston in Huntingdonshire and, in July, of Sevenoaks in Kent (G 11:90). Perhaps an even

[17] See K. W. Gransden, *John Donne* (London: Longmans, Green and Co., 1954), p. 40.

more impressive recognition of his considerable powers and talents as a preacher came when the Masters of Lincoln's Inn invited Donne to serve as Reader in Divinity; this he did from October 1616 to February 1622.

Donne, whose new appointment called upon him to preach before the learned and critical congregation at Lincoln's Inn twice every Sunday during the academic terms, was in every way equipped for his task. He knew the character of his hearers, having been a student at Lincoln's Inn during his youth. He knew also the language of law, a knowledge enabling him frequently to press home his religious teaching and exhortation in legal metaphor. And he possessed a wide experience and learning outside a purely religious and theological framework, a fact which must have commanded the high respect of an academic group. We need only read those extant sermons preached at Lincoln's Inn to be assured of Donne's fitness for his position and his success in it.

Anne Donne died on August 15, 1617, her death resulting from the stillbirth of the twelfth child of her fifteen and a half years of marriage. We know little enough about Donne's family life, less about Anne herself. The inscription which Donne composed for her stone pays tribute to a most excellent and beloved woman, a most loving and chaste wife, a most dutiful and forbearing mother. There is no questioning the depth of affection which Donne felt for his wife, an affection so movingly expressed in two of the farewell poems which he doubtless addressed to her, "Sweetest love, I do not goe,/For wearinesse of thee," and "A Valediction: forbidding mourning." Still greater is the tribute paid to Anne in the sonnet, "Since she whom I lov'd hath payd her last debt," in which Donne asserts that her very being had given him such a foretaste of divinity as to lead him to seek God. Following Anne's death, Donne apparently settled with his seven surviving children in lodgings affectionately placed at his disposal by the administrators of Lincoln's Inn (G II:110). The next few years seem relatively uneventful, except for a leisurely and relaxing trip to the Continent from May 1619 until early in 1620.

Donne became Dean of St. Paul's Cathedral on November 19, 1621. Walton attributes to King James a quaintly worded invitation to Donne, who, having been summoned by his King, was purportedly addressed in this manner: " '*Dr.* Donne, I have invited you to Dinner; and, though you sit not down with me, yet I will carve to you of a dish that I know you love well; for knowing you love *London,* I do therefore make you Dean of *Pauls;* and when I have dined, then do you take your beloved dish home to your study; say grace there to your self, and much good may it do you' " (W:55). The appointment was a master stroke, with great advantages for both Donne and England. The heart of the nation's life was London, a city which could nourish well Donne's theological, political, and aesthetic interests; and in London Donne could be most widely heard by persons from all walks of life, nobles and commoners alike. There was no pulpit in England, except perhaps that at Paul's Cross,[18] which influenced the life of the nation as profoundly as that of St. Paul's Cathedral. On February 11, 1622, Donne resigned his Readership in Divinity at Lincoln's Inn amid feelings of mutual good will. To the library of the Inn Donne presented his own six-volume edition of the Vulgate Bible; the administrators of the Inn resolved that Donne would have the continued use of his lodgings there and would be afforded the privileges of the institution (G II:154-155). In his first major preaching assignment, Donne had acquitted himself with distinction.

[18] For an interesting study of Paul's Cross, see Millar MacLure, *The Paul's Cross Sermons, 1534-1632* (Toronto: University of Toronto Press, 1958).

The next few years were marked by some important preaching duties, by a near fatal illness, and by the additional responsibility of the vicarage of St. Dunstan's in the West. In the late summer of 1622, Donne was commissioned to come to the assistance of his monarch. James, disturbed by the independence of some of the Puritan preachers, had issued a brief treatise entitled *Instructions to Preachers*, which sought to regulate what could and what could not be preached from English pulpits. The Puritans were incensed, and Donne was called upon to defend the King's position. The sermon in which he did so, delivered at Paul's Cross on September 15, 1622, stated clearly the Anglican view of the proper relationship between Church and State, attempted a complete justification of the *Instructions*, and pleased James to the extent that it was published and elicited his comment that " 'it was a piece of such perfection as could admit neither addition nor diminution' " (G II:160-161).[19] Two months later Donne preached what was to become his second published sermon, this time to the Virginia Company, and argued again how central to Anglicanism was the interdependence of Church and State.

In the late months of 1623 Donne was overcome by an illness more serious than any he had hitherto experienced. Out of this illness, or out of his reflections upon it, grew what has come to be his most popular prose work, his *Devotions upon Emergent Occasions*, published in 1624. Fully aware of the proximity of death, Donne's habitually introspective mind was brought to its greatest powers of self-examination, and in these moving and magnificent devotions he brings to the reader a step-by-step account of the progress and regress of his malady—from his first awareness of its approach, to the coming of the physician (and

---

[19] During his sixteen-year ministry Donne enjoyed good relations with his monarchs. For two brief ripples on the habitually serene waters, see G II:194-195 together with W:56-57, and G II:242-246.

then the physicians) and the medical efforts to combat the disease, to the period of crisis and sleeplessness, to the tolling of the bells announcing the deaths of others, to the successful purging of his poisoned body, to the final warning to fortify himself against a relapse. A passage of particular relevance to the student of the sermons is found in the Nineteenth Expostulation, where Donne makes clear the basis of much of his Scriptural exegesis, his way of treating his texts both literally and figuratively:

"My *God*, my *God*, Thou art a *direct God*, may I not say, a *literall God*, a *God* that wouldest bee vnderstood *literally*, and according to the *plaine sense* of all that thou saiest? But thou art also (*Lord* I intend it to thy *glory*, and let no *prophane misinterpreter* abuse it to thy *diminution*) thou art a *figuratiue*, a *metaphoricall God* too: A *God* in whose words there is such a height of *figures*, such *voyages*, such *peregrinations* to fetch remote and precious *metaphors*, such *extentions*, such *spreadings*, such *Curtaines* of *Allegories*, such *third Heauens* of *Hyperboles*, so *harmonious eloquutions* [sic], so *retired* and so *reserued expressions*, so *commanding perswasions*, so *perswading commandements*, such *sinewes* euen in thy *milke*, and such *things* in thy *words*, as all *prophane Authors*, seeme of the seed of the *Serpent*, that *creepes*, thou art the *doue*, that flies."[20]

Recovered from his illness, Donne received in March 1624 the charge of St. Dunstan's in the West. His years at St. Dunstan's brought him the friendship of Isaak Walton, whose *Life of Dr. John Donne*, idealized as it may be, is the foundation stone for any study of Donne's life. Its chronology is defective; its portrait of Donne's sanctity is probably overly effusive; its neglect, whether consciously or in ignorance, of some of the less palatable expressions of

[20] *Devotions Vpon Emergent Occasions, and seuerall steps in my Sicknes* (London, 1624), pp. 479-481.

Donne's temperament is notable. Even so, our indebtedness to Walton is immense.

In 1625 the plague made one of its customary and dreaded visitations to London. Donne, removing himself and his family from the center of the plague's activity, took up lodgings at Chelsea, home of Sir John Danvers, who had married the widowed Magdalen Herbert in 1608. That the Dean made good use of his time at Chelsea is shown in the postscript to a letter written from there on November 25, 1625: "I have revised as many of my sermons as I had kept any note of, and I have written out a great many, and hope to do more. I am already come to the number of eighty, of which my son, who, I hope, will take the same profession or some other in the world of middle understanding, may hereafter make some use" (G 11:225). The younger Donne may well have made some use of his father's sermons in his own preaching career. But he made far greater use of them when he edited over one hundred and fifty in the three great folio volumes—the *LXXX Sermons* of 1640, the *Fifty Sermons* of 1649, and the *XXVI Sermons* of 1661. To Donne's stay at the Danvers' we may also attribute the growth of a friendship with a man who was, like himself, a blessing to the life of English poetry and of the Anglican Church—George Herbert. Donne was back in London at the beginning of 1626.

The remaining five years of Donne's life, gratifying as they may have been in some respects for the man then judged to be without a peer in the English pulpit, were nevertheless years of many personal sorrows, for he heard the tolling of the bell for some of those who had been most dear to him. The Countess of Bedford, who had served as patron during some of the bleaker periods of his life, died on the last day of May 1627. In the first week of June, the lovely Magdalen Lady Danvers, who had possessed Donne's deepest affection and had been the inspiration for some of his fine poetry, also passed out of his life. In March 1628, Sir Henry Goodyer, Donne's most faithful correspondent, died, soon to be followed by Christopher Brooke, who had stood affectionately and illegally by Donne in the secret marriage to Anne More. Donne was assailed not only by bereavement but by ill health. During the last six months of 1629 he was incapacitated and unable to carry on his cherished preaching duties. He returned to the pulpit early in 1630, but became gravely ill again in the summer of that year. Thus we are brought to those months immediately preceding Donne's last sermon, months which he spent with his daughter Constance and her husband, Samuel Harvey, at Aldborough Hatch in Essex. Letters written in January 1631, so shortly before Donne's final journey into the pulpit, record the progress of his malady; an excerpt from a letter to Mrs. Cokain tells of his condition:

"I have never good temper, nor good pulse, nor good appetite, nor good sleep. Yet I have so much leisure to recollect myself, as that I can think I have been long thus, or often thus. I am not alive, because I have not had enough upon me to kill me, but because it pleases God to pass me through many infirmities before He take me either by those particular remembrances to bring me to particular repentances, or by them to give me hope of His particular mercies in heaven. Therefore have I been more affected with coughs in vehemence, more with deafness, more with toothache, more with the vurbah (?uvula), than heretofore." (G ii:269-270)

Six weeks later Donne was in the pulpit at Whitehall.

Walton gives us a general account of the latter part of Donne's life. He tells us that it was a "continued study," that Donne "usually preached once a week" or oftener,[21]

[21] Such activity, of course, would not be true of his periods of illness.

and that as soon as he finished one sermon he turned to preparation of the next one, choosing his text, organizing his material, consulting the relevant writings of the Church Fathers, and then committing the sermon to memory (W:67). Walton also comments briefly on the pastoral life of a man whose ministerial activity, in contrast to George Herbert's, is usually thought of in terms of its preaching rather than its pastoral work. We are told that Donne frequently visited the afflicted; that he displayed many evidences of charity to prisoners, penurious scholars, and others whose financial needs were known to him; and that his willing and successful efforts at reconciliation frequently resolved the family difficulties of his friends (W:70-71).

Following the preaching of "Death's Duel," the five remaining weeks of Donne's life were devoted to meticulous preparations for death, which, it seems, he faced with equanimity. A conversation which Walton records as taking place the day after the sermon indicates Donne's assurance that he had been truly called to the priesthood: " '. . . looking back upon my life past,' " he says, " 'I now plainly see it was his [God's] hand that prevented me from all temporal employment; and that it was his Will I should never settle nor thrive till I entred into the Ministry." The conversation ends on a note of joyful hope; after a word about his sins, he concludes: " '. . . yet, I know he [God] looks not upon me now as I am of my self, but as I am in my Saviour, and hath given me even at this present time some testimonies by his Holy Spirit, that I am of the number of his Elect: *I am therefore full of unexpressible joy, and shall dye in peace*' " (W:76-77).

Walton's account of Donne's last days is dramatically told (W:75-82). The Dean's conversations, his meditations on this world and the next, his summoning of good friends to his bedside for a final farewell and benediction, his instructions to his servants that affairs be put in order—

[33]

all of this we might expect. But of a more striking nature is that macabre and wonderful tale of the preparation of his monument. Persuaded by his physician, Dr. Simeon Foxe, to have a monument made before his death, Donne went imaginatively to work. He "sent for a Carver to make for him in wood the figure of an *Vrn*," and requested that a board of his own height be brought to him with the carving. Summoning a painter, he had some charcoal fires lighted in his study, took off his clothes, and had a winding-sheet placed around him and fitted as it later would be on his corpse. And thus he stood on the urn, "his eyes shut, and with so much of the sheet turned aside as might shew his lean, pale, and death-like face, which was purposely turned toward the East, from whence he expected the second coming of his and our Saviour Jesus." The picture drawn, Donne had it placed by his bed that he might reflect upon it until his death. Upon his death, his executor, Dr. Henry King, commissioned a marble monument to be sculptured in imitation of the picture. This monument, bearing above it Donne's self-composed epitaph, stands in St. Paul's Cathedral, where Donne's body rests.

To Isaak Walton may be entrusted the last words of this brief chapter on the life and death of John Donne: "Thus *variable*, thus *vertuous* was the Life; thus *excellent*, thus *exemplary* was the Death of this memorable man" (W:82).

CHAPTER TWO

Dr Donne Views his Calling

THE PRIEST

When God plac'd *Adam* in the world, God enjoyed *Adam* to fill the world, to subdue the world, and to rule the world; when God plac'd him in Paradise, He commanded him to dress Paradise, and to keep Paradise; when God plac'd his children in the land of promise, he enjoyned them to fight his battails against Idolatry, and to destroy Idolators; to every body some errand, some task for his glory . . . . (D viii:177)

FOR some years before his ordination in 1615, John Donne seemed to be casting about for "some errand." As early as June 1607 Thomas Morton had sought to persuade him "to wave . . . [his] Court-hopes, and enter into holy Orders" (W:33) and had offered him a benefice of his own. But Donne was not ready. His reply to Morton was a gracious and an unequivocal negative: he feared that the known irregularities of his life might bring dishonor upon the office; he was not clear in his conscience that an acceptance would be motivated primarily by his desire to serve to the glory of God (W:34-35). The outer course of Donne's life from the time of Morton's proposal to that day in January when he did "enter into holy Orders" has been traced; the inner course—the conscious motivations which he may have kept to himself and the subconscious ones which escaped even his powers of introspection—this course can be drawn less clearly. It is possible that Donne through to his death pursued an "errand," to use his term, which would rebound to his own glory rather than that of God; but his words and deeds suggest, at least to me, that his decision of 1615 was what he honestly felt to be a response to God's call.

The quotation which heads this chapter is an expression of what is known as the doctrine of calling or of vocation, a doctrine central to Biblical thought and, with certain variations, prominent in most political and social philosophies. An understanding of it is important in this present context since it is related both to Donne's entrance into the priesthood and to his concept of the role of the priest. In the Judeo-Christian tradition, as Donne's remarks about Adam would indicate, God is viewed as calling every man, each in his own way, to his service and to his Kingdom. Thus Adam was called to fill, subdue, and rule the world; his failure to respond obediently to the call resulted in his exclusion from the Paradise which he had been commanded to dress and keep. Abraham was called from his native land to go forth and people the earth with God's chosen ones. Moses was later called from his shepherding to be the leader of his people in their exodus from Egypt and to climb Mount Sinai for the revelation of the Law. The whole of Biblical history is a series of calls by God to his creatures. And Donne was, of course, familiar not only with the Old and the New Testament records of God's calls, but also with the extension of the doctrine of calling enunciated by Luther and then by Calvin. Luther, convinced that Rome had misinterpreted the doctrine by setting the priesthood above other Christian callings and by affirming that priests were possessed of a higher degree of God's righteousness and favor than others, insisted that the faithful housewife in the kitchen or laborer in the fields had as fully blessed and Christian a vocation as the preacher of the Word and celebrant of the sacraments.

The concept of vocation is not confined to the Bible; one of its classical expressions is found in Plato's *Republic*. It is true, of course, that Plato did not envisage a Judeo-Christian God calling every man to a specific task, but he was convinced that every man had his peculiar skill and that the health of the body politic depended upon a discovery of that skill and a putting it to use; the New Testament parable of the talents would doubtlessly have received his favor. Every man in the *Republic* was to have his particular place, and the decay of Plato's Utopia would have its source in the pretensions of a man to do anything other than that for which he was best fitted. This belief that an orderly world was dependent upon every man's doing what he was intrinsically best able to do was a part of the philosophical thought of western civilization at least from fifth-century Greece through the Age of the Enlightenment.[1] In Donne's own time one clear expression of this conviction was found in Shakespeare's *Troilus and Cressida,* when Ulysses tells Agamemnon that the Greeks can attribute their lethargy at the Trojan gates to the fact that rightful order has been discarded—"The specialty of rule hath been neglected." When the planets forget their rightful order, the sea rages and the earth shakes; when men forget their proper place and degree, the human community is shaken: "Take but degree away, untune that string," Ulysses laments, "And hark what discord follows!" And certainly the center of eighteenth-century philosophical thought affirmed that the whole creation was compounded of an unbroken continuum stretching from the angels of heaven through man, animal, vegetable, and mineral, a chain of spirit and matter which attested to the architectural skill and supernatural foresight of the Creator.

Donne's remark about Adam and his duties is found in a Lenten sermon on St. Stephen, delivered at Whitehall on February 29, 1628. The significance of the text—"And when he had said this, he fell a sleep" (Acts 7:60)—is that

[1] For the most thorough exposition of this concept of order, see Arthur O. Lovejoy, *The Great Chain of Being* (Cambridge, Massachusetts: Harvard University Press, 1936).

Stephen, to whose final words and martyr's death the text refers, so followed God's call to him in this life that he passed from this natural world in a death that was but a sleep, a rest from his earthly afflictions and a rest that would culminate in his resurrection into glory. Donne urges each member of his congregation faithfully to carry out the duties of his particular calling, pointing out, with St. Stephen as an example, that a man's response to his calling will determine the nature of his death and of his eternity. He illustrates his contention by drawing concrete pictures of two dying men, one whose slovenly life leads to a death which is a nightmare, the other whose disciplined existence leads to the sleep of Stephen. Donne speaks directly to the first man, sketching the horror of the last moment: "To see the Blood of Christ, imputed, not to thee, but to thy Sinnes; To see Christ crucified, and not crucifyed for thee, but crucified by thee; To heare this blood speake, not better things, then the blood of *Abel*, but lowder for vengeance then the blood of *Abel* did" (D viii:189). And how contrasting is the future of the man who follows the way of Stephen; that man will enter the gate and dwell in the house "where there shall be no Cloud nor Sun, no darkenesse nor dazling, but one equall light, no noyse nor silence, but one equall musick, no fears nor hopes, but one equal possession, no foes nor friends, but one equall communion and Identity, no ends nor beginnings, but one equall eternity" (D viii:191).

To question the view that every man has in this world his own specific place and the responsibility for carrying out its duties is to question the wisdom and economy of the Creator himself. And many are Donne's rebukes against idleness, against deafness to one's calling. "He that undertakes no course," he writes, "no *vocation*, he is no part, no member, no limbe of the body of this world; no eye, to give light to others; no eare to receive profit by others" (D iv:160). At another time, describing the world as a theater in which every man has been assigned a role, and as an organ in which every man should play a part, he berates the man who would be a mere spectator at the theater or an idle listener to the organ. This particular passage Donne concludes with a touch of sarcasm which seldom finds its way into his sermons: "Thinkest thou to eat bread, and not sweat? Hast thou a prerogative above the common Law of Nature? Or must God insert a particular clause of exemption for thy sake?" (D 1:207-208).

It is God's will "that every man should embrace a Calling, and walk therein; they who do not so, pervert Gods order" (D vii:149). To reject one's vocation is thus demonic, is a sin against the proper structure of the created world. To this concept of order Donne turns illuminatingly in a sermon on the text of Psalms 32:9: "Be not as the horse, or the mule, who have no understanding; whose mouth must be held in with bit and bridle, lest they come neere unto thee." He points out that a person is ordered to maintain his proper place in the creation and not to descend into a lower nature. To degenerate into beastliness is to offend the creation, and it is man alone of all created beings and objects who does so. Tigers and wolves, herbs and plants, the sea, the earth, and all the other planets— all these maintain their order and carry out their function, "and onely Man himselfe disorders all, and that by displacing himselfe, by losing his place." (D ix:371-373)

For man not to act out his assigned role in this complex and wonderful creation was to John Donne, as to many before and after him, simply suicidal. The person who bends no ear and no hand to his calling is no man, is nothing. And the man who chooses to be nothing in this world will be nothing in the next. He must realize not only that he possesses an individual life, a unique place in the world of space and time, but that he is called also to a social life, a life in the world of men: ". . . he may no more take himself away from the world, then he may make himself away out of the world. For he that dies so, by withdrawing himself from his calling, from the labours of mutual society in this life, that man *kills himself,* and God calls him not" (D 1:209-210). Or, to put it another way, this time on the authority of St. Basil and St. Chrysostom, the man who abstains from the "labours of mutual society" is like the ant, which labors only for itself; but the person who has some sense of social responsibility is like the bee, which labors for others (D iii:232). In his first sermon as Vicar of St. Dunstan's in the West, when he had his own calling very much on his mind, Donne preached much the same doctrine: ". . . every man is bound to marry himselfe to a profession, to a calling: God hath brought him from being *nothing,* by creating him, but he resolves himselfe into nothing againe, if he take no calling upon him" (D vi:84-85).

It is to his first two sermons to this congregation at St. Dunstan's that we now turn. Donne's insistence upon the importance of accepting a vocation is clear, and it is of interest to note precisely what he felt to be the proper nature and function of his own calling, the priesthood. Donne was called to St. Dunstan's in the spring of 1624 and, on April 11 and 25, he preached on the ideal relationship between a minister and his congregation. The central image of the first sermon in his new benefice is, appropriately, that of marriage: just as a spiritual marriage exists between Jesus Christ and the bride which is the entire Christian Church, so does one exist between each individual minister and his particular parish. Implicit in any healthy marriage are the qualities of honor and labor; in the union between minister and congregation, the congregation must show him due honor and respect, and he in turn must be willing to shoulder for them certain labors. God, in his mercy, calls a min-

ister to a particular congregation and calls upon him to
preach the Word and administer the sacraments, by means
of which his charges are brought to a holy obedience and
an honorable service to the Lord. The minister, married as
he is to his flock, should exercise the power and authority
which befit a husband's relationship to his wife, and yet remember that his every act should be rooted in love. Au-
thoritatively and lovingly, the preacher must denounce the
sins of his parishioners, thus leading them to that conviction of sin which brings the soul to repentance. As God's
original intentions for marriage were to provide man and
woman mutually with a helpmate and to provide for the
procreation and education of children, so are priest and parish to find mutual comfort in one another, and so is the
priest as husband to assist in the regeneration of God's children that they may inherit Heaven. If that spirit of love
which should bind together every husband and his wife
exists between shepherd and sheep, if it comes to exist between John Donne and his St. Dunstan's congregation, then
he will be able to reprove them without bitterness, and
they will be able to accept his rebukes in the loving spirit
with which they are given. (D vi:81-94)

By the end of the second sermon, delivered just two
weeks later, the people of St. Dunstan's had a real sense of
what to expect of their new vicar and of themselves, for
Donne was never more explicit about his views on the minister's role than in those early days at Isaak Walton's church.
His text of April 25—"Come ye children, hearken unto
me, I will teach you the fear of the Lord" (Psalm 34:11)
—served well to show what Donne felt to be at the very
center of his calling. At this center was the sermon, the
proclamation of the Word, for to teach the fear of the
Lord is to preach the Word of the Lord. If either the
Psalmist or Donne should be challenged as to his right to
a hearing, his right to teach such weighty matters and to

preach such mysteries, he must answer that any one who
has been called by the Lord to his ministry comes in the
name of the Lord—a fully sufficient authority. The Word
of the Lord, Holy Scripture, is open for all to see, but not
for all to understand, and it is the called one who may open
the eyes and ears of understanding. Donne goes on to make
an interesting distinction between a man's calling or office
or rank and his person. It is an unfortunate perversity, he
asserts, when a congregation will not heed a preacher unless they like him as a person, when they "more respect
the *man*, then the *Ministery*, and his *manner* of delivering
it, then the *message* that he delivers." Donne carries his
argument a step further when he writes that "what names
soever we brought into the world by our extraction from
this or that family, what name soever we took in our *baptisme*, and contract between God and us, that name, in
which we come to you, is . . . *The Ministers of Christ, The
Stewards of the Mysteries of God. . . .*" The congregation
must simply have faith that God does not call those who
are not fit, or, if he does call them, that he will make fit
ones of the unfit. Donne's examples of men in the latter
classification are well chosen—Moses, Jeremiah, and Isaiah.
When Moses complained that the Israelites had not listened to him and that the Pharaoh would not listen to him
of uncircumcised lips, the Lord circumcised Moses' lips and
provided Aaron as his prophet and spokesman. When Jeremiah lamented that he could not speak for God because he
was a child, the Lord provided him with the power of
speech. When Isaiah woefully protested that he was a man
of unclean lips dwelling among a people of unclean lips,
the Lord sent a seraph bearing a live coal in his hand; and
when the coal was laid upon Isaiah's mouth, taking away
his iniquity and purging his sin, he was ready to go forth
proclaiming the Lord's way. In short, the congregation at
St. Dunstan's must entrust to God the preparing of his

ministers, and if ministers—John Donne among them—do possess some of the infirmities common to all mankind, the parishioners must be content to overlook the weaknesses and focus their attention on the fact that these men have been called by the Lord. (D vi:102-104)

Evidence that Donne considered carefully the duties of his calling extends well beyond his initial sermons at St. Dunstan's. For the most part he proceeds by metaphor to enumerate the many qualities and responsibilities of the man who has been summoned by God to call others to his Kingdom through diligent and obedient service on this earth. Not only is the preacher a husband to his congregation: he is an archer, a watchman, a trumpeter, a harmonious charmer; he possesses the most desirable qualities of a lion, an ox, an eagle, and a man; he is an earthquake, a son of thunder, the fall of waters, the roaring of a lion.

In one of his many sermons on the Thirty-eighth Psalm, Donne describes the preacher as the hand that shoots the arrows of the Lord. The text is the second verse—"For thine arrowes stick fast in me, and thy hand presseth me sore." Arrows, in Biblical terms, are the metaphorical equivalent of God's indignation, the expression of his wrath. Donne tells us that "these arrows which are lamented here, are all those miseries, which sinne hath cast upon us" (D ii:55). But convinced as he is that the punishments of God are primarily medicinal, he asserts that the arrows are not simply a cause for lamentation, for they are more corrective than punitive; to be sure they are arrows which are miseries, but they are also arrows which drew tears of repentance from Mary Magdalene and from Peter, arrows that cast one down that he might be raised up. They are delivered by God through the mouths of his servants, his preachers; consequently, every preacher who is moved by the Holy Ghost becomes "the deliverer of Gods arrows" (D ii:68).

In another sermon the minister is at once watchman, trumpeter, and harmonious charmer. Donne is indebted to Ezekiel 33:7 for the watchman metaphor, and he employs it to emphasize the necessary vantage point which a minister must have if he is to "shake, and shiver, and throw down the refractory and rebellious soul, whose incredulity will not admit the History, and whose security in presumptuous sins will not admit the working and application of those Merits and Mercies which are proposed to him" (D 11:164). God makes of his ministers watchmen, placing them upon watchtowers that they may take advantage of their high position to look down upon the vast panorama of all the sins of this world. With his view of this corruption the preacher is to blast upon his tuba or trumpet, terrorizing his people by waking them to a conviction of their sins. The trumpet blast and the ensuing terror are not enough, however, for terror alone could lead to a despair of God's mercies. And so, in the second movement of this homiletic symphony, the preacher "shall become *Carmen musicum*, a musical and harmonious charmer, to settle and compose the soul again in a reposed confidence, and in a delight in God: he shall be *musicum carmen*, musick, harmony to the soul in his matter; he shall preach harmonious peace to the conscience. . . ." (D 11:164-167)

Donne seemed particularly fond of discoursing on his profession before the congregation at St. Dunstan's. He did not speak his last word on the matter in those spring sermons of 1624; on Trinity Sunday, 1627, he described in the most metaphorical detail the proper nature of the minister, using as his text Revelation 4:8: "And the foure beasts had each of them sixe wings about him, and they were full of eyes within; and they rest not day and night, saying, Holy, holy, holy, Lord God Almighty, which was, and is, and is to come." The division is in two parts: what the creatures were, and what the creatures did. Donne has found thirty interpretations of what the creatures signify: scholars have identified them as the four monarchies, the four patriarchs, the four doctors of the Church, the four cardinal virtues, the four elements, the four quarters of the world. But to him they are the four evangelists and, by extension, all ministers of the Gospel. The verse before the text describes the four beasts as having the faces, in order, of a lion, a calf or an ox, a man, and an eagle. Donne follows St. Ambrose in suggesting that the four creatures actually make up one creature, and he goes on, in a striking passage, to insist that "every Minister of God is to have all, that all foure had; the courage of a *Lion*, the labouriousness of an *Oxe*, the perspicuity and cleare sight of the *Eagle*, and the humanity, the discourse, the reason, the affability, the appliableness of a *Man*" (D VIII:41). The minister must have a courage which will shield him from the rigors of persecution and the temptations of preferment. He must achieve the industriousness of an ox, being neither "over-growne, nor stall-fed," and he must be careful that his labors are expended upon those pursuits which clear the understanding, strengthen the conscience, and edify the souls of his congregation to their salvation. He must have the clear vision of an eagle, enabling him to see and move against the sins of his parishioners and to look into the brilliant light of God's truth rather than being diverted by the false and schismatic tendencies of his day. And he must possess the gentleness, persuasiveness, and reasonableness of man, always seeking to distinguish between the fundamental matters and the more flexible matters of Christian faith and practice, always succoring the reason and understanding as well as the faith of his parishioners, and always seeking to lead them to their reconciliation with God. (D VIII:37-43)

The beasts identified, literally and symbolically, Donne can now discourse, again allegorically, on their wings, which are beneficial both to their possessors and to those who receive the beasts' ministrations. They serve to raise the minister above the entanglements of this earth and at the same time to enable him to care for the souls of his people. With a reference to Deuteronomy 32:11—the verse telling of the eagle which stirs up her nest, flutters over her young, spreads her wings, and bears her young upon them—Donne draws his analogy. The minister resembles the eagle in that he too must stir the attention of his congregation; then flutter, indeed clap, his wings thunderously as he proclaims the Lord's judgments on sinners; then spread his wings over his people to assure them that God's wrath is countered by his mercy; then take them, bearing them aloft so that they may see their Lord in Heaven soliciting their cause before God the Father. The Deuteronomic text having served to clarify the propriety of engrafting wings upon a minister, Donne turns to Isaiah 6:2 to account for the necessity of six wings. Isaiah in his vision beheld the seraphim standing above the Lord, each with six wings, two to cover his face, two to cover his feet, and two with which to fly. The seraphim of Isaiah, Donne affirms, are to be identified with the beasts of John. And like the seraphim, the ministers of God are to cover their faces, not so completely as to hide their identity or stifle the voice of pure doctrine, yet enough to manifest their inability fully to look upon the great mysteries of God. As their covered faces are directed primarily to God and indicate their modest disposition not to pry too curiously into God's mysteries, so are their covered feet directed primarily to the congregation; a man's feet are symbolic of his actions, and their covering should deter the congregation from searching immodestly into all the actions of the minister. God would not have his children pay such rapt attention to the prophet's feet that they fail to hear and heed the inspired words which flow from his mouth. It is to the minister's two middle wings that the congregation should pay most attention, for it is these wings which effect the preaching of the Word and the celebrating of the sacraments, the nurturing of all those bodies and souls under the minister's care. (D VIII:43-49)

These remarkable six-winged beasts are also "full of eyes," a happy fact, since the wings of a minister would be of little value either to himself or to his congregation had he not the eyes to show him where to fly. For he must not only fly but know his proper direction; he must not be a victim of blind obedience, but must exercise a wise and discriminating judgment in carrying out the duties of his office; he must have the eyes, lacking in his Roman brethren, by which he may "discerne be-tweene Religion and Rebellion, betweene a Traytor and a Martyr." The good minister is full of eyes: eyes in his tongue that, distinguishing between the presumptuous and the downcast, it may reprove the former and inspirit the latter; eyes in his ears that they may be sensitive enough to listen "neither to a superstitious sense from Rome, nor to a seditious sense of Scriptures from the Sepa-ration"; eyes in his hands that they may have the vision to serve no master but God; and spiritual eyes in his bodily eyes that they may view with charity the deeds of others. Finally, the good minister is full of eyes within, by means of which he may watch over the salvation of his own soul as well as the souls of other men. (D VIII:49-50)

The beasts now having been fully identified, Donne can turn to the second part of his sermon: what do the beasts do? Above all, the beasts—and the ministers whom they symbolize—speak; they spend their lives declaring the glory of God. Every Christian should heed Donne's in-struction: "Be thou *Verbum* too, A Word, as God was; A Speaking, and a Doing Word, to his glory, and the edi-

fication of others." Moreover, God's spokesmen should
be as assiduous and constant as the beasts of the text, who
"rest not day and night." Their rest, their Sabbath, will
come only when all the cares of this world are behind
them, and their rest will then be eternal. And what are
they to proclaim day and night? They are to proclaim the
Trinity, which, as John and Isaiah and all expositors agree,
is confessed in the threefold repetition, *"Holy, holy, holy."*
They are also to declare God's eternity and the coming
Judgment Day, which are expressed by the words *"which
was, and is, and is to come."* The more blessed a man is,
the more he is called upon to declare the glory of God
to other men; and the man who is called to be priest,
enjoying as he does a large measure of the Lord's blessing,
must always speak his praise. (D VIII:51-60)

Even with our notice of the six-winged, many-eyed,
ever-proclaiming beasts we have not come to the end of
Donne's metaphoric variation. The ministers of God possess still additional powers, sweepingly enumerated in the
following passage: ". . . His ministers are an *Earth-quake*,
and shake an earthly soule; They are the *sonnes of thunder*,
and scatter a cloudy conscience; They are the fall of waters,
and carry with them whole Congregations; 3000 at a
Sermon, 5000 at a Sermon, a whole City, such a City as
Niniveh at a Sermon; and they are as the roaring of a
Lion, where the Lion of the tribe of Juda, cries down the
Lion that seekes whom he may devour . . ." (D VII:396).

In the sermons there is ample evidence of Donne's conviction that every man is called by God to some vocation
and way of life, and of his eagerness to make clear his understanding of the nature and obligations of his own
calling. His persistence in analyzing his calling is of one
piece with the careful self-examination which we find in
his *Devotions*, in much of his religious poetry, and in some
of his love poetry. When in the sermons he turns to his

descriptions of the priesthood, he does so with a nice sense of dramatic presentation, making full use of a wide range of metaphor, and with a readiness to play upon various allegorical interpretations of Scripture. Donne was fully aware of the nature of his calling and the holiness of its offices.

THE TEMPLE

One of the many remarkable characteristics of Donne's sermons is the quality of their teaching. As insistent as Richard Hooker on the reasonableness of religion and equally opposed to a blind faith, he wishes his congregation to be as "full of eyes" as St. John's four six-winged beasts. And if he was persistent in making clear to himself and to his people the nature of his calling, he was equally persistent in expounding the nature of that body to which all Christians are called, the Church. The Articles of Religion to which Donne and his fellow Anglicans subscribed had, following John Calvin, succinctly defined the Church as "a congregation of faithful men, in the which the pure Word of God is preached, and the Sacraments be duly ministered according to Christ's ordinance in all those things that of necessity are requisite to the same" (Article xix). The faithful men of every particular congregation are directly related to those of every other congregation, all being members of the same one body, catholic and indivisible. Donne approvingly quotes Tertullian's statement that "the whole Church of God is one household"; all individual congregations which "agree in the unity of that doctrine which the Apostles taught, and adhere to the supreme head of the whole Church, Christ Jesus" are members of that household (D iii:138). No Romanist would have disputed him on this, though there were some significant disagreements in their respective interpretations of the apostles' teachings.

The word *Church* designates not only a body of believers, either in terms of a single group of persons united in one parish or the entire body of the Communion of Saints, wherever they may be found. It also denotes a building consecrated to the glory of God. The sermon from which we learn most about Donne's views regarding the church as a place of worship was preached in the spring of 1619 at Lincoln's Inn, where plans were under way to build a chapel, where funds were needed, and where gifts might be expected to come more readily from those who understood that a chapel was more than the building materials which went into its making. After some early general remarks on the virtue of charity, Donne speaks specifically of the application of this virtue to the building of a sanctuary. Directing himself first to those persons who might argue that God can be worshiped at any place and that lavish expenditures on chapels or churches are unnecessary, Donne astutely accepts their argument and then goes on to give it full documentation, furnishing his hearers with a host of examples to prove that God indeed can be and has been worshiped in many strange and seemingly unpromising places. Any man who properly prepares himself and reverently disposes himself may lift up his prayers to God and hear his answer. Job's church was a dunghill; Hezekiah's a bed; Jeremiah's a dungeon; Jonah's the belly of a whale; Daniel's the den of lions; Shadrach, Meshach, and Abednego's a fiery furnace; Peter's and Paul's a prison; and the repentant thief's the Cross itself. But if these examples show that God is confined to no one place and may go where he will to meet his worshipers, they in no way alter the fact that God is to be found by most people in that place where he has promised primarily to manifest himself—in a building known as a church. And, Donne continues, it has been the admirable custom from the days of primitive Christianity to build churches to the glory of God. (D II:213-218)

Having established the fact that the church has been traditionally the focal point of man's worship, Donne goes on to suggest its rich and manifold nature, both as a society of people and as a place, by enumerating some of the names by which it has been known. First it was called *Ecclesia*, meaning company or congregation. The importance of this particular name lies in its indication that men generally worship in a body and that, though "every earnest, and zealous, and spiritually valiant Man, may take hold of it [the Kingdom of Heaven]," the fact remains that Christ has promised to be present whenever two or three are gathered together in his name. Another designation is *Dominicum*, meaning Lord's possession, a name which should be kept in mind particularly by Rome, where the Papal hierarchy would seemingly seek to usurp the place of the Lord. Still other names are *Domus Dei*, God's dwelling house, and *Basilica*, his court. But none of these names signifies the full meaning of the church quite so adequately as the word *Temple*, derived from *Tuendo*. "*Tueri*," writes Donne, "signifies both our beholding, and contemplating *God* in the Church: and it signifies Gods protecting, and defending those that are his, in his Church." (D II:220-221)

The Church is to Donne all these things and more, as we learn when we turn to some of his more arresting metaphoric equivalents. In his earliest extant sermon he describes it as "the Magazine of his [Christ's] graces" (D I:167). A decade later he uses a musical image, defining the Church as "the *Trumpet* in which God sounds his *Judgements*, and the *Organ*, in which he delivers his *mercy*" (D VI:283). It is a fold, an ark, a net, a city, a kingdom (D VI:152); it is typified by Noah's ark, and as the clean beasts of the ark outnumbered the unclean, so

do the elect of the Church outnumber the lost (D VI:155).
The Holy Ghost comforts us with the assurance that the
Church is "A Jordan to wash thine originall leprosie in
Baptisme; A City upon a mountaine, to enlighten thee
in the works of darknesse; a continuall application of all
that Christ Jesus said, and did, and suffered, to thee" (D
VII:232).

Donne had a word for those who might argue that
they could carry on their worship without benefit of church
attendance. Though private or family worship is, of course,
to be encouraged, yet it is no substitute for the prayers,
the teaching, and the celebration of the sacraments which
take place when the members of the body come together
in community worship:

"Chamber-prayers, single, or with your family, Chamber-
Sermons, Sermons read over there; and Chamber-Sacra-
ments, administred in necessity there, are blessed assist-
ants, and supplements; they are as the almes at the gate,
but the feast is within; they are as a cock of water without,
but the Cistern is within; *habenti dabitur*; he that hath
a handfull of devotion at home, shall have his devotion
multiplyed to a Gomer here; for when he is become a part
of the Congregation, he is joynt-tenant with them, and
the devotion of all the Congregation, and the blessings
upon all the Congregation, are his blessings, and his devotions" (D VII:292).

That such exhortations to church attendance were needed
in Donne's day is made clear through two of the most
authoritative documents of his Church. Richard Hooker,
in his *Of the Laws of Ecclesiastical Polity*, distinguished
between private prayer and public and enumerated the
greater advantages of the latter: congregational worship
is worthier than private devotions "as a whole society . . .
exceedeth the worth of any one"; public prayers are more

comforting because "the things we ask publicly are approved as needful and good in the judgment of all, we hear them sought for and desired with common consent"; not only is congregational worship of greater benefit to each individual who partakes in it but "the whole Church is much bettered by our good example."[2] In addition, *The Second Tome of Homilies*, that collection of religious exhortations which served as a guide to sound doctrine and right practice in the Church of England, in speaking of Christ, his apostles, and the Church Fathers, states "That albeit they certainely knew that their prayers were heard in what place soeuer they made them, though it were in caues, in woodes, and in deserts, yet (so oft as they could conueniently) they resorted to the materiall Temples, there with the rest of the congregation, to ioyne in prayer and true worship."[3]

The ultimate question to ask about any doctrine of the Church is its view of the relationship between Church and salvation: in what ways is the Church a means to or an instrument of redemption? is salvation possible outside the bounds of the Body of Christ? is church membership in itself an assurance of salvation? Donne turns to these questions many times, never more effectively or movingly than in a sermon on the text of Matthew 21:44: "Whosoever shall fall on this stone, shall be broken; but on whomsoever it shall fall, it will grinde him to powder."

[2] Book v, chapter xxiv, sections 1-2. All quotations from Hooker are from the Reverend John Keble's edition of *The Works of that Learned and Judicious Divine Mr. Richard Hooker* (Oxford at the University Press, 1836). For the convenience of those who may wish to consult another edition, I have referred to the Book, chapter, and section of *Of the Laws of Ecclesiastical Polity.*

[3] *The Second Tome of Homilies, of Svch Matters as Were Promised, and entituled in the former part of Homilies. Set out by the authority of the late Queenes Maiestie: and to be read in euery Parish Church agreeablie* (London, 1623), p. 128. *The Second Tome* is bound with and follows *Certaine Sermons or Homilies appointed to be read in Chvrches, In the time of the late Queene Elizabeth of famous memory* (London, 1623).

Every man is subject to one of the two classifications of the text: as sinner, he either falls or is fallen upon. The stone is Christ, who is to be found in the Church; the man who faithfully embraces the Church will not be free from sin, but the fall which his sin occasions will be intercepted by the stone or the Christ to whom he entrusts his salvation: ". . . for this man that fals there [in the Church], fals not so desperately, as that he feeles nothing between hell and him, nothing to stop at, nothing to check him by the way, *Cadit super*, he falls upon some thing; nor he falls not upon flowers, to wallow and tumble in his sinne, nor upon feathers, to rest and sleep in his sinne, nor into a cooling river, to disport, and refresh, and strengthen himself in his sinne; but he falls upon a stone, where he may receive a bruise, a pain upon his fall, a remorse of that sinne that he is fallen into . . ." (D II:190). To put it another way, the nurture of the Church is instrumental in bringing man to a conviction of his sin. Whereas the person not nourished by the teaching and discipline of the Church will respond to his sin only as a pleasant diversion to be pursued, the faithful church member will find his fall broken by the stone which is Christ, by the sharp recognition of how far short he comes of the righteousness which is God's will for man. His fall is a fortunate one, bringing with it that remorse and contrition which lead to repentance and to being pieced together again. The instruments of this salvation are the instruments of the Church—"the Word . . . the Sacraments, and other medicinall institutions of Christ in his Church." But the sinner whose fall is not intercepted by such "medicinall institutions" will fall until, at the Last Judgment, he will in turn be fallen upon by the stone, ground into powder, and forever denied that peace which may be reached through the Church of Jesus Christ. (D II:188-196)

Donne did not, however, take the next step and declare

that there was no salvation outside the Church. He maintained a nice balance in regard to this problem, neither minimizing to the members of his congregation the tremendous blessing which the Church was as a means of salvation to them, nor peremptorily denying salvation to all those who may never have had the opportunity to know Christ through the Word and the sacraments. In his Easter sermon of 1622 on the doctrine of the resurrection, he hints that some of the Church Fathers may in their tenderness have been too enthusiastic in their views regarding the salvation of pagans, but he at the same time rebukes those who would too severely limit the extent of God's mercy. His position is essentially twofold: the Christian congregation, to which God has revealed himself through Christ and his Church, must seek its salvation only through the institution ordained for that purpose; but the Christian must not inquire too curiously into the ways in which God may extend his mercy to others:

"To me, to whom God hath revealed his Son, in a Gospel, by a Church, there can be no way of salvation, but by applying that Son of God, by that Gospel, in that Church. Nor is there any other foundation for any, nor other name by which any can be saved, but the name of Jesus. But how this foundation is presented, and how this name of Jesus is notified to them, amongst whom there is no Gospel preached, no Church established, I am not curious in inquiring. I know God can be as mercifull as those tender Fathers present him to be; and I would be as charitable as they are. And therefore humbly imbracing that manifestation of his Son, which he hath afforded me, I leave God, to his unsearchable waies of working upon others, without farther inquisition." (D IV:78-79)

The frequency of Donne's references to this problem indicates the importance he attributed to it. In one sermon he states that God had many single sheep, persons like Job and Naaman, who were never brought into his flock, and that such examples should dissuade the Christian from affirming that "God *could* not, in the largenesse of his power, or *did* not, in the largenesse of his mercy, afford salvation to some, whom he never gathered into the Christian Church" (D x:170). In another he assures his congregation that some of the many mansions in God's house will be occupied by gentiles and heathens (D II:253). In still another he compares university and Church, pointing out that though the university is the usual place for the acquisition of knowledge, yet some have grown learned elsewhere; and that though the Church is God's customary place for revealing himself, yet some have been enlightened by God outside the Church (D VIII:226).

Such byways to the Kingdom, however, are not open to the Christian congregation, and foolish and presumptuous is the man who, disdaining the Church, seeks to improve upon God's redemptive plan. The Christian should look upon Noah's ark as an image of the Church: the stalwart individual who depends on his own morality and righteousness, who prays outside the Church and not in the name of Jesus, has as much chance of salvation as the strongest of swimmers who, in Noah's time, was not on the ark—both can only sink deeper and deeper into the waters of death (D IX:319). Donne reproves the person who would set himself up as a "little Church," as a microcosm of God's own Church, telling him that if he has no more corn, oil, or milk than grows in himself, he will starve; that if he has no more seals of grace or absolution of sin than he can give himself, he will perish (D VII:232-233). For the Christian the only way to the Church Triumphant is through the Church Militant; indeed, the two are one, with the Church of this earth serving as the porch leading

into the chancel which is the dwelling place of the risen
Communion of Saints (D vii:340).

The sermon which speaks perhaps most eloquently about
the glory of the Church was delivered at St. Paul's on
Christmas day, 1628, on the text, "Lord, who hath beleeved
our report?" Donne preaches on the three uses of the verse
found in Isaiah 53:1, John 12:38, and Romans 10:16.
The first appearance of the verse is a part of the Suffering
Servant passage in which Isaiah prophesies the coming of
Christ; the second refers not to a future Christ, but to the
Lord's miraculous acts on this earth; and the third to the
evidences of his continuing presence in the Church which
he established. (D viii:293-294) Donne's central argument is that God has progressively revealed himself more
fully and unmistakably. To those who could not read
God in Nature or through the Law engraved on their
hearts, he sent his prophets, inspired to proclaim the coming of Christ. To those for whom this was not enough, he
sent the Incarnate Word, whose miracles bore witness to
his Sonship. But for some, not even the words or works of
Christ were or are enough. "Therefore," Donne tells his
congregation, "we have a clearer, that is, a nearer light
then the written Gospell, that is, the Church." The Church
is a "nearer light" because it is the continuing witness of
Christ, the present assurance that Jesus of Nazareth was
the Son of God, empowered to save mankind. It is in the
Church that those priests called by God preach the Word
so that men may hear and, hearing, may believe and, believing, may call upon God for their salvation. (D viii:306-
308)

Powerful and blessed as the Church is, mere membership, or attendance, or outward profession of faith is not
enough for salvation; there is no magical process through
which a man's exposure to the church roll, the church
building, the congregation, the sermon, or the sacraments

will enable him to stand in comfort at the Last Judgment. Hooker in touching upon this subject had made good use of the ark metaphor; he wrote that, so far as we know, we are as lost without the Church as Noah's contemporaries were without the ark; but the ark was more certain than the Church in the sense "that whereas none of them which were in the one could perish, numbers in the other are cast away, because to eternal life our profession is not enough."[4] And Donne casts a more terrible and dramatic warning at those who rest at ease simply because they enjoy nominal church membership: ". . . for a Child may drowne in a Font, and a Man may be poysoned in the Sacrament, much more perish, though in a true Church" (D vi:61).

It is no wonder that Donne calls upon his congregation to take with full seriousness their commitment to the Church, to prepare themselves through meditation for its services, and to maintain an attitude of devotion during its time of worship. The man who comes to church in body only, leaving his soul behind, comes but to his own funeral; and if he comes seeking only earthly praise for his presence, then his reward, appropriately, will be "to be *laid in the earth.*" More than once Donne rails against those who are inattentive or who show disrespect through failing to uncover their heads or to kneel in prayer. But those who come to God's Church humbly and devoutly "come to be *Canonized,* to grow *Saints.*" (D vi:100-101) Donne never lets his auditors forget that the Church ordained for the salvation of mankind is holy ground, to be approached with awe and thanksgiving.

THE WRITTEN WORD

The priest will possess the noblest characteristics of lion, ox, eagle, and man in vain, and the Church, the power of a trumpet and the harmony of an organ in vain, unless

[4] *Works of . . . Hooker,* Book v, chapter lxviii, section 6.

they can turn to some sure authority for their pronouncements and judgments. Their ultimate authority is, of
course, God, of whose being they must be assured and
whose will they must know. Man's knowledge of God and
of his will, which cannot come in this life with a person-
to-person directness, is unfolded in one of two ways,
through God's works or through his Word, through Nature or through Scripture. One of Francis Bacon's persua-
sive arguments for the study of the physical universe is
that such an activity leads to a knowledge of God. Affirming that the Scriptures express God's will and that the
world of creatures attests to his power, Bacon goes on to
say that "the later [latter] is a key unto the former; not
only opening our understanding to conceive the true sense
of the Scriptures, by the general notions of reason and
rules of speech; but chiefly opening our belief, in drawing
us into a due meditation of the omnipotency of God, which
is chiefly signed and engraven upon his works."[5] And
Donne realizes that there was a time when man did not
have the Scriptures on which to rely for a knowledge of
God: "There is an elder booke in the World then the
Scriptures; It is not well said, in the World, for it is the
World it selfe, the whole booke of Creatures . . ." (D
III:264). It was a traditional Christian argument, first expressed in Chapter One of Paul's Epistle to the Romans,
that the creation left the atheist without excuse, for proof
of an Almighty Creator lies in the created universe to be
observed by all men. Yet a purely natural theology, the
knowledge of God which man gains through an observation of the natural world alone, is not in itself sufficient to
bring man to the kind of knowledge of God which carries
with it the comforting assurance of the Creator's power to

[5] *The Advancement of Learning* (1605), *The Works of Francis
Bacon,* collected and edited by James Spedding, Robert Leslie Ellis, and
Douglas Denon Heath (London: Longmans & Co. and others, 1857-
1874), III, 301.

redeem. Bacon writes that we must *"not presume by the contemplation of nature to attain to the mysteries of God."*[6] Calvin argues, furthermore, that since man's original power to perceive God through Nature has become dimmed as a result of his fall, he now needs the Scriptures to serve as spectacles for a clear perception of God; what sufficed for the vision of innocent man is insufficient for fallen man.[7] Donne agrees that a natural theology is not enough:

"The voyce of the Creature alone, is but a faint voyce, a low voyce; nor any voyce, till the voyce of the Word inanimate it; for then when the Word of God hath taught us any mystery of our Religion, then the booke of Creatures illustrates, and establishes, and cherishes that which we have received by faith, in hearing the Word: As a stick bears up, and succours a vine, or any plant, more precious then it selfe, but yet gave it not life at first, nor gives any nourishment to the root now: so the assistance of reason, and the voyce of the Creature, in the preaching of Nature, works upon our faith, but the roote, and the life is in the faith it selfe; The light of nature gives a glimmering before, and it gives a reflection after faith, but the meridianall noone is in faith" (D vi:143).

Thus the book of Creatures and the book of the Word complement each other; the latter, speaking more clearly to man's understanding and faith, is an extension of the former: ". . . the Scriptures are but a paraphrase, but a comment, but an illustration of that booke of Creatures" (D iii:264).

It is to Scripture that priest and Church must turn for the authority behind their teaching and proclamations; and since "Holy Scripture containeth all things necessary to salvation," as the Sixth of the Thirty-nine Articles

---

[6] *Ibid.*, iii, 266.
[7] *Institutes of the Christian Religion*, Book i, chapter vi, section i.

phrases it, then the Bible is sufficient in itself as the ultimate authority for all fundamental matters of religion.
Donne's view of the nature of Scripture and of its proper
interpretation is, of course, of immense importance. He
follows the tradition of the Christian Church in looking
upon the Old Testament as a prophecy of and preparation for the New, which is "a performance of those promises, a fullfiling of those Prophecies, a revelation of those
types and Figures, and an accomplishment, and a possession
of those hopes and those reversions" (D 1:298). The reason
Isaiah, Jeremiah, Ezekiel, and Daniel are called the greater
prophets is not that they wrote more than the twelve so-
called lesser prophets, but that they spoke more of the
coming of Christ and the Christian Church and were thus
closer to the New Testament writers than were the other
prophets (D x:140). Donne refers on various occasions to
the relationship between the two Testaments, summing
up his position perhaps most succinctly in a sermon on the
text of Galatians 3:27: "For, all yee that are baptized into
Christ, have put on Christ." Following Paul, as we might
expect, Donne affirms that the Jews' greatest happiness lay
in their possession of a law which could serve as a schoolmaster to lead them to Christ. But once a man gains faith
in Christ he no longer needs the schoolmaster. "The law
of *Moses* therefore," Donne continues, "binds us not at
all, as it is *his Law*; Whatsoever binds a Christian, in that
law, would have bound him, though there had been no
law given to *Moses*." The ceremonial part of the Law,
consisting of rituals which were types or figures of things
to come in the Christian era, is dead to the Christian, since
the greater realities have now come. The judicial part of
the Law was perfect for the time of Moses, but to think
that all people must follow those laws because God gave
them to one nation makes no more sense than to think that
all men should wear the skins of beasts because God clothed

Adam and Eve in such fashion. The moral part of the
Law, abridged in the Ten Commandments, has always
been written in the hearts of men and would be binding
even if Moses had never written it. (D v:151-152) In
another sermon Donne states that the Gospel, prefigured
though it was in the Law, was like a sealed letter to the
Jew, who was entrusted to carry the letter to the Christian;
when the Christian opens the letter he sees that what was
once prophecy has now become history (D viii:351).

Such an argument is no more a disparagement of the
Old Testament than the belief that the Old Testament
represents an advance over the "booke of Creatures" is a
disparagement of God's creation. God has simply chosen
to reveal himself by degrees. Among the "booke of Creatures" and the two Testaments there are no contradictions;
all move in the same direction, with an increasing clarity
of revelation as we progress from creation to Gospel. Perhaps the best example of this movement in clarity is illustrated in the progressive revelation of the Trinity, so
central to Christian faith. The Trinity is revealed most
clearly in the New Testament, but there are previous evidences of it, not only in the Old Testament but even in
the natural world. A close study of the human soul will
demonstrate how a Trinity may be inferred from the creation. St. Bernard saw *"A Trinity from the Trinity"* in the
three faculties of the soul—the understanding, the will,
and the memory (D ii:72-73). And Donne observes that
man's understanding (analogous to the Father), begets
discourse or ratiocination (analogous to the Son), from
which powers proceed conclusions (analogous to the Holy
Ghost). This argument by analogy, Donne admits, is but
one example of a number of "poore and faint expressions
of the Trinity," but the fact remains that such meditation
on the natural order will help prepare us for a higher
order of revelation, "That comming out of that Schoole,

thou mightest profit the better in that University, having well considered Nature, thou mightest be established in the Scriptures" (D iii:264). Donne also finds various evidences of the Trinity in the Old Testament, and he at different times calls attention to the use of the plural in the verse "Let *us* make man in *our* image," a plural referring to the Trinity. But he admits that such arguments are more in the nature of confirmations for those who already believe in the Trinity, through the light of the New Testament, than of arguments which may convince those who do not already believe. Though Donne is not always perfectly consistent, he is saying in essence that if we but had eyes to see we could perceive—or at the least infer—the triune God through the world of his creation; that failing that, then once we have come to know God through his fullest revelation in the New Testament, we will see that the New Testament message is confirmed through Nature and the Old Testament. The complementary character of God's revealing powers is nowhere better shown than in the following passage: ". . . This distinguishes the two Testaments, The Old is a Testament of *fear*, the New of *love*; yet in this they grow all one, That we determine the Old Testament, in the New, and that we prove the New Testament by the Old; for, but by the Old, we should not know, that there was to bee a New, nor, but for the New, that there was an Old; so the two Testaments grow *one Bible* . . ." (D vi:112).

The Old Testament Apocryphal books posed something of a problem to the churches of the Renaissance. The Roman Church afforded them canonical status; a Puritan like Thomas Cartwright, on the other hand, would not have had them even read in church.[8] The Anglican Church, in its customary middle position, affirmed through the Sixth

---

[8] See Richard Hooker, *Works of . . . Hooker*, footnote 58 to Book v, chapter xx, section 1.

of the Thirty-nine Articles that "the Church doth read (the Apocryphal books) for example of life and instruction of manners; but yet doth it not apply them to establish any doctrine." Hooker, describing his Church's position as one which held "not the Apocrypha for sacred (as we do the holy Scripture) but for human compositions, the subject whereof are sundry divine matters,"[9] would have them read in church for the profitable instruction of the congregation. Donne, of course, adopts the same position. Since the sixty-six canonical books of the Bible state the fundamental doctrines of the Church and are in themselves sufficient for salvation, he looks with considerable disfavor on the Roman practice of elevating the Apocryphal books to the level of the canonical books, viewing this as a part of the customary Papist disposition to undervalue Scripture (D VII:120). To canonize a book which does not belong in the canon is to him a more serious danger than to reject a book which properly belongs there (D IV:218; D VIII:-135). On the other hand, Donne would place the authors of the Apocryphal books above the philosophers (D IV:-333), and he finds a very salutary use for them in the Church. They are not foundations for the establishment of doctrine, but they are of assistance both in establishing the kind of behavior which befits one who wishes to be faithful to the Articles of the Church and in throwing some interpretive light on certain knotty passages in the Old Testament (D VII:385-386).

A greater problem than the relationship between the two Testaments or between canonical and Apocryphal books is the manner of interpreting the words of Scripture. How, for example, is the interpreter to determine whether the Holy Ghost would be understood literally or figuratively? This dilemma was not peculiar to the Renaissance but has extended from the Jewish Philo and the early

[9] *Ibid.*, Book V, chapter xx, section 11.

Church Fathers to our own time. Many of the Church Fathers, St. Augustine among them, interpreted large portions of the Bible, the Old Testament in particular, allegorically, in part because the literal meaning of a passage would often seem unbecoming to or at odds with what must manifestly have been God's intention.[10] But if the literal meaning was deemed unacceptable, one can imagine to what lengths allegorical interpretation, sometimes resting in part upon an overly fertile and ingenious imagination, might go. Donne thinks it wise, wherever possible, to maintain the literal sense of Scripture (D x:194), and he is in this respect in the good company of Hooker, who holds "it for a most infallible rule in expositions of sacred Scripture, that where a literal construction will stand, the farthest from the letter is commonly the worst."[11] One extended statement of Donne's position appears in the introductory paragraph of a sermon preached on a text from the Book of Revelation.[12] He tells us that in Genesis, the danger is to depart from the letter; in Revelation, of adhering too closely to the letter. And he continues in a very significant passage:

"The literall sense is always to be preserved; but the literall sense is not alwayes to be discerned: for the literall sense is not alwayes that, which the very Letter and Grammer of the place presents, as where it is literally said, *That Christ is a Vine*, and literally, *That his flesh is bread*, and literally, *That the new Ierusalem is thus situated, thus built, thus furnished*: But the literall sense of every place,

[10] For a succinct account of the history of Scriptural Interpretation, see articles by Robert M. Grant, John T. McNeill, and Samuel Terrien in *The Interpreter's Bible*, ed. George Arthur Buttrick, Nolan B. Harmon, and others (New York and Nashville: Abingdon-Cokesbury Press, 1951-1957), I, 106-141.

[11] *Works of . . . Hooker*, Book V, chapter lix, section 2.

[12] For still another statement about literal and figurative Scriptural interpretation, see the relevant passage from Donne's *Devotions upon Emergent Occasions*, quoted above, p. 30.

[65]

is the principall intention of the Holy Ghost, in that place: And his principall intention in many places, is to expresse things by allegories, by figures; so that in many places of Scripture, a figurative sense is the literall sense, and more in this book [Revelation] then in any other." (D vi:62)

Donne is, among other things, urging us to recognize a metaphor when we see one.

Donne's most interesting and significant application of this view on Scriptural interpretation is found in the last of three sermons which he preached on the text of 1 Corinthians 15:29: "Else, what shall they doe which are baptized for the dead? If the dead rise not at all, why are they then baptized for the dead?" The Roman Church used this verse as a proof text for its beliefs in prayer for the dead, Purgatory, and indulgences. If Donne would reject these beliefs he must do so by showing that the Holy Ghost was not saying in this verse what the Roman commentators—Cardinal Bellarmine in particular—attributed to him. And when we note that the difference between Bellarmine and Donne rests on the difference between a figurative and a literal reading, we can understand the great importance of the nature of one's reading—it is directly related to and responsible for the doctrine of the Church.

The interpretation of this particular verse from 1 Corinthians revolves around the question of whether baptism is here to be understood literally or figuratively. Donne insists that any doctrine should always rest on the sound foundation of the literal sense of Scripture. But Bellarmine in this case does not accept the literal sense of the Sacrament of Baptism, but the figurative sense of a baptism of tears. The tears in turn signify the penance, discipline, and mortification which the living undergo for the sake of the dead; such suffering on the part of the living will accrue to the benefit of the dead, hastening their departure from their own purgatorial suffering. This specific example of Roman interpretation Donne uses to substantiate a general charge which he brings against their commentators. He states that when they are disinterestedly engaged in Scriptural exposition, then they "doe very often content themselves with the true sense of those places which they handle, and hunt after no curious, nor forced, nor forraine, nor unnaturall senses." But when they are engaged in controversy, they are more interested in trying to validate their argument than in remaining true to unbiased interpretation, particularly when matters of profit are involved. Since prayers and sacrifices for the dead imply a purgatorial state which would benefit from such activity, and since profitable indulgences could be sold to those who further wished to free the dead ones from their misery, it follows that Bellarmine's figurative interpretation is of great practical value to the revenue of his Church. (D vii:190-192) *Quod erat demonstrandum*! However we may assess the logic of Donne's argument, we can see how well it demonstrates the importance of the interpreter's decision to read Scripture either literally or figuratively.

There are also other indications of Donne's view of Scripture. Living as he did before the days of literary and historical criticism of the Bible, he assigned the authorship of both Proverbs and Ecclesiastes to Solomon (D 1:237; D iii:47-48), believed Matthew to be prior to Mark (D v:240), and thought the Fourth Gospel to be chronologically the last book of the Bible (D iii:348). He shared with Christian expositors of all ages a fondness for typology, and he carried into homiletical practice his view, already quoted, that the New Testament is "a revelation of those Types and Figures" of the Old Testament. Thus David's sling is a type of the Cross, and the stone with which he slew Goliath a type of Christ (D ii:187). Jacob is also a figure of Christ: Jacob's blessing from Isaac pre-

figures Christ's adoration by the Magi, and Jacob's banishment from his home prefigures Christ's banishment into
Egypt (D 1:278-279). In a sermon on the text of Luke
23:34—"Father forgive them, for they know not what
they do"—Donne, noting that this prayer is recorded in
Luke only, takes occasion to comment on the relationship
among the four Gospels. The Gospel writers are in harmony because the Holy Ghost directed the writing of all
four of them; furthermore, if the Spirit "directed one of
them to say any thing, all are well understood to have said
it." But although there are no contradictions among the
four writers, there are differences, and these are to be attributed to the fact that each wrote at a particular time and
with "a private reason peculiar to each of them." Matthew
wrote for the Eastern Church, and Mark for the Western.
Luke, disturbed by the errors in some of the many accounts
of the life of Christ written before his Gospel, wrote "to
cut off an excesse and superfluitie"; he was the most learned
of the Gospel writers and profited through his companion-
ship with Paul. John wrote to refute the heresies of Ebion
and Cerinthus, and he was more expert than his predeces-
sors in his teaching about Christ's divinity and his reporting
of Christ's sermons. Luke alone remembered that Malchus'
ear, cut off by Peter, was healed, a memory accounted for
by the fact that Luke was a physician. And to this same
fact we can attribute his memory of the text of this sermon,
the prayer of Christ, "which is the Physick and *Balsamum*
of our Soule," the sort of thing which would be remembered by a physician, all of whose words are "Physick for
a languishing soule." (D v:239-242)

To the literary skill of the Holy Ghost, who inspired the
human hands which penned the words of Scripture, Donne
responds with an enthusiasm befitting a poet. The writers
of Scripture are unsurpassed in their eloquence; no Greek
or Latin author has matched their tropes and figures

[68]

(D II:170-171). *"David* is a better *Poet* then *Virgil,"* and
"The power of *oratory,* in the force of perswasion, the
strength of conclusions, in the pressing of *Philosophy,* the
harmony of *Poetry,* in the sweetnesse of composition, never
met in any man, so fully as in the Prophet *Esay* [Isaiah]"
(D IV:167). Those who have failed to see that the Holy
Ghost carried out his work "not only with a propriety, but
with a delicacy, and harmony, and melody of language;
with height of Metaphors, and other figures . . . and not
with barbarous, or triviall, or market, or homely language," probably have done so because they read the Bible
in translation and were thus deprived of the majesty and
elegance of the original tongues (D VI:55-56).

Donne, convinced that the Holy Ghost was as precise
as he was eloquent and that he had weighed his every
word carefully before committing it to Scripture, felt im-
pelled to pursue the interpretation of Scriptural texts with
the greatest assiduity. He had, consequently, to be familiar
with the original Hebrew and Greek texts, as well as the
Greek Septuagint, the Latin Vulgate, the views of the
Church Fathers on the proper translation of various texts,
and the English translations of the Bible, particularly the
Bishops' Bible, the Geneva Bible, and the King James
Bible. Evidences of his consummate care to be faithful to
the original meaning and intention of the text are many.

Thus when Donne preaches on the text of Psalm 90:14
—"O satisfie us early with thy mercy, that we may rejoyce
and be glad all our dayes"—he argues that *rejoyce* and *be
glad* are not synonymous. The Holy Ghost, though not
penurious, is not superfluous either, and he exercises in his
use of language a fine economy which prevents him from
falling into unnecessary repetition. To *rejoyce* is a translation of the Hebrew word *Ranan,* which signifies the outward expression of inner joy. There may be times when a
person is not able to abandon himself to such a visible in-

dication of his joy, but the purely inner joy denoted by the Hebrew word *Shamach*, translated *to be glad*, may be the righteous man's possession at all times (D v:287-291). Similar respect for the Spirit's sensitivity to language is shown in two sermons preached on the Penitential Psalms. Commenting on Psalm 51:7—"Purge me with hyssope, and I shall be cleane; wash me, and I shall be whiter then snow"—Donne distinguishes between the two actions. *To purge* means in this case to "un-sin," to give one a fresh start, to forgive him and take him into the Church; this particular kind of cleansing is that infusing of God's grace which makes us capable of receiving his mercies. But the *wash me* of the text goes beyond this action; it signifies not merely the "un-sinning" of a person, not simply the new beginning, but rather that additional power to eschew backsliding; it is that sanctification which enables a person, once he has been redeemed, to persevere in God's way (D v:307-314). Similarly in his sermon on the text of Psalm 6:1—"O Lord, rebuke me not in thine anger, neither chasten me in thy hot displeasure"—Donne is careful to correct St. Jerome, who affirmed that both clauses come to the same thing, except for the fact that *anger* refers to a sentiment expressed in this world, and *hot displeasure* to one in the world to come; and to correct St. Augustine, who, seeing no essential difference between *rebuke* and *chasten*, felt that if there was any distinction, then *rebuke* was the stronger word. Donne goes into considerable detail to affirm that to be rebuked means only to be chidden, whereas to be chastened means to be beaten. But there is a difference between simply being rebuked and being rebuked *in anger*, and David is not fearful of the Lord's rebuke but of his rebuke in anger, which may lead to damnation. Both *chasten* and *hot displeasure* signify that damnation; they both "expresse the eternity of Gods indignation, even to the binding of the soule and bodie in eternall chaines of darknesse." *Chasten* denotes a binding and a bondage; *hot displeasure*, poison itself. Thus a rebuking in anger on this earth will lead to a chastening in hot displeasure, an eternal damnation in the world to come. (D v:331-337)

Another text which receives elaborate attention is that of Psalm 2:12: "Kisse the Son, lest he be angry." Donne's remarks on the first part of the text, "Kisse the Son," well exemplify the careful study he has made of the various translations:

"The Chalde paraphrase (which is, for the most part, good evidence) and the translation of the Septuagint, (which adds much weight) and the currant of the Fathers (which is of importance too) doe all read this place, *Apprehendite disciplinam, Embrace knowledge*, and not *Osculamini filium, Kisse the sonne*. Of the later men in the Roman Church, divers read it as we do, *Osculamini*, and some farther, *Amplectimini, Embrace the sonne*. Amongst the Jews, *Rabbi Solomon* reads it, *Armamini disciplina, Arme your selves with knowledge*; And another moderne man, reads it, *Osculamini pactum, Kisse the Covenant*; And, *Adorate frumentum, Adore the Corne*, and thereby carries it from the pacification of Christ in heaven, to the adoration of the bread in the Sacrament. Clearly, and without exception, even from *Bellarmine* himselfe, according to the Originall Hebrew, it ought to be read, as we reade it, *Kisse the Sonne*." (D iii:314-315)

And Donne goes on to discuss relevant remarks by Luther, Calvin, and Pellicanus.

Donne never feels more called upon to be exhaustive in presenting all the possible meanings of a word than when he is considering names. Two fascinating excursions upon which he occasionally embarks in this respect are his disquisitions on the names of man and on the names of God.

In his sermon on the text of Psalm 38:3—"There is no soundnesse in my flesh, because of thine anger, neither is there any rest in my bones, because of my sinne"—Donne underlines the meaning of the verse by showing that the various Biblical words signifying *man* are words denoting misery, the condition which led to the Psalmist's mournful outburst. In fact, man is a microcosm primarily in the sense that he embodies within himself all the world's miseries. The Holy Ghost, who possesses a sure sense of appropriate naming, has given man four names in the Hebrew language. The name *Adam*, which means man, "signifies but *Redness*, but a *Blushing*: and whether we consider their [Adam's and Eve's] low materials, as it was but *earth*, or the *redness* of that earth, as they stained it with their own blood, and the blood of all their posterity, and as they drew another more precious blood, the blood of the Messias upon it, every way *both* may be *Adam*, both may *blush*." God also calls mankind *Ish* (Genesis 2:24), a name which signifies crying, an activity which marks a person's entrance into the world. A third Hebrew name for man is *Gheber*, which, to be sure, signifies *greatness*, but a greatness which bears a curse: "It signifies a Giant, an *oppressour*, Great in power, and in a delight to doe great mischiefs upon others, or *Great*, as he is a *Great mark*, and easily hit by others." The fourth name is *Enosh*, meaning *misery*. In short, "*Adam* is *Blushing*, *Ish* is *lamenting*, *Geber* is *oppressing*, *Enosh* is *all* that. . ." (D ii:78-79). Donne returns more than once to a discussion of the four Hebrew names for *man*, showing a consistency in his treatment of *Adam*, *Ish*, and *Enosh*, but usually insisting upon a more elevated meaning for the word *Gheber* than is found in the quotation above, though even the man who possesses all of the good attributes signified by the word *Gheber* is encompassed by the misery of man's fallen condition. For example, preaching on Lamentations 3:1—"I am the man, that hath seen affliction, by the rod of his wrath"—Donne notes that the Hebrew word here is *Gheber*, "which denotes excellency, Excellency in *virtue*, (his minde rectified) Excellency in *wealth*, (his estate enlarged) Excellency in *power*, (his authority extended) Excellency in *favour*, (all seas calm on the top, and foordable at the bottome to him). . . ." But, Donne continues, even this man has seen affliction and has suffered the misery of being under God's wrath. (D x:198; see also D ii:200-201 and D ix:61-62)

If the various names which the Holy Ghost has given to man or mankind would serve to describe his miserable condition, then the names by which God is known would, for the most part, designate his power. Donne is never more elaborately precise than when he is trying to make clear the meanings of the Scriptural names of God. Preaching on the text of Psalm 55:19—"Because they have no changes, therefore they fear not God"—he takes pains to denote the nature of the God who is not feared. In this verse God is not named *Jehovah*, which signifies an absolutely transcendent God, one removed from man rather than one in close relationship to him, one whose essence is emphasized rather than his existence; the name *Jehovah* is "unexpressible and unutterable . . . incomprehensible and unimaginable." Nor is the name *Adonai*, meaning *The Lord*, a name suggesting absolute power, a power which sometimes seems to border on the arbitrary, where the curse of damnation bears no relationship to a man's sin and the gift of salvation no relationship to his faith. The name is not *Tzebaoth*, meaning *The Lord of hosts*, which connotes a warring God armed with the destructive weapons of famine, war, pestilence, and malice. The God of the Psalmist is in this verse *Elohim*, "which, though it be a name primarily rooted in power and strength, (for *El* is *Deus fortis*, The powerful God; and as there is no love

without fear, so there is no fear without power) yet properly it signifies his Judgment, and Order, and Providence,
and Dispensation, and Government of his creatures."
(D 1:234-235; see also D vii:65-67)

As we might expect, Donne also evinces an interest in
Moses' inquiry about God's name "I am that I am"
(Exodus 3:14). Donne moves into his discussion of this
verse by affirming that man alone of all creatures is interested not only in the present but in the future. Man can
therefore be called a future creature, as God can be called
a future God. God's name in Exodus signifies *Essence* or
Being. As Ambrose said, "*Verum nomen Dei, Semper esse,*
Gods proper name is *Allwayes Being*." Donne continues:

". . .*Being* is the *peculiar* and *proper* name of *God*. But
though it be so cleere, that that *Name* of *God* in *Exodus*
is *Being*, yet it is not so cleere, whether it be a *present*, or a
future Being. For, though most of the *Fathers* expressed,
and our *Translators* rendered in the *present*, *Sum qui sum*,
I am that I am, and, *Goe, and tell Pharaoh that he whose*
name is I am, hath sent thee; yet in the *Originall*, it is
plaine, and plaine in the *Chalde Paraphrase*, that that name
is delivered in the *future*, *Ero qui ero*, *I shall bee that I*
shall be, and, *Goe, and tell Pharaoh that he whose name*
is I shall bee, hath sent thee. *God* cals upon man, even in
the consideration of the name of *God*, to consider his *future*
state." (D viii:75-76)

Still another example of Donne's preoccupation with
Scriptural variations for the name of God is found in a
sermon on the text of Job 13:15: "Loe, though he slay me,
yet will I trust in him." Donne points out that it is in the
third verse of the chapter that Job names or describes the
being to whom he is referring. Job conceives him "to be
Shaddai, that is, *Omnipotens, Allmighty; I will speake to*
the Allmighty, and I desire to dispute with God." The

word *Shaddai* is used frequently in Scripture and has many significations. In the Septuagint translation of Proverbs 19:26, the word signifies *dishonor*. Isaiah uses the word in the sense of *depredation*; Jeremiah in the sense of *destruction* and *devastation*. It is used once in Proverbs to denote *deceit*, and once in Psalms to designate the *devil*. To note all of these meanings of *Shaddai* is to realize that it is God who visits all calamities upon us, not that we may be reduced to despair, but that we may realize that all misfortunes are purposeful: "I cannot feel an affliction, but in that very affliction I feel the hand (and if I will, the medicinall hand) of my *God*." By bringing the calamity to man "and calling that calamity by his owne name, *Shaddai*, he would make that very calamity a candle to thee, by which thou mightst see him." *Shaddai* is the Lord who gives and the Lord who takes away. (D III:190-192) In this way Donne explains how a name which may initially seem so far removed from the nature of God is appropriately and "medicinally" used.[13]

But let us not infer from these high praises of the Holy Ghost's eloquence and precision that we should turn to Scripture primarily to glorify these virtues or to seek rhetorical counsel. For all its literary excellence and secular wisdom, the Bible is ultimately to be read for one reason: it is the Word of God to our salvation. And Donne reminds us that his beloved David, in whose Psalms we find such an abundance of knowledge in all arts and of learning of all kinds, boasts in his dying words "not that he had delivered himself in strong, or deepe, or mysterious Arts, that was not his Rock; but his Rock was the Rock of Israel, His way was to establish the Church of God upon fundamentall Doctrines" (D IX:252-253).

Donne has his favorites among the Biblical books, as-

[13] For a discussion of the names of Jesus Christ, see, for example, D VII:308-309; of Mary, D IX:192-193.

serting early in his preaching career that he prefers the
Psalms of David for a first course in his spiritual diet and
the Epistles of St. Paul for a second. He takes comfort in
the fact that St. Augustine also bore a special devotion to
the Psalms, as did St. Chrysostom to the Epistles, and he
points out further that his own predilection for these books
may be occasioned in part by their being written in literary
forms to which he is most accustomed. (D II:49) More
than once he cites with approval the judgment of St. Basil,
who said of the Book of Psalms that, if all the other Scriptural books could perish, the Psalms would be sufficient for
catechising all believers and for converting all non-be-
lievers (D IV:91; D VI:292). His affection for Paul's letters he displays once in an unusual way. Preaching on a
text from I Timothy, he states that though the Holy Ghost
possessed all the authors of the Scriptures, yet in Paul's
Epistles there is, as Irenaeus said, "The vehemence, the
force of the holy-Ghost." And, as Chrysostom said, the
letters written in prison (of which I Timothy is one) "have
most of this holy vehemence." Furthermore, of all the
Epistles, I Timothy, which instructs a bishop to propagate
the Gospel, is the most vehement of all! (D I:286) Toward the end of his life Donne spoke with equal enthusiasm of the Sermon on the Mount, finding in the three
chapters thereof "All the Articles of our Religion, all the
Canons of our Church, all the Injunctions of our Princes,
all the Homilies of our Fathers, all the Body of Divinity
. . ." (D IX:173-174).

One of the most effective characteristics of Donne's
sermons, as will later be argued in greater detail, is their
constant and immediate application of all divine matters
to the lives of the men and women who heard them. In
his remarks about the Bible he impresses upon his people
the advantage they enjoy over the Papists of being able to
read Scripture in their homes, and he recalls to them

Christ's admonition that they search the Scriptures as the authority for their way of life. He points out to them the comforting conviction that God will neither judge nor condemn them on the basis of anything they never saw or knew, and that the sole criterion of judgment will be the Word of the Bible. "The *Scripture* is a Judge, by which God himself will be tryed. As the Law is our Judge, and the Judge does but declare what is Law, so the Scripture is our Judge, and God proceeds with us according to those promises and Judgements, which he hath laid down in the Scripture." (D VIII:281-282) Such an argument should certainly suffice to send a man to the Bible, for its terrifying and joyful significance could hardly be more pertinently emphasized. And on Christmas Day, 1627, Donne commended the Scriptures in an even more positive way to all who would seek their salvation: "As much as Paradise exceeded all the places of the earth, doe the Scriptures of God exceed Paradise. In the midst of Paradise grew the *Tree of knowledge*, and the *tree of life*: In this Paradise, the Scripture, every word is both those Trees; there is Life and Knowledge in every word of the Word of God." (D VIII:131)

The ultimate authority, then, to which the Church must turn for all its teaching is the Bible, the Word of God brought to man through the activity of the Holy Spirit. The person most sensitive to the meaning of the Scriptural books is the priest who has been called to interpret them to his congregation; the place in which the priest pronounces his interpretation is the Church; the form through which the written Word is interpreted in the Church is the spoken word, the sermon.

THE SPOKEN WORD

There is no salvation but by faith, nor faith but by hearing, nor hearing but by preaching; and they that thinke meanliest of the Keyes of the Church, and speake faintliest of the Absolution of the

Church, will yet allow, That those Keyes lock, and unlock in Preaching; That Absolution is conferred, or withheld in Preaching, That the proposing of the promises of the Gospel in preaching, is that binding and loosing on earth, which bindes and looses in heaven. (D vii:320)

No words of Donne sum up any better than these his conviction of the indispensability of the sermon and, consequently, the weighty responsibility of the preacher. The passage may recall the intensity of Paul's remarks about the preacher and the spoken word in his Epistle to the Romans (10:13-14): "For whosoever shall call upon the name of the Lord shall be saved. How then shall they call on him in whom they have not believed? and how shall they believe in him of whom they have not heard? and how shall they hear without a preacher?" The analogy used by Donne to suggest the relationship between written Word and spoken word, between Scripture and sermon, is that of honey and honeycomb. Honey is collected in and distributed from the honeycomb; similarly, the Word of God is gathered in and proclaimed by the preacher. Noble as the preacher's role may be, the congregation must always distinguish between him and the Holy Ghost, just as they distinguish between the honeycomb and the honey. The minister is never the source of the saving Word, though he is God's instrument to proclaim it. But not even the proclamation is the end of the process of redemption, since neither a mere reading nor a mere hearing of the Word has intrinsic value; each Christian must apply the teaching of the Word to his life before it has any efficacy for him. (D viii:271-273)

Preaching is a distinctly Christian institution, unknown in the days before Jesus and established through his command, recorded in the last chapter of Mark, that his disciples go into the world and preach the Gospel to all creatures (D iv:194). And though God may provide other ways of salvation for other people, he has given to the Christian Church no other way of bringing salvation to its members than through "the manifestation of Christ Jesus in his Ordinance of preaching" (D v:45). And how eloquently Donne announces its virtues. Every word from the lips of the preacher is "a drop of the *dew of heaven*, a dram of the *balme of Gilead*, a portion of the bloud of thy Saviour" (D III:364). Even the Creation was not such a mighty act as that miracle by which men are saved through the preaching of the Word; for the act of Creation evoked no resistance, since there was nothing to offer resistance, but the sermon is resisted by man's inherited disposition to sin (D VII:300-301). Hooker too was able to summon a convincing eloquence when he spoke of the gift of preaching: ". . . sermons [are] as keys to the kingdom of heaven, as wings to the soul, as spurs to the good affections of man, unto the sound and healthy as food, as physic unto diseased minds."[14]

Though Donne follows both Calvin and the Thirty-nine Articles in viewing the Church as that institution where the Word is truly preached and the sacraments duly administered, he speaks more frequently and more fully of the saving power of the sermon than of that of the sacraments. It is true that he esteems both of them necessary, and on one occasion he writes that they go together as thunder and lightning: preaching is the thunder which clears the air and drives away the clouds of ignorance; the sacrament is the lightning which is the presence of Christ himself (D IV:105). But his greater emphasis on the sermon is perhaps explained by the following explicit distinction, made when he is speaking of Christ's own work on earth. He points out that Christ preached "long before he instituted the Sacraments," and that "Sacraments were instituted by Christ, as subsidiary things, in a great part, for

[14] *Works of . . . Hooker*, Book v, chapter xxii, section 1.

our infirmity, who stand in need of such visible and sensible assistances" (D x:69).

Donne's sermons are interlarded with remarks about the proper manner and matter of preaching. He asks of others the same meticulous care in preparation which he obviously devoted to his own sermons; impatient with those who have the mistaken confidence to preach extemporaneously, he points out that it is somewhat late to prepare a sermon when the Psalm is being sung (D ii:171). The sermon should be neither too complex for the understanding of the congregation's least perceptive mind nor too banal for the patience and attention of its most active intellect (D ix:215).[15] At the same time, individual members of a congregation must not be too restive or uncharitable if the sermon seems not quite at their proper level of understanding; if the minister preaches "in the mountaine," the plain dweller must not be offended, and if he preaches "on the plaine," the mountain dweller must not think himself superior to the sermon (D vii:330-331). Perhaps most importantly, the preacher should know his congregation well enough to rouse his parishioners to a conviction of their particular sins, and yet he must, in pronouncing the Lord's judgments on sin, season his pronouncement with an equal emphasis on God's merciful and forgiving nature (D iii:363-365).

Donne also takes pains to inform his congregation what a sermon is not. For one thing, it is not a lecture, for "a Sermon intends *Exhortation* principally and *Edification*, and a holy stirring of religious affections, and then *matters of Doctrine*, and points of *Divinity* . . ." (D viii:95).

---

[15] Quite appropriate here is a remark by Thomas Fuller about the sermons of William Perkins: "His sermons were not so plain but that the piously learned did admire them, not so learned but that the plain did understand them." From Book ii, chapter x—"The Life of Mr. Perkins"—of *The Holy State, and The Prophane State* (1642), ed. James Nichols (London: printed for Thomas Tegg, 1841), p. 81.

Or, as he expresses it at another time, the minister turns more to edification than to speculation; he preaches "for the saving of soules, and not for the sharpning of wits" (D VIII:42). The hour of preaching is not the time for him to play the prima donna either, to use the sermon as an occasion for the display of his own talents. He should employ with discrimination that secular learning which he possesses, taking care not to show it off too much in his delivery of the Word of God (D x:146-147). He must not mistake ostentation for solidity, must not follow the foolish man who, "having made a Pye of Plums, without meat, offers it to sale in every Market, and having made an Oration of Flowres, and Figures, and Phrases without strength, sings it over in every Pulpit . . ." (D VII:329). The sermon is not to be a political or social manifesto. Preachers must not be so obsessed with contemporary concerns that they forget the centrality of Christ, must be careful not to "make the emergent affaires of the time, their *Text*, and the humors of the hearers their *Bible*" (D IV:276), must not surrender to "such itching Ears, as come to hear popular and seditious Calumnies and Scandals, and Reproaches, cast upon the present State and Government" (D IV:91). To put it more positively and admonishingly, at the center of the Bible is *"Christ Jesus, and him crucified*; and whosoever preaches any other Gospell, or any other thing for Gospell, let him be accursed" (D IV:231).

Whatever the manner and matter of preaching, it is a vain activity unless the hearers of the Word become also doers of the Word. The preacher may first look to himself and know that his own best comment on his text is a good life. For the sermon does not end with the benediction, and members of a congregation cannot assess a preacher accurately until the Saturday following the sermon, at which time they can praise the sermon if they note that he has lived it during the week (D v:263). A minister's preaching may be merely his speech, whereas his good life is his eloquence (D IX:156). Speaking of the effectiveness of preaching, Donne once remarks: "Twenty of our Sermons edifie not so much, as if the Congregation might see one man converted by us" (D II:275-276); or, as he says on another occasion: "God makes sometimes a plaine and simple mans good life, as powerfull, as the eloquentest Sermon" (D VIII:150). Such a life is indeed eloquent testimony that the Word of God has been heard.

To Protestants who were encouraged to read their Bibles at home, it was particularly necessary to emphasize the value of the sermon as a guide to sound interpretation. We may gather from Donne's remarks that a number of persons were inclined to neglect the sermon and depend on their own private reading of the Bible. Parts of Scripture are beyond the understanding of the lay reader, even beyond the understanding of the minister, who with his congregation must await the fulfillment of certain prophecies before they will become clear to him. But surely the man called by God will have a better comprehension of his Word than men of other callings, and one should consult a minister for divine matters in the same way that he might turn to a physician or a lawyer when in medical or legal perplexities (D IV:219-223). Donne is touchy about those who intrude their way into the callings of other men, particularly those laymen who censure or question the doctrines proclaimed by Church and clergy (D II:278-279). He points out that the Holy Ghost often makes clear the power of God through the mouth of the preacher (D v:-69), and he once told his congregation at St. Paul's that "The men from whom we are to receive testimony of the sense of the Scriptures, must be men that have witnesses, that is, a visible and outward *calling in the Church of God*" (D IV:218). He expresses the same sentiment in other ways: "The Scriptures are Gods Voyce; The Church is his Eccho" (D vi:223); the meaning of Scripture must be seen through "the eye of the Church" (D iii:210). These remarks show the mutual interdependence of priest, Church, Scripture, and sermon; all work together as co-operating instruments for the salvation of mankind. The priest gains his knowledge of the redemptive way through Scripture; and his sermon, delivered in the Church, is the means of communicating this saving knowledge. All of these strands are brought together in a sermon preached at Whitehall on April 30, 1626. In a passage providing a convenient summary for the argument of this entire chapter, Donne asserts that the act of calling to salvation needs a voice as well as a Word, and that for a Christian community to be kept alive the Word of Scripture must constantly be sounded from the pulpit through the voice of the preacher:

"Now, this *calling*, implies a voice, as well as a Word; it is by the Word; but not by the Word read at home, though that be a pious exercise; nor by the word submitted to private interpretation; but *by the Word preached*, according to his Ordinance, and under the Great Seal, of his blessing upon his Ordinance. So that *preaching* is this *calling*; and therefore, as if Christ do appear to any man, in the power of a miracle, or in a private inspiration, yet he appears but in weakness, as in an infancy, till he speak, till he bring a man to the hearing of his voice, in a setled Church, and in the Ordinance of preaching: so how long soever Christ have dwelt in any State, or any Church, if he grow speechless, he is departing; if there be a discontinuing, or slackning of preaching, there is a danger of loosing Christ." (D vii:157)

Such notice as we have now taken of Donne's many remarks about his calling will give some sense of the seriousness with which he viewed his work. Reflecting upon the nature and responsibilities of his profession with considerable care, he makes clear to both himself and his hearers the manner in which the priest and the Church, the Bible and the sermon, are related to the ultimate question of man's salvation. Donne's indisposition to call for blind faith is nowhere more evident than in his persistent attempt to clarify and justify the whole apparatus ordained by God for the calling of men to salvation. The principal institution of salvation is the Church, the body of Christ, called into being by the Word of God found in Scripture; the priest is a person called by God to interpret his Word and to preach the good news of salvation. It is probable that few clergymen have ever been so consciously aware as was Donne of the precise nature of their vocation. That he felt the nature of his profession to be worthy of such intensive investigation suggests his sense of its grandeur. And what we know of his work during the last sixteen years of his life suggests that he dedicated himself fully to his divine calling, the responsibilities of which he knew so well.

CHAPTER THREE

"Golden Chrysostome . . . Alive Againe"

Mee thinkes I see him in the pulpit standing,
Not eares, or eyes, but all mens hearts commanding,
Where wee that heard him, to our selves did faine
Golden Chrysostome was alive againe. . . .

THUS wrote Richard Busby in his elegy "In memory of John Donne." The comparison to St. John Chrysostom (Chrysostom means "golden-mouthed"), the remarkably eloquent fourth-century Greek Father, is apt. When John Donne took holy orders in 1615 he brought to the altar of God many talents, certainly one of the greatest of which was his control of language. His eminence as a priest does not rest on the sanctity of his life, and we do not sense in him the kind of holiness that would seem to have marked his very distant kinsman, Thomas More, or, in his own time, Nicholas Ferrar or George Herbert. Nor was he in any sense a great or an original theologian. But awesome indeed to a person who reads and re-reads the 160 extant sermons are the cumulative effect of the style and the unbroken evidence of the most painstaking literary craftsmanship. Though the precise relationship of the published discourses to the preached sermons is a matter of some uncertainty, it seems probable, as I shall hope to show, that the printed sermons come close to preserving what he actually preached and, in most cases, contain certain additions to or elaborations of what was preached.

There is both external and internal evidence that Donne was not accustomed to entering the pulpit without the most careful preparation, that he had his sermons well in mind before the time of delivery.[1] Walton's comment on the assiduous scholarly activity of Donne's later life has already been noted; we are told that the Dean usually preached at least once a week and that, after each sermon, "he never gave his eyes rest, till he had chosen out a new Text, and that night cast his Sermon into a form, and his Text into divisions; and the next day betook himself to consult the Fathers, and so commit his meditations to his memory, which was excellent" (W:67). There is substantial internal evidence as well, from his earliest sermons to his latest, that Donne throughout his career manifested the care to which Walton attests. As one evidence we have the well-ordered sermons themselves; as another we have Donne's many strictures, already mentioned briefly, against inadequate preparation or extemporaneous preaching. Firm as his conviction was that God's ministers speak through the inspiration of the Holy Ghost, he was equally firm in insisting that the minister meet the Spirit on some middle ground. The one extemporaneous sermon which won his hearty approval was a brief one, the words of the repentant thief on the Cross to the unrepentant one: "Fearest not thou God, being under the same condemnation?" "This Thief," writes Donne, "had premeditated nothing. But he is no more a precedent for extemporal preaching, then he is for stealing. He was a Thief before, and he was an extemporal preacher at last: But he teaches no body else to be either" (D 1:260). On the contrary, that recorder of God's Word, the Holy Ghost, would put into the preacher "a care of delivering God's messages, with consideration, with meditation, with preparation; and not barbarously, not suddenly, not occasionally, not extemporarily, which

---

[1] For some interesting observations on seventeenth-century sermon preparation and methods of delivery, see John Sparrow, "John Donne and Contemporary Preachers," *Essays and Studies by Members of the English Association* (Oxford at the Clarendon Press, 1930 on binding, 1931 on title page), XVI, 144-178.

might derogate from the dignity of so great a service"
(D II:171). Those preachers who "resolve in a minute,
what they will *say*, out-go Gods Spirit, and make too much
hast" (D VI:104). Actually a sermon's preparation must
begin years before its delivery, because good preaching
requires not only careful phrasing and order but a sound
knowledge of the tradition and doctrine of the Church.
Donne writes that if he resorts to extemporaneous preaching, then

"I shall come to an extemporall faith, and extemporall
religion; and then I must looke for an extemporall Heav-
en, a Heaven to be made for me; for to that Heaven which
belongs to the Catholique Church, I shall never come, except I go by the way of the Catholique Church, by former
Idea's, former examples, former patterns, To beleeve according to ancient beliefes, to pray according to ancient
formes, to preach according to former meditations. God
does nothing, man does nothing well, without these Idea's,
these retrospects, this recourse to pre-conceptions, pre-de-
liberations." (D VII:61)

The fact that Donne thought through his sermons with
such care before delivering them and the fact, attested by
Walton, that he had an excellent memory increase the
probability that the written text is a fairly accurate reflection of the spoken text. It is also probable that there is a
greater fidelity in those sermons written shortly after their
delivery than in those written after a longer interval. The
earliest evidence of the former practice is seen in a dedicatory letter to the Countess of Montgomery, prefacing a
sermon preached before her on February 21, 1619; Donne,
sending a copy of the sermon to the Countess shortly after
it was preached, speaks of "writing this Sermon which
your Ladiship was pleased to hear before" (D II:179).[2]

[2] For the dating of the sermon and of the letter, see D II:23, 25.

The six sermons published during Donne's lifetime were also written out shortly after their delivery. Evidence of a somewhat more tardy composition is found in the heading for two sermons on the text of Matthew 4:18-20: "*At the Haghe Decemb. 19. 1619. I Preached upon this Text. Since in my sicknesse at Abrey-hatche in Essex, 1630, revising my short notes of that Sermon, I digested them into these two*" (D II:269). One may in a case like this reasonably doubt the verbatim quality of the written sermon!

It seems certain that Donne, in writing out his sermons, elaborated upon the preached version. He speaks on many occasions of a customary one-hour sermon, once fitting his fourfold division to the quarter hours—"These foure steps, these foure passages, these foure transitions will be our quarter Clock, for this houres exercise" (D VI:64); and once apologizing for a longer discourse—"Be not weary, if at any time your patience be exercised some minutes beyond the threescore, sometime beyond the houre in these exercises . . ." (D IX:316). But very few of his printed sermons could be delivered in an hour, and we may assume that additions were made. The pulpit at Paul's Cross perhaps faced sinners of a more stubborn cast, for the sermons there customarily ran to two hours,[3] a fact of which Donne apparently took full advantage on September 15, 1622, when he preached his long sermon defending King James's *Directions for Preachers*. Relevant to Donne's practice of writing at greater length than he preached is the testimony of Thomas Playfere, whose sermons were published in 1623; in a dedicatory epistle, speaking of a sermon delivered in 1604, he writes that he preached as much of it "as filled up the ordinary time of an houre: but that was scarce halfe the Sermon. I vttered no more, to auoid the Offence of the hearer; I wrote no lesse, to procure the profit of the reader. . . . I thought

[3] Millar MacLure, *Paul's Cross Sermons*, p. 8.

good in publishing this Sermon rather to inlarge it to the comprehension I had conceiued and meditated in my minde, then to scant it according to that strict compasse of time which I was tied to in the pulpit."[4]

Only a fraction of the many sermons which Donne preached is extant, but it is comforting to know that those which we have are in the form in which he would wish us to have them. We will recall that, in describing his summer activity at Chelsea during the plague year of 1625, Donne spoke of his revising many of his sermons and writing out a great many others. And we have Henry King's statement to Walton that Donne "three days before his death delivered into my hands those excellent Sermons of his now publicke: professing . . . that it was by my restless importunity, that he had prepared them for the Press . . ." (W:14-15). We can assume that Dr. Donne is represented as he would wish to be, that we possess the sermons which he esteemed most highly, and that we possess them in a text which bears his imprimatur.

STRUCTURE

In this chapter on Donne's style I should like to discuss the structure, rhetoric, imagery, and tone of the sermons. And in turning to the characteristics of the sermons' structure, we might first ask to what degree Donne's organizational principles were influenced by the fourfold method which characterized medieval Scriptural interpretation. For some centuries before his time, preachers and Biblical commentators had customarily read and interpreted Scripture on four levels: the literal, allegorical, tropological, and anagogical.[5] The literal would entail simply a recapitu-

---

[4] Quoted by W. Fraser Mitchell, *English Pulpit Oratory from Andrewes to Tillotson* (London: Society for Promoting Christian Knowledge, 1932), p. 27.

[5] See H. Flanders Dunbar, *Symbolism in Medieval Thought and Its Consummation in The Divine Comedy* (New Haven: Yale University Press, 1929), especially pp. 18-21.

lation of the Biblical passage under discussion. The allegorical would note the manner in which the text went
beyond its literal and particular truths and pointed to a
universal truth, one which applied not only to the Scriptural situation or character under scrutiny but to all occasions and to all men. The tropological interpretation would
expound the moral to be derived from the text. The
anagogical would proclaim the mystical or spiritual or
ultimate significance of the passage. A working example
of this fourfold procedure could be applied to Abraham's
aborted sacrifice of Isaac. Taking this narrative as the
substance of his sermon, a preacher might begin by a literal
telling of the story itself, placing it in its historical context, and then proceed to the allegorization by suggesting
that Abraham stands for any man called upon to render
absolute obedience to God, regardless of the nature of
God's command. The tropological or moral lesson might
be that a man so called upon must bow to God's command,
even though the Lord may demand the most painful of
sacrifices. The anagogical or spiritual truth could be that
God provides for all those who follow his will, that the way
to union with God is through sacrifice. Or the preacher
might proceed from another interpretation, urging that
Abraham in his willingness to sacrifice represents God the
Father's willingness to sacrifice his son and that Isaac is
a Christ figure.

Familiar as he was with the fourfold method of interpretation, Donne seldom paid strict adherence to it in
organizing his sermons. The sermons which come closest
to bearing the imprint of this method are those six on
the Thirty-eighth Psalm preached at Lincoln's Inn in the
spring or summer of 1618. In one of these, with the third
verse as text—"There is no soundnesse in my flesh, because
of thine anger, neither is there any rest in my bones, because of my sinne"—Donne in his "Divisio" points to a

threefold interpretation of the text and a threefold division
for his sermon:

"Which words [the text] we shall first consider, as they
are our present object, as they are historically, and literally to be understood of *David*; And secondly, in their
retrospect, as they look back upon the first *Adam*, and so
concern *Mankind collectively*, and so you, and *I*, and all
have our portion in these calamities; And thirdly, we shall
consider them in their *prospect*, in their future relation to
the *second Adam*, in *Christ Jesus*, in whom also all mankinde was collected, and the calamities of all men had their
Ocean and their confluence, and the cause of them, the
anger of God was more declared, and the cause of that
anger, that is sin, did more abound, for the sins of all the
world were *his*, by imputation; for this Psalm, some of our
Expositors take to be a *historicall*, and *personall* Psalm,
determin'd in *David*; some, a *Catholique*, and *universall*
Psalm, extended to the whole condition of *man*; and some
a *Propheticall*, and *Evangelicall* Psalm, directed upon
Christ" (D 11:75).

The retrospective interpretation, which concerns mankind collectively and is catholic and universal, would cor-
respond to the allegorical portion of the fourfold division;
the prospective, which concerns man's relationship to Christ
and is prophetic and evangelical, is the anagogical interpretation. Though there is no specific section marked out
as tropological or moral, various portions of the sermon
are, of course, tropological in nature; the concluding lines
are a direct statement of the moral:

"We have done; *Est ars sanandorum morborum medicina,
non rhetorica*; Our physick is not eloquence, not directed
upon your *affections*, but upon your *consciences*; To *that*
wee present this for physick, *The whole need not a Physician*, but the sick doe. If you mistake your selves to be *well*,

or think you have physick enough at home, knowledge enough, divinity enough, to save you *without us*, you need no Physician; that is, a Physician can doe you no good; but then is this Gods physick, and Gods Physician welcome unto you, if you be come to a remorsefull sense, and to an humble, and penitent acknowledgement, that you are sick, and that *there is no soundnesse in your flesh, because of his anger, nor any rest in your bones, because of your sins*, till you turn upon *him*, in whom this anger is appeas'd, and in whom these sins are forgiven, the Son of his love, the Son of his right hand, at his right hand Christ Jesus. And to this glorious Sonne of God, &c." (D 11:93-94)

The three sermons based on the text of Psalm 38:4 follow a somewhat similar structural plan, as evidenced, for example, by this statement of organization from the "Divisio" of the first of these discourses: "First then, all these things are *literally* spoken of *David*; By *application*, of us; and by *figure*, of Christ. *Historically, David; morally*, we; *Typically*, Christ is the subject of this text" (D 11:97).

But Donne's sermons do not as a rule show any strong influence of the fourfold method of interpretation. More typical of his structural procedure is the organization of his first extant sermon, preached on April 30, 1615, at Greenwich, on the text of Isaiah 52:3: "Ye have sold your selves for nought, and ye shall be redeemed without money." The sermon consists of an introduction, a division, and the main parts referred to in the division. The introduction enumerates the three principal interpretations placed by expositors upon the text. Some have felt that the verse refers to the deliverance of the Jews from their captivity by the Babylonians, with the Persian King Cyrus serving as the redeemer; others that it looks forward to the freeing of the early Christian Church from persecution through the redeeming action of the fourth-century Roman Emperor Constantine; still others that it points to the redemption by Jesus Christ of the whole world from its bondage to sin and death. Accepting the third interpretation as the most useful and proper, Donne then moves on to a careful analysis of the principal words of the text. I quote the following passage, not because it is of any considerable intrinsic interest, but because it well exemplifies Donne's frequent habit of seeking to define precisely the key words in the text on which he is preaching: ". . . the word in which our action is expressed, which is *Machar*, *vendidistis*, ye have sold, signifies in many places of Scripture, *dare pro re alia*, a permutation, an exchange of one thing for another; and in other places it signifies *Dedere*, upon any little attempt to forsake and abandon our defences, and to suffer the enemy easily to prevail upon us; so also it signifies *Tradere*, not onely to forsake our selves, but to concur actually to the delivering up of our selves; and lastly, it signifies *Repellere*, to joyn with our enemies in beating back any that should come to our relief, and rescue" (D 1:152). This analysis is followed by a detailed discussion of the words "nought," "without money," and "redeemed."

In this way Donne introduces his text to his hearers, summarizing its various interpretations and defining painstakingly the meaning or meanings of all the key words. The introduction is followed by a "Divisio," a statement of the main sections into which the sermon is to be divided. This first extant sermon Donne divides into two main parts: "*Exprobrationem*, and *Consolationem*: First, an exprobration, or increpation from God to us, And then a consolation, or consolidation of the same God upon us." The first main part is then subjected to a twofold subdivision: ". . . in the exprobration, God reproches to us, first, our Prodigality, that we would sell a reversion, our possibility, our expectance of an inheritance in heaven; And then, our cheapness, that we would sell that, for nothing." The first subdivision, discussing our prodigality, is in turn subdivided into three parts, each of which describes one of the penalties or misfortunes befalling the prodigal. (D 1:154-155) From sermon to sermon, the number of divisions varies, as does the degree of subdividing, but Donne's early Greenwich sermon serves basically as a convenient model, structurally, of virtually all his sermons. An interesting exception is a sermon preached on Christmas Day, 1627, in the "Divisio" of which Donne writes: "From this Branch, this Text, *O my Lord send, I pray thee, by the hand of him, whom thou wilt send*, we shall not so much stand, to gather here and there an Apple, that is, to consider some particular words of the Text it selfe, as endeavour to shake the whole tree, that is, the Context, and coherence and dependance of the words . . ." (D VIII:132).

Given the length and the structural and intellectual complexity of the sermons, the careful textual division, as well as the explicit transitions from one section to the next, must have been helpful to Donne's hearers, as they are to his readers. One of Donne's favorite analogies is the comparison of a sermon's organization to the structure of a building, and in his use of this metaphor he acknowledges a spiritual indebtedness: "The Holy Ghost seemes to have delighted in the Metaphore of *Building*. I know no figurative speech so often iterated in the Scriptures, as the name of a *House*. . . ." (D VII:302) The "Divisio" of one of his sermons concludes with the sentence: "So have you the designe, and frame of our building, and the severall partitions, the roomes; passe we now to a more particular survey, and furnishing of them" (D IV:146). The three divisions of another sermon are compared, respectively, to a building, its foundation, and its prospect (D VI:40); and those of still another to the foundation of a building,

the building itself, and its outhouses or furniture (D
VII:168). And the opening sentence of his last sermon,
"Death's Duel," is the key to its organization: "Buildings
stand by the benefit of their *foundations* that susteine and
support them, and of their *butteresses* that comprehend and
embrace them, and of their *contignations* that knit and
unite them: The *foundations* suffer them not to *sinke*, the
butteresses suffer them not to *swerve*, and the *contignation*
and knitting suffers them not to *cleave*" (D x:230).

The organization of some of Donne's sermons, or at
least of large sections of them, is determined by what we
might call his scholarly apparatus, resulting from his in-
voking of authority. When he turns to a controversial
matter, whether a point of Scriptural interpretation or
theological doctrine, and wishes to present a history of
the controversy, he will sometimes reproduce at length
the testimony of Scripture, of the Church Fathers, of more
recent theologians and commentators, and, occasionally, of
poets and philosophers. Such a procedure, of course, is a
determining factor in the structure of his discourse. A
typical example is found in a sermon preached on February
20, 1618, on the text of Luke 23:40: "Fearest not thou
God, being under the same condemnation?" The point
at issue is whether the repentant thief, like the unrepentant
one, had moments before reviled Christ. Donne first ap-
peals to Scripture itself: Luke does not say that both
thieves reviled Christ; John does not say that either of
them did; Matthew and Mark say that both of them did.
The sermon then moves to a discussion of the Church
Fathers. Athanasius finds both thieves guilty of reviling
the Lord; Origen agrees, asserting that such a situation
affords God opportunity to manifest his mercy and his
justice. To Chrysostom the repentant thief's vilification
of Christ makes the reconciliation more striking than it
would otherwise be. Hilary, in accord with the earlier

Fathers, finds the repentant thief a type of those elect persons who fall away from God in times of crisis and later are reconciled. Theophylact sees the two thieves as types of the Jews and Gentiles, both of whom reproached Christ, and St. Jerome also finds both men guilty. Only St. Augustine goes against the tradition, denying that the repentant thief vilified Christ. It is Donne's judgment that Augustine erred. (D 1:257-259)

A far more sustained example of the way in which Donne's appeal to authority, his reliance on a scholarly method, determines his organization is found in two sermons preached at St. Paul's on May 21 and June 21, 1626, on the text of 1 Corinthians 15:29:[6] "Else, what shall they doe which are baptized for the dead? If the dead rise not at all, why are they then baptized for the dead?" The sermons comprise an elaborate study of (1) the manner in which the Church of Rome has, through textual misinterpretation, fallen into three heresies—beliefs in the efficacy of prayer for the dead, in the doctrine of purgatorial suffering, and in the efficacy of indulgences—heresies which a true reading would have obviated; and of (2) the proper interpretation of the text. The structure of the various sections of these two sermons is based in great part on the orderly tracing, from theologian to theologian, of the development of the Roman heresies.

Donne opens the first sermon by stating that, despite diverse expositions of the text, all scholars have agreed that it refers to the resurrection, and he outlines his plan to consider "how these words have been mis-applyed by our Adversaries of the Romane Church, and then the severall Expositions which they have received from sound and Orthodoxall men . . ." (D VII:165). The "Divisio" calls for three parts, one on each heresy, with each section

[6] The sermon preached on the evening of Easter Day, 1626, had also been on the same text.

organized according to the historical development of the
heresy. In the manifold instructions and directions given
by God to Moses and Aaron, there is no reference to any
encouragement of prayer for the dead. "In all the Law,"
Donne continues, "no precept for it . . . In all the History
no example . . . In all the Gospell no promise annexed
to it . . ." (D vii:168). It was from the Gentiles that Jews
and Christians alike were first influenced by the practice
of such prayer. Tertullian first acknowledged it as a custom of the Christian Church. Both Aerius and Epiphanius
opposed it, but without measurable success. Chrysostom,
finding no Scriptural basis for the custom, yet affirmed that
it was an "Apostolicall Constitution." Augustine encouraged
the practice, though the nearest thing to Biblical authority
that he could find for it was in the apocryphal Maccabees.
Thus the first main section of the sermon gets under way.
When Donne moves on to Part Two, in which he argues
that the Roman concept of Purgatory is also without Scriptural basis, the roll call of authorities is ever more impressive. His argument is developed through calling on the
testimony of Plato, Tertullian, Eusebius, Vergil, Lactantius, Hermes, Clement of Alexandria, Origen, St. Ambrose, St. Hilary, St. Augustine, St. Gregory, St. Dionysius
the Areopagite, Luther, Chemnicius, Sextus Senensis, and
St. Bernard, as well as various canonical and apocryphal
writers. Donne then levels his guns at the Roman doctrine
of indulgences, pursuing to the end of the sermon the
scholarly references which mark it throughout.

The next sermon, on the same text, contains more of
the same, with its first part carrying on the argument
against the textual interpretations made by the writers of
the Roman Church, Cardinal Bellarmine in particular,
and with the second presenting the "sounder and more
Orthodoxall Divines" who teach us "what to embrace and

follow" (D vii:190). Numbered among these divines are Luther, Melancthon, Piscator, and Calvin. Donne's practice of quoting many authorities on both sides of an argument was, of course, a common one of his time, and we need for an example go no further than his contemporary and fellow Anglican clergyman, Robert Burton, in whose *The Anatomy of Melancholy* we can see to what lengths the practice could be carried. Donne's own vast learning is unquestionable,[7] and it is interesting to note how large sections of many of his sermons do depend for the order of their argument on his marshaling of innumerable critical authorities.

The over-all structure of a sermon was not a matter of particular controversy in the seventeenth century, though George Herbert in Donne's own time and Joseph Glanvill a half-century later both inveighed against the disposition of some preachers to divide their discourses into too many splinters. In his *A Priest to the Temple*, Herbert approves a twofold division, to include a statement of the text's meaning and some observations on the text as a whole, and he derides the practice of "crumbling a text into small parts, as, the Person speaking, or spoken to, the subject, and object, and the like. . . ."[8] And Glanvill, urging that the "divisions be not numerous, minute, and nice," goes on to affirm that there is no worse vanity in preaching than that "of dividing Texts into indivisibles; and mincing them into single words; which makes them signifie nothing. . . ."[9] But Donne was no great offender in this respect, and the sermons of Lancelot Andrewes, whose divisions were many,

[7] But see Don Cameron Allen, "Dean Donne Sets His Text," *ELH: A Journal of English Literary History*, x (September 1943), 208-229.

[8] *The Works of George Herbert*, ed. F. E. Hutchinson (Oxford at the Clarendon Press, 1941), pp. 234-235.

[9] [Joseph Glanvill], *An Essay Concerning Preaching: Written for the Direction of A Young Divine; and Useful also for the PEOPLE in order to Profitable Hearing* (London, 1678), p. 46.

hardly signified nothing; the targets of Herbert and Glanvill were in all probability preachers of considerably less stature.

RHETORIC

In any case, critical arguments of the time were far less occupied with structural matters than they were with rhetoric. The proper rhetorical qualities of sermons—and other prose writings—were matters debated with frequency and with heat. The scientific impulse of the age, with its suspicion of the truth or value of the poetic imagination, strongly influenced the literary styles of the century. Roger Ascham's earlier admonition, that "Ye know not what hurt ye do to learning, that care not for words, but for matter,"[10] must have been heeded, for Francis Bacon, just thirty-five years later, felt called upon to issue a counterwarning. In *The Advancement of Learning* (1605), he informed the world that one of the main causes of learning's sad estate was that men had recently begun "to hunt more after words than matter; more after the choiceness of the phrase, and the round and clean composition of the sentence, and the sweet falling of the clauses, and the varying and illustration of their works with tropes and figures, than after the weight of matter, worth of subject, soundness of argument, life of invention, or depth of judgment."[11] After such a demolishingly inclusive criticism, Bacon goes on to single out Car of Cambridge and Ascham as among the foremost English culprits and to lament their near deification of Cicero and Demosthenes. As George Williamson has pointed out, Bacon argues that "eloquence is a hindrance to the advancment of learning,

---

[10] *The Whole Works of Roger Ascham*, ed. Rev. Dr. John Allen Giles (London: John Russell Smith, 1864-1865), III, 211.

[11] *The Works of Francis Bacon*, III, 283. See also A. C. Howell, *"Res et Verba*: Words and Things," *ELH: A Journal of English Literary History*, XIII (June 1946), 131-142.

but not to the use of learning,"[12] and it is well to note that pulpit rhetoric was not the object of Bacon's attack. But as the century moved on, attacks on the language of preachers became abundant, until ministers were cast in the role of chief offenders against the proprieties of speech. The full force of the attack on pulpit eloquence was not felt until the Restoration, a good generation after Donne's death, though John Dryden assigns to the clergy a guilt of long standing. In his *Defence of the Epilogue*, published in 1672, speaking somewhat disparagingly of a certain mode of wit which he detected in Sidney, Jonson, and other writers of Jonson's time, Dryden states his belief that this unhappy style made its way during the Elizabethan Age into the pulpit, "where . . . it yet finds the benefit of its clergy; for they are commonly the first corrupters of eloquence, and the last reformed from vicious oratory. . . ."[13]

Details of the seventeenth-century contention over stylistic practices have been traced in many scholarly articles and books,[14] and I will do no more than sketch the main outlines of the argument. The century called for more matter and less wit, more things and fewer words, more plainness and less fancy. Thomas Fuller (1642) condemns those divines who eschew "clearness and plainness" in their writings, asserting that "Some affect this darkness, that they may be accounted profound; whereas one is not bound to believe, that all the water is deep that is muddy."[15]

[12] *The Senecan Amble* (London: Faber and Faber Limited, 1951), p. 153.

[13] *Essays of John Dryden*, ed. W. P. Ker (Oxford at the Clarendon Press, 1900), I, 173-174. For a number of references in this section I am indebted to J. E. Spingarn's introduction to his edition of *Critical Essays of the Seventeenth Century* (Oxford at the Clarendon Press, 1908-1909), I, xxxvi-lxviii.

[14] George Williamson's *The Senecan Amble*, the most thorough book on the subject, cites a number of relevant scholarly studies.

[15] *The Holy State, and The Profane State*, p. 59.

John Wilkins devotes part of his *Ecclesiastes, or, A Discourse concerning the Gift of Preaching As it falls under the Rules of Art* (1646) to the problem of style; he speaks against "*Rhetorical* flourishes" and is convinced that the "greatest learning is to be seen in the greatest plainness."[16] Thomas Hobbes, writing of the abuses of speech (1651), condemns those who "use words metaphorically; that is, in other sense than that they are ordained for; and thereby deceive others."[17]

It was in the 1660's and 1670's that the attack on eloquence, pulpit and otherwise, reached its peak. Thomas Sprat, in his *History of the Royal Society* (1667), speaks out against "luxury and redundance of *speech*," "specious *Tropes* and *Figures*," "vicious abundance of *Phrase*," "trick of *Metaphors*," and "volubility of *Tongue*." Members of the Society, he goes on, have been "most rigorous in putting in execution, the only Remedy, that can be found for this *extravagance*: and that has been, a constant Resolution, to reject all the amplifications, digressions, and swellings of style: to return back to the primitive purity, and shortness, when men deliver'd so many *things*, almost in an equal number of *words*. They have exacted from all their members, a close, naked, natural way of speaking; positive expressions; clear senses; a native easiness: bringing all things as near the Mathematical plainness, as they can: and preferring the language of Artizans, Countrymen, and Merchants, before that, of Wits, or Scholars."[18]

Restoration preacher Robert South attacked pulpit eloquence from the pulpit. Preaching on April 30, 1668, on the text of Luke 21:15—"For I will give you a mouth and wisdom, which all your adversaries shall not be able

[16] I have quoted from the 1659 edition (London), p. 128.
[17] *Leviathan* (Oxford at the Clarendon Press, 1909), p. 25.
[18] Pp. 111-113. I have quoted from the 1667 edition as duplicated in the volume edited by Jackson I. Cope and Harold Whitmore Jones (Saint Louis: Washington University Studies, 1958).

to gainsay nor resist"—South urged his fellow preachers to speak with "Great clearness and perspicuity," with "unaffected plainness and simplicity." He affirmed that Biblical truth should be presented "in the plainest and most intelligible language," and declaimed against "fustian bombast," "highflown metaphors and allegories," and "scraps of Greek and Latin."[19]

Certain treatises of the 1670's single out the clergy as bearing a heavy responsibility for the sad state of contemporary rhetoric. John Eachard, in *The Grounds & Occasions of the Contempt of the Clergy and Religion Enquired into* (1670), recommends a careful study of English in the curriculum of young students, feeling as he does that the contempt of the clergy is motivated in part by their mutilation of language. It is his judgment that "most of that Ridiculousness, phantastical Phrases, harsh and sometimes blasphemous Metaphors, abundantly foppish Similitudes, childish and empty Transitions, and the like, so commonly uttered out of Pulpits, and so fatally redounding to the discredit of the Clergy, may in a great measure be charg'd upon the want of that [an intensive study of English] which we have here so much contended for."[20] He belabors "high tossing and swaggering Preaching," commends "Matter plain and practical" and "plain words, usefull and intelligible instructions," offers as a model of intelligibility the Sermon on the Mount, and assails pulpit metaphors which roam "away presently to both the *Indies*, rake Heaven and Earth, down to the bottom of the Sea, then tumble over all Arts and Sciences, ransack all Shops and Ware-houses, spare neither Camp nor City, but that they will have them."[21] And in Joseph Glanvill's *An Essay Concerning Preaching* (1678) we find a

[19] *Sermons Preached upon Several Occasions* (Oxford at the Clarendon Press, 1823), IV, 149-151.
[20] London, p. 32.
[21] *Ibid.*, pp. 38, 39, 41, 46.

like sentiment. "There is," he writes, "a bastard kind of eloquence that is crept into the Pulpit, which consists in affectations of wit and finery, flourishes, metaphors, and cadencies." How well he speaks for his age in the concluding sentence to his section on rhetorical plainness: "Thus I have described to you the first Rule and Character of Preaching: it should be PLAIN."[22]

It was not until after Donne's death that the demand for a plain style began in earnest. To what extent Donne's sermons may have been in the minds of those who clamored for a new style is uncertain. Writers from Fuller through Glanvill were surely more concerned with the preachers of their day, including Jeremy Taylor perhaps,[23] than with men like Andrewes and Donne. Yet the great success and fame of Andrewes and Donne must have influenced the clergy of the next generation. Since the critics spoke generally, seldom identifying the villains, we cannot be certain which preachers were considered most responsible for the prevailing pulpit rhetoric, or which ones were thought to be carrying it to its greatest lengths in the generation following Donne. But a reading of Donne's sermons and then of the criticisms by, say, Wilkins or Eachard or Glanvill, would lead one to believe that Donne must have pleased the London of James I and Charles I more than he did his readers of the following decades. And what, indeed, are the marks of Donne's style?

Judging from the few explicit remarks Donne makes about style, we may infer that his ideals were closer to Bacon's than to Ascham's. In a sermon on the text of Philippians 3:2—"Beware of the concision"—Donne remarks: "Language must waite upon matter, and *words* upon

<hr/>

[22] Pp. 23, 28. See also J. E. Spingarn's edition of *Critical Essays in the Seventeenth Century*, II, 276-277.

[23] W. Fraser Mitchell points out that Robert South's sermon on the text of Luke 21:15, mentioned above, was directed against Jeremy Taylor; see *English Pulpit Oratory*, pp. 13, 316.

things . . . The matter, that is, the doctrine that we preach, is the forme, that is, the Soule, the *Essence*; the language and words wee preach in, is but the Body, but the *existence*." At the same time, the language of the early verses of chapter three of Philippians, Donne tells us, is carefully and artistically chosen; indeed, Paul makes a fine marriage of content and expression: ". . . in elegant language, he incorporates, and invests sound and important Doctrine; for, though he choose *words* of musicall sound, *Circumcision* and *Concision*, yet it is a matter of weighty consideration that he intends in this Concision." (D x:112) In another sermon, in words that might almost be mistaken for those of Sprat himself, Donne tells his congregation that he will expound his text "with such succinctness and brevity, as may consist with clearness, and perspicuity, in such manner, and method, as may best enlighten your understandings, and least encumber your memories" (D iv:92).[24] That the rhetoric is not the sermon Donne makes clear when he reproves the man who "heares but the Logique, or the Retorique, or the Ethique, or the poetry of the Sermon," and urges him to hear above all "the Sermon of the Sermon" (D vii:293). Nor is he so intent upon the sermon intrinsically as to forget that it is to be preached to a group of human beings and not to remain in a vacuum. "As God gave his children such Manna as was agreeable to every mans taste, and tasted to every man like that, that that man liked best," he writes, "so are wee to deliver the bread of life agreeable to every taste, to fit our Doctrine to the apprehension, and capacity, and digestion of the hearers" (D ii:276). The sermon to him was not primarily a literary enterprise, but a careful exposition of Scripture and a passionate exhortation to hear and do the Word of God.

[24] George Williamson states that the stylistic aims expressed in this quotation are "typically Senecan"; *The Senecan Amble*, p. 243.

But for all that, Donne never forgot or neglected his own literary artistry. He knew with Sir Philip Sidney that a discourse is effective in proportion to its ability to teach *and* delight. And he was not, like Bacon, primarily concerned with the advancement of learning; he was, instead, intent upon proclaiming what, once and for all, has been revealed. He was not dispassionately seeking to come to know that which is not known; he was not doing his work in the laboratory of scientific empiricism. He was seeking to lay hold upon man's heart and mind with the passionate persuasion that God has made known what is necessary for the soul's salvation. Whatever priority he may give "the Sermon of the Sermon," he knew that this is really not enough.

It is difficult, I think, to describe with precision what makes for greatness in prose style, but I should like to begin the study of Donne's style with some remarks on its rhythm. A great part of the beauty of his prose stems from his acute sensitivity to sentence structure, a kind of architectonic in which he knows just how far to go with parallel constructions without allowing them to become monotonous, and knows exactly what devices to use to prevent a rhythm too regular and a pace too unvaried. A good example of such art is found in his description of the terrors of a man who is spiritually ill: "Every fit of an Ague is an Earth-quake that swallows him, every fainting of the knee, is a step to Hell; every lying down at night is a funerall; and every quaking is a rising to judgment; every bell that distinguishes times, is a passing-bell, and every passing-bell, his own; every singing in the ear, is an Angels Trumpet; at every dimnesse of the candle, he heares that voice, *Fool, this night they will fetch away thy soul*; and in every judgement denounced against sin, he hears an *ito maledicte* upon himselfe, *Goe thou accursed into hell fire*" (D II:84).

If the hearer or reader can momentarily detach himself from the macabre spectacle, he will be impressed primarily by the parallel structure. Marked by the repetition of the word *every*, the parallelism is yet saved from monotony by the simple and effective device of having the word *every* twice preceded by the conjunction *and*, once by the preposition *at*, and once by the preposition *in*; to strip each main clause of the initial conjunctions and prepositions would be to destroy the rhythmical effectiveness of the passage. The parallelism is further carried out by repetition of the word *hears*, followed by the two Biblical quotations of what the wretched man does hear. There is still another quality of this passage, namely a certain brittleness and terseness, which sets it off from a more flowing and relaxed prose used sometimes by Donne in his successful attempts to be as varied stylistically as possible. As we read of this poor sinner, we find the prose a long step not only from that which Donne uses at other times but also from the habitually more complex and grand sentences of Richard Hooker and of others whose style bore the strong influence of Cicero; indeed, it is closer to the style that one associates with Bacon's essays (particularly those of the 1625 edition), a style usually designated as Senecan. It is a prose which makes more sparing use of subordinate clauses and of connectives between main clauses than does Ciceronianism. One effect of Senecanism is to quicken the pace or, at least, to give the impression of quickening, a fact which in turn heightens the dramatic quality. And so we see that Donne's passage moves quickly from its first ague to everlasting hell-fire; his Lincoln's Inn congregation must have been frighteningly disconcerted by the rapidity with which damnation may overtake a human being.

It is well to look now at a longer passage which also shows Donne's sure control over rhythm. One is again struck by the parallelism, but soon becomes aware that it is tempered again and again by an asymmetry which at once precludes monotony and heightens the effectiveness of what symmetry there is. Donne's skill lies in his ability to play large blocks of the passage over against other major sections in parallel order but at the same time to see to it that within the larger parallel sections there are smaller parts in asymmetrical order. Up to a point Donne follows the parallel practices of the euphuistic writings of such men as Lyly, but his style is made considerably more effective by his constant avoidance of playing off too exactly the individual clauses and phrases within one larger block against those in another:

"Here then Salvation is eternall Salvation; not the outward seals of the Church upon the person, not visible Sacraments, nor the outward seal of the person, to the Church, visible works, nor the inward seal of the Spirit, assurance here, but fruition, possession of glory, in the Kingdome of Heaven; where we shall be infinitely rich, and that without labor in getting, or care in keeping, or fear in loosing; and fully wise, and that without ignorance of necessary, or study of unnecessary knowledge, where we shal not measure our portion by acres, for all heaven shall be all ours; nor our term by yeers, for it is life and everlasting life; nor our assurance by precedent, for we shal be safer then the Angels themselves were in the creation; where our exaltation shal be to have a crown of righteousness, and our possession of that crown shal be, even the throwing it down at the feet of the Lamb; where we shal leave off all those petitions of *Adveniat regnum,* thy Kingdom come, for it shal be come in abundant power; and the *da nobis hodiè,* give us this day our dayly bread, for we shal have all that which we can desire now, and shall have a power to desire more, and then have that desire so enlarged, satisfied; And the *Libera nos*, we shall not pray to be delivered from evil, for no evil, *culpæ* or *poenæ*, either of sin to deserve punishment, or of punishmen for our former sins shal offer at us; where we shall see God face to face, for we shall have such notions and apprehensions, as shall enable us to see him, and he shall afford such an imparting, such a manifestation of himself, as he shall be seen by us; and where we shall be as inseparably united to our Saviour, as his humanity and divinity are united together: This unspeakable, this unimaginable happiness is this Salvation, and therefore let us be glad when this is brought neer us" (D ii:266).

The structure of this passage describing eternal salvation is determined by the enumeration of those things which eternal salvation is and those things which it is not. Reading the paragraph up to the first *where*, we will note that the construction is governed by the adverbs *not. . .nor. . .not* and the conjunction *but*. Had Donne carried out the initial parallelism in perfectly symmetrical fashion, he would have written the following far less effective and less rhythmical passage: ". . .not the outward seals of the Church upon the person, not visible Sacraments, nor the outward seal of the person to the Church, not visible works, nor the inward seal of the Spirit upon the person, not assurance here, but. . . ." Donne thus gets off to a good start, yet the most skillful use of rhythm and asymmetry begins with the initial *where* and continues to the end of the paragraph. The variation in phrasing can best be seen by noting those connective words that follow each *where*, providing the transitions from one phrase or clause to the next and binding together the various sections. Thus we find: "where we shall. . .and that without. . .or. . .or. . .and. . .and that without. . .or. . ."; "where we shal not. . .for. . .nor. . .for. . .nor . . .for. . ."; "where our exhaltation shal be. . .and. . .shal

be. . ."; "where we shal. . .for. . .and. . .for. . .and. . .and
. . .and. . .for. . .either. . .or. . ."; "where we shall. . .for
. . .as. . .and. . .as. . ."; "and where we shall. . .as. . .as. . . ."
To read the passage aloud is to feel the full impact of the
rhythm and to sense the effect which Donne's rhetoric
must have had on those who sat before him.

If their rhythmical quality is one of the outstanding
characteristics of Donne's sermons, their metaphysical style
is another. By *metaphysical style* I mean the use of such
devices as the epigrammatic statement, the paradoxical
affirmation, the startling comparison, and the concrete,
dramatic picture. Though these practices depend in great
part, of course, on the subject matter, they may be termed
stylistic in that they are devices for presenting the subject
matter in a particularly arresting manner. The practices
frequently overlap; a passage may be at once epigrammatic
and paradoxical, or paradoxical and startling, and so forth.
It would require the ingenuity and verbosity of a Polonius,
with his "pastoral-comical, historical-pastoral, tragical-his-
torical, tragical-comical-historical-pastoral," to suggest
Donne's manifold combinations. We might note a few of
them.

First, let us look at a short passage the principal force of
which comes from its terse, clipped, pithy, epigrammatic
quality: "It is a lesse miracle to raise a man from a *sick bed*,
then to hold a man from a *wanton bed*, a litentious bed;
lesse to overcome and quench his fever, then to quench his
lust. *Joseph* that refused his *mistris* was a greater *miracle*
then *Lazarus* raised from the dead." (D IV:152) The
rhetoric might be Bacon's; the thought is unmistakably
Donne's. A closely allied form of writing is one built upon
a series of paradoxical affirmations, each of which, though
theologically sound, seems more outlandish than the preceding one: "*Adam* sinnd, and *I* suffer; I *forfeited* before
I had any *Possession*, or could claime any *Interest*; I had a

Punishment, before I had a *being*, And *God* was displeased with *me* before *I* was *I*; I was built up scarce 50. years ago, in my Mothers womb, and I was cast down, almost 6000. years agoe, in *Adams* loynes; I was *borne* in the last *Age* of the world, and *dyed* in the first" (D VII:78).

Both of the quoted passages are marked by their extravagance of statement; the first is distinguished by its epigrammatism, the second by its paradox. And there is still another kind of extravagance of statement found in Donne, one which is spun to greater length, depending for its effectiveness not so much on epigram or paradox as on a series of startling comparisons, a mounting dependence on hyperbole. Sometimes such a passage will progress through a description of the unknown by means of the known; and the known, usually expressed in some superlative degree, is found even in its greatest extremity to fall short of the unknown which Donne is seeking to suggest to the imagination of his hearers. A superb twentieth-century example of such a procedure is found in Father Arnall's sermon on eternity in James Joyce's *A Portrait of the Artist as a Young Man*. And one outstanding example of Donne's technique is also found in a description of eternity; the passage contains most of the distinguishing marks of his style—parallel structure, repetition of key words, rhythmical control, and the kind of hyperbolic comparison which would recapture any attention which might have wandered. Preaching on the text of John 14:2—"In my Fathers House are many Mansions; if it were not so, I would have told you"—Donne points out that the word *Mansions* "signifies a *Remaining*," and he then goes on to hint at the nature of this everlasting quality; it is

"A state but of one Day, because no Night shall over-take, or determine it, but such a Day, as is not of a thousand yeares, which is the longest measure in the Scriptures, but of a thousand millions of millions of generations: *Qui nec præceditur hesterno, nec excluditur crastino,* A day that hath no *pridie,* nor *postridie,* yesterday doth not usher it in, nor to morrow shall not drive it out. *Methusalem,* with all his hundreds of yeares, was but a Mushrome of a nights growth, to this day, And all the foure Monarchies, with all their thousands of yeares, And all the powerfull Kings, and all the beautifull Queenes of this world, were but as a bed of flowers, some gathered at six, some at seaven, some at eight, All in one Morning, in respect of this Day. In all the two thousand yeares of Nature, before the Law given by *Moses,* And the two thousand yeares of Law, before the Gospel given by Christ, And the two thousand of Grace, which are running now, (of which last houre we have heard three quarters strike, more then fifteen hundred of this last two thousand spent) In all this six thousand, and in all those, which God may be pleased to adde, *In domo patris,* In this House of his Fathers, there was never heard quarter clock to strike, never seen minute glasse to turne. No time lesse then it selfe would serve to expresse this time, which is intended in this word *Mansions*; which is also exalted with another beame, that they are *Multa, In my Fathers House there are many Mansions."* (D vɪɪ:138-139)

Still another quality of Donne's prose is the highly dramatic practice of calling upon his hearers to imagine themselves placed in some concrete, specific situation. Louis Martz, in *The Poetry of Meditation,* has shown to what extent this detailed picturing of a scene is a predominant characteristic of the Renaissance literature of meditation. A fine example of this practice is found in a sermon preached on April 1, 1627, before the King at Whitehall; the text is Mark 4:24: "Take heed what you heare." The last paragraph of the sermon is cast in the form of an imaginary conversation between Satan and a member, indeed all members, of Donne's congregation on the verge of death. The scene is the deathbed, to which Donne transports his hearers. Here Satan is to be found recalling to the dying man's memory the sins of his life, with the hope of bringing him to the despair which is spiritual death. Satan, Donne tells his congregation, will appear to each of them "when thine eares shall be deafe, with the cryes of a distressed, and a distracted family, and with the sound, and the change of the sound of thy last bell." The dreadful experience is more than auditory: ". . .thou shalt see, or seem to see his [Satan's] hand turning the streame of thy Saviours bloud into another channell, and telling thee, here's enough for *Jew* and *Turke*, but not a drop for *thee*." And Satan does more than *speak* of past sins: he holds up a mirror of despair, in which are reflected the multitude of sins which have beset the man's life. The focus of action then shifts, as the demonic temptations are countered by the reply of the dying man who, rather than taking heed of Satan's words, paints a vivid picture of the nature of his own redemption. "Take heed what you heare," Donne admonishes, and tell your tempter to return to you a minute after your physical death. For the faithful one, the man who has not been reduced to a despair of Christ's redemptive power and love, will then be able to draw a picture of the glory which awaits him and may thus retort to Satan: ". . .come a minute after my soule is departed from this body, come to me, where I shall be then, and when thou seest me washed in the bloud of my Saviour, clothed in the righteousnesse of my Saviour, lodged in the bosome of my Saviour, crowned with the merits of my Saviour, confesse, that upon my death-bed, thou wast a lyer, and wouldest have been a murderer, and the Lord shall, and I, in him, shall rebuke thee." The peroration is a final assurance of eternal victory to the man who withstands the Adversary:

"Heare what that bloud says for you, in the eares of the Father, and then no singing of the flatterer, no lisping of the tempter, no roaring of the accuser, no thunder of the destroyer shall shake thy holy constancy. Take heed what you heare, remember what you have heard; and the God of heaven, for his Sonne Christ Jesus sake, by the working of his blessed Spirit, prosper and emprove both endeavours in you. Amen." (D vii:412-414) The concrete placing of the deathbed scene; the tension between Satan's beckoning and the dying man's faith, with the inducement to despair played off against the envisaged redemptive action of Christ's blood; and the final exhortation to hear and to take heed—all of these make for a pictorial and moving prose passage.

Of the many concrete scenes which Donne draws, there is just one more to which I should now like to refer. The passage is from a sermon on the text of 1 Timothy 3:16, in which Christ is said to be seen by the angels. Donne is contrasting what the angels do see when they behold the risen Christ with what it is hoped they will not see when they look down and behold Christ within the person of a living man; once again the effectiveness arises from the vivid contrast. They behold the risen Christ "sate down in glory at the right hand of his Father; all sweat wip'd from his Browes, and all teares from his Eyes; all his Stripes heal'd, all his Blood stanch'd, all his Wounds shut up, and all his Beauty returned there. . . ." Donne then speaks of what he hopes the angels will *not* see when they direct their attention to this earth: ". . .when they look down hither, to see the same Christ in thee, may [they] not see him scourged again, wounded, torn and mangled again, in thy blasphemings, nor crucified again in thy ir-religious conversation." (D iii:218)

Passing mention should be made of Donne's use of al-literation and other sound devices, perhaps even more

popular since the days of Lyly than before and familiar
in the sermons of Andrewes. Donne shows moderation in
this respect, though a few of his flights may be recorded.
He has a certain fondness for the "s" sound: ". . . a Sea
of sinking and swallowing in the sadnesse of spirit . . ."
(D III:127); again, and this time in reference to the letter "Y": "We bind our selves to the stake, to the stalk,
to the staff, the stem of this Symbolical Letter . . ." (D
IX:174). He once combines the alliterative "s" with the
terminal "ings": ". . . he flings, and slings, and stings the
soul of the sinner . . ." (D I:174); and he once makes
full use of the terminal "tion": "Expectation, Acceptation,
Acclamation, Congratulation, Remuneration, in a fair proportion" (D II:175). But there are few such noticeable
displays in his text.

IMAGERY

The reader of Donne's sermons is certainly moved by
their rhetorical power; he is perhaps even more impressed
by their sure sense of imagery. From his poetry Donne
carries over into his prose a startling and exciting metaphoric skill, and with no loss of either intensity or com-
prehensiveness. He writes in one of his early sermons
that "the Prophets, and the other Secretaries of the holy
Ghost in penning the books of Scriptures, do for the most
part retain, and express in their writings some impressions,
and some air of their former professions; those that had
been bred in Courts and Cities, those that had been Shep-
heards and Heardsmen, those that had been Fishers, and
so of the rest; ever inserting into their writings some
phrases, some metaphors, some allusions, taken from that
profession which they had exercised before . . ." (D I:236).
To apply the same argument to the preacher which is here
made about the prophet would be to conclude that Donne
had been bred in many places, so large is the range from

which his metaphors are drawn, and so few the areas of experience that his imagery leaves untouched.[25] Perhaps the most convenient approach to a study of Donne's imagery would entail a fourfold division: first, notice of those passages in which comparisons are made, rather briefly, between the religious experience and some familiar area of secular experience; second, examination of the way in which references to various parts of the human body are used metaphorically or symbolically; third, analysis of Donne's occasional practice of structuring a sermon almost entirely around one central analogy; finally, study of the two images used most extensively throughout the sermons, those of light and water.

First, then, we may consider the analogies in which the nature of a religious experience is made clearer through its comparison to a more familiar secular experience. And a discussion of these analogies calls in turn for a subdivision. Donne uses such comparisons at times to make clear the spiritual condition of the sinful man, at times to suggest the nature of God's redemptive activity, and at times to illustrate some of the many other aspects of the relationship between God and man. I will begin with references to a few, quite differing analogies which seek to make clear the condition of the sinful man, comparisons drawn from the areas of law, commerce, and medicine. In his first extant sermon, on the text of Isaiah 52:3—"Ye have sold your selves for nought, and ye shall be redeemed without money"—Donne, wishing to describe the nature of spiritual prodigality by comparing it to what is in fact known about temporal prodigality, enumerates the legal punishments which fall upon a man judged wasteful of his temporal estate and shows their relationship to the limitations placed upon the spiritual prodigal. The first penalty

[25] See Milton Allan Rugoff, *Donne's Imagery: A Study in Creative Sources* (New York: Corporate Press, Inc., 1939).

is that he who "is a Prodigall, in the Law, cannot dispose of his own Estate; whatsoever he gives, or sells, or leases, all is void, as of a mad-man, or of an Infant." The sinful man, the spiritual prodigal, is similarly frustrated in any transaction, since he is rendered irresponsible by his debilitating sinfulness. Secondly, the man who has been legally declared a prodigal can make no will. In like manner the sinner who squanders his spiritual gifts is unable to will his soul to God, his body to a church, or his material goods to designated persons; for he is burdened with the indebtedness under which his sins have placed him, and the devil may lay rightful claim to him. Thirdly, as the prodigal has no claim on his father's property, so the unrepentant sinner may expect nothing of the bounty of God's grace. (D 1:155-156) There is, in one of the Lincoln's Inn sermons, another striking legal image, used this time to describe the status of the faithful persons who arrive at the gate of heaven, "where all Clients shall retain but one Counsellor, our Advocate Christ Jesus, nor present him any other fee but his own blood, and yet every Client have a Judgment on his side, not only in a not guilty, in the remission of his sins, but in a *Venite benedicti*, in being called to the participation of an immortal Crown of glory" (D 11:249).

At another time Donne uses a commercial image to clarify the sinful nature of man's estate. Through Adam's fall, all mankind was sold to the devil; through the shedding of Christ's blood, mankind was redeemed. But man through his actual, day-to-day sins has sold himself to Satan once again, a fact which Donne expresses with considerable wit: "In *Adam* we were sold in *grosse*; in our selves we are sold by *retail*" (D 11:115). And on another occasion a medical image describes the human condition. When the human heart receives a wound it is incurable, since its perpetual motion and constant beating prevent the physician from working upon it. So it is with the spiritual heart *"fully set to do evil"*; so unsettled is its condition, so brisk is the motion of its sinful activity, so extensive is the presence of sin, that there is simply "no room for a Cure." (D 1:179-180)

Donne turns to various other secular areas to make clear by analogy the nature of God's redemptive action. He finds rich quarry, for example, in agricultural imagery. In discussing Christ's love for man, Donne writes that the Lord "loves us most for our improvement, when by his ploughing up of our hearts, and the dew of his grace, and the seed of his word, we come to give a greater rent, in the fruites of sanctification than before" (D 1:241). And speaking of the Kingdom of God within the human being, he asserts that it is *"planted* in your *election; watred* in your *Baptisme; fatned* with the *blood* of Christ Jesus, *ploughed* up with many *calamities*, and tribulations; *weeded* with often *repentances* of particular sins . . ." (D 11:337). Marine imagery also illustrates God's redeeming action. True it is, Donne writes, that Christ alone could still a tempest, but man can at the least ride out a storm if he will anchor his confidence in God's being:

"It is well for us, if, though we be put to take in our sayls, and to take down our masts, yet we can hull it out; that is, if in storms of contradiction, or persecution, the Church, or State, though they be put to accept worse conditions then before, and to depart with some of their outward splendor, be yet able to subsist and swimme above water, and reserve it selfe for Gods farther glory, after the storme is past; onely Christ could becalm the storme; He is a good Christian that can ride out, or board out, or hull out a storme, that by industry, as long as he can, and by patience, when he can do no more, over-lives a storm, and does not forsake his ship for it, that is not scandalized with that State, nor that Church, of which he is a member, for those abuses that are in it" (D III: 185).

In these different ways Donne seeks to impress upon his hearers the condition of the sinful man and the nature of God's redemptive activity. But it is necessary, in order to feel something of the scope of Donne's imagery, to see how he describes some of the many other aspects of the relationship between God and man. Attempting, for example, to persuade his congregation that God asks only for human gratitude in response to his infinite love, Donne uses a clockmaking image, though not in a Cartesian sense: the clockmaker works diligently upon the various wheels so that the bell may ring and the hand inform others of the time; so God has bestowed his merciful work on us, hoping only that we may make a declaration of his mercies and thus win others to his love (D VI:42). The sense of joy felt by the Lord when man shows his gratitude through good works is conveyed by a music analogy. Heaven and earth together are like a musical instrument: touch a string at the bottom of an instrument, and the vibrant motion carries to the top; in like manner, the good deeds done by man on earth are felt by Christ in heaven (D III:59). God is affected not only by man's works, but by his prayerful words as well, a fact Donne chooses to convey through an image of war. The words are likened to the shots from a cannon, in the paths of which God graciously stations himself:

"The words of man, in the mouth of a faithfull man, of *Abraham*, are a Canon against God himselfe, and batter down all his severe and heavy purposes for Judgements. Yet, this comes not, God knows, out of the weight or force of our words, but out of the easinesse of God. God puts himselfe into the way of a shot, he meets a weak prayer, and is graciously pleased to be wounded by that:

God sets up a light, that we direct the shot upon him, he enlightens us with a knowledge, how, and when, and what to pray for; yea, God charges, and discharges the Canon himself upon himselfe; He fils us with good and religious thoughts, and appoints and leaves the Holy Ghost, to discharge them upon him, in prayer, for it is the Holy Ghost himselfe that prayes in us." (D III:152-153)

Among Donne's most effective analogies to suggest the relationship between God and man are those involving a map or a circle. A flat map, on which East and West are at the greatest possible distance from each other, is like a flat soul, one which is dejected and despairing. The soul sees itself lost in the West, symbolizing death, and at the greatest distance from salvation, signified by the East or by Christ—"The name of Christ is *Oriens, The East....*" West can be made to touch East by pasting the map on a round body; and the soul's West can be made its East if it will but "apply. . .[its] trouble. . .to the body of the Gospel of Christ Jesus," and respond to its offer of salvation. (D VI:59) Donne's poetic expression of the same idea, found in "Hymne to God my God, in my sicknesse," is a familiar one:

> As West and East
> In all flatt Maps (and I am one) are one,
> So death doth touch the Resurrection.

Man's existence may also be viewed as a circle, in which death and new life may be seen in their true relationship. Nowhere is this concept more clearly illustrated than in one of Donne's references to the martyrs, whose death and rebirth are described through a pattern not of one, but of two circles:

"Their death was a birth to them into another life, into the glory of God; it ended one Circle, and created another;

for immortality, and eternity is a Circle too; not a Circle where two points meet, but a Circle made at once; This life is a Circle, made with a Compasse, that passes from point to point; That life is a Circle stamped with a print, an endlesse, and perfect Circle, as soone as it begins. Of this Circle, the Mathematician is our great and good God; The other Circle we make up our selves; we bring the Cradle, and Grave together by a course of nature." (D ii:200)

When Donne wishes to distinguish among the different ways in which God has acted toward the Gentiles, the Jews, and the Christians, he also resorts to metaphor. In one sermon God's varying degrees of revelation are compared to the three meals of the day. He first enlightened the Gentiles, and he did so purely through his creation, through the light which comes from observing the workings of the natural world; the gift of such knowledge is analogous to the breaking of a fast, to a breakfast, but not to a full meal. God's gift to the Jews lay primarily in the revelation of the Law, more efficacious than the light of Nature, and yet meant for only certain people, for the Jewish nation; this gift is analogous to a dinner rich in bounty but prepared for only certain guests. God comes in his fullness only in the third meal, in the supper which is attended by Jesus Christ himself. In this third meal Christ first comes to us in his Spirit and then invites us to partake of supper with him in the Sacrament of Holy Communion; by such means we are brought to the blessedness of the Kingdom of Heaven. (D vii:301)

We find an unusual metaphoric practice in the course of two sermons preached on the text of Matthew 4:18-20, in which we are told of Jesus walking by the Galilean Sea and calling upon Peter and Andrew, who were casting their fishing nets, to follow him and become "fishers of men." The first sermon is a discussion of what Peter and Andrew were like when Jesus found them; the second of what they became through discipleship to their Lord. Of great importance to both discourses is Donne's metaphoric or symbolic use of the word *net*, particularly since this word assumes the precisely opposite symbolic meaning in the second sermon from what it held in the first. When Jesus first came upon the fishermen, their nets, used to gather fish, would have been deterrents to their allegiance to Christ; consequently, in answer to Jesus' call, "they straightway left their nets, and followed him" (D 11:269). Their doing so indicates that the faithful man must put aside any worldly consideration which might hinder him from his primary calling to follow Christ. Toward the end of the sermon Donne writes that faithful men "must leave themselves without nets, that is, without those things, which, in their own Consciences they know, retard the following of Christ. Whatsoever hinders my present following, that I cannot follow to day, whatsoever may hinder my constant following, that I cannot follow to morrow, and all my life, is a net, and I am bound to leave that" (D 11:286). But in the second sermon on the same text, in which Donne is discussing the later Peter and Andrew, the disciples of Christ, the word *net* assumes an opposite meaning. For when they become "fishers of men" and not of fish, the net symbolizes not a retarding force, but the Gospel itself, and the similarities between a net and the Gospel of Jesus Christ are written out in some detail. The Gospel is like a net in that it has leads, that is, pronouncements of God's judgments which have the power of sinking down the rebellious heart; it also has corks which serve to raise the contrite spirit above the waters of tribulation. Like a net the Gospel has knots, hindering knots if a man spends too much time on obscure and ambiguous passages, an understanding of which is not necessary for his salvation anyway; but also knots which bind him to God if he accepts the fundamental and clear Biblical teachings. The fisherman loses control of

his net if he casts it too far from him, and yet finds it useful
if he draws it to him; the Scriptures will become useless
"if thou cast and scatter them upon Reason, upon Philosophy, upon Morality, to try how the Scriptures will fit all
them, and beleeve them but so far as they agree with thy
reason; But," Donne continues as he draws his elaborate
analogy to its close, "draw the Scriptures to thine own
heart, and to thine own actions, and thou shalt finde it
made for that; all the promises of the old Testament made,
and all accomplished in the new Testament, for the salvation of thy soule hereafter, and for thy consolation in
the present application of them." (D II:307-308) Thus
there are really two images, antithetic in character, one in
which a net is a possible hindrance to salvation, the other in
which it is the very way of salvation.

Before turning to the metaphoric uses of various parts of
the human body, I should like to examine one more image,
one which does not fit exactly into any of the aforementioned analogical categories. In a sermon on the text of Ecclesiastes 12:1—"Remember now thy Creator in the dayes
of thy youth"—Donne turns to a discussion of God as Creator, a topic central to his *Essays in Divinity* and one which
fascinated him throughout his ministry. Within the sermon there is an extended analogy between the six days of
creation and the various conditions, qualities, and stages
of a man's religious life. As the first day was the making
of light, so the first day of our spiritual regeneration is the
knowledge which we have of God through the revealing
light of the Gospel. On the second day God made the
firmament, symbolizing the proper bounds to be placed on
human faculties; those waters above the firmament represent the unrevealed mysteries never meant to be fathomed
by man's understanding, which should limit itself to those
fundamental truths, belief in which is necessary for salvation. God's decree on the third day that the waters be

gathered together in one place is paralleled by the fact that the Church is the gathering place for the waters of life, that is, for "all the doctrine necessary for the life to come." The creations of the fourth day, the sun and the moon, are to be viewed, respectively, as indicative of God's love to us in the light of our temporal prosperity and of his "comfortable promises in the darkness of adversity." The creation of the creeping things and the flying things of the fifth day denotes on the one hand the propriety of our imitating the humility of the lowly and, on the other, the exhaltation which we may feel in winging ourselves away from the temptations of this world. Finally, the fact that man, the creation of the sixth day, is formed of the earth and the breath of God should constantly remind us of both our mortality and our immortality. Each day of creation is thus to be viewed in its symbolic relationship to the proper religious life of any child of God. (D II:240-243)

Throughout his preaching career Donne made extensive metaphoric use of virtually every part of the human body. The effectiveness of such imagery rests in large part upon its concreteness and familiarity. Occasionally he will construct a compound image, sometimes pairing off two of his bodily images and, on at least one occasion, using a triple image. He tells us several times that the Devil in his office of tempter works on both the eye and the ear of man; when Satan tries us with visual temptations, our eye is "the window to the heart," and when he works upon us through lascivious discourses, our ear is "the door to our heart" (D I:179). The eye, hand, and ear are once taken together, as Donne preaches that "The instrument and Organ of Nature was the eye; The Natural Man finds God in that he sees, in the Creature. The Organ of the Law, which exalted, and rectified Nature, was the Hand; *Fac hoc &* *vives*; perform the law, and thou shalt live. So also, the Organ of the Gospel is the Ear, for faith comes by hearing. . . ." (D VIII:343) The word *eyes* is used also to denote a person's capacity for understanding. Reference has already been made to Donne's imaginative exegesis of Revelation 4:8, which states that the four six-winged beasts "were full of eyes within"; the ministers of God, symbolized by the beasts, are gifted with eyes so that they will not, like the priests of Rome, be victims of blind obedience (D VIII:49-50). The eye of the Lord is to be viewed as an organ of guidance, as we learn from God's promise to the Psalmist that he will guide him with his eye; indeed the whole work of the Church may be equated with God's face, and thus the congregation may be said to see God face to face "in the Service, in the Sermon, in the Sacrament. . .there is an eye in that face, an eye in that Service, an eye in that Sermon, an eye in that Sacrament, a piercing and an operating Spirit, that lookes upon that soule, and foments and cherishes that soule, who by a good use of Gods former grace, is become fitter for his present." These eyes lead to conversion and to union with God. (D IX:366-367)

On March 24, 1617, to celebrate the fourteenth anniversary of King James's monarchy, Donne preached on the text of Proverbs 22:11: "He that loveth pureness of heart, for the grace of his lips, the king shall be his friend." In the course of the sermon Donne tells us that when the word *lips* is not used in a purely literal sense in Scripture, it is sometimes "enlarged to all manner of expressing a mans ability, to do service to that State in which God hath made his station" (D 1:206). The *"grace of lips"* indicates a man's capacity for public service, an ability not to be viewed with pride but to be used to the good of his nation (D 1:209). At another time Donne admonishes preachers not to proclaim God's word "with uncircumcised lips," that is, not without the eloquence which should mark so sacred an occasion (D VIII:147).

"There is no *phrase* oftner in the *Scriptures*," Donne once asserted, "then that *God* delivered his people, in the *hand* of *Moses*, and the *hand* of *David*, and the *hand* of the *Prophets*: all their Ministeriall office is called the *Hand* . . ." (D VI:245). The expression *clean hands* denotes justice in one's relationship with other men; unless a man's hands are kept clean through integrity or washed clean through repentance, that is, unless his relationship with other men is as it should be, then he will enjoy no satisfactory communion with God—"there is no pure prayer without clean hands." (D IX:216-220) In another sermon, bringing together once again a pair of images, Donne writes that a man's heart is the source of all good and holy purposes, and that his hand "is the execution and Declaration of those good purposes, produc'd into the eyes of men. . ." (D I:188).

The most elaborate consideration of the metaphoric significance of *feet* is found in a sermon on the text of Canticles [Song of Solomon] 5:3: "I have washed my feet, how shall I defile them?" Our feet represent our actions in this world; their washing indicates a cleansing of our ways. Man stands upon the two feet of nature and custom, one of which is lame through our inheritance of Adam's sin, the other through our indulgence in habitual sins. The covering of the feet signifies an unclean action—witness King Saul's covering of his feet in the cave; a washing of the feet is symbolic of that examination of our actions which leads to repentance and may be equated with tears of repentance. A true witness of God must keep his feet clean, for only then may he serve as the Lord's instrument, as an effective example to all those who look upon him. (D V:171-181) Reference has been made to the six-winged seraphim, two of whose wings cover their feet, and we will recall Donne's equation of the seraphim with God's ministers, and his statement that a minister's feet are covered so that a congregation may not pry so curiously into the ways of his life that it is distracted from the proclamation of Scripture which flows from his lips (D VIII:47-48). There are still other references to the word *feet*: the beauty which impels men to love us lies in our feet, that is, our actions (D II:173); the ministers of God are his feet (D III:323).

Donne's marriage sermons also have their share of bodily analogies, usually to suggest the proper relationship between husband and wife. True to the Biblical and seventeenth-century view that the wife is the weaker vessel, and yet one not to be unduly debased, Donne points to Eve's creation as an indication of woman's true status: "She was not taken out of the *foot*, to be troden upon, nor out of the *head*, to be an overseer of him; but out of *his side*, where she weakens him enough, and therefore should do all she can, to be a Helper" (D II:346). Of a more extended nature is the following blueprint for marital bliss: "The husband is the Helper in the nature of a foundation, to sustain and uphold all; The wife in the nature of the roof, to cover imperfections and weaknesses: The husband in the nature of the head from whence all the sinews flow; The wife in the nature of the hands into which those sinews flow, and enable them to doe their offices. The husband helps as legges to her, she moves by his motion; The wife helps as a staffe to him, he moves the better by her assistance." (D III:247) Speaking of marital arguments, Donne explains succinctly that "our flesh is the wife, and the spirit is the husband, and they two will never agree" (D V:208).

A passage taking issue with contemporary cosmetic and beautifying practices laments the fastidious labor expended on our skins, described as "the Records of velim. . .the parchmins, the endictments, and the evidences that shall condemn many of us, at the last day." God's law which is written in our hearts, his image which is imprinted in our souls, his character and seal which come to us in our baptism—all of these gifts are "bound up in this velim, in this parchmin, in this skin of ours, and we neglect book, and image, and character, and seal, and all for the covering." (D III:103-104) The body which is enclosed in this frail parchment is characterized as the grave of the soul (D VI:75) and as a "House of Clay" and a wall of mud (D VI:356). But a later description of the function of our bones would persuade us to look upon the body in the more exalted status of the Temple of the Holy Ghost: our bones are the "Beames, and Timbers, and Rafters of these Tabernacles, these Temples of the Holy Ghost, these bodies of ours" (D V:352). If we would be angelic, let us see to it that our bodies be kept within narrow bounds: "The attenuation, the slendernesse, the deliverance of the body from the encumbrance of much flesh, gives us some assimilation, some conformity to God, and his Angels; The lesse flesh we carry, the liker we are to them, who have none. . ." (D VII:106).

The breasts, the womb, and the belly also fall within Donne's compass. In discussing the Trinity, he asserts that our conceptions of Father, Son, and Holy Ghost "are so many handles by which we may take hold of God, and so many breasts, by which we may suck such a knowledge of God, as that by it wee may grow up into him" (D III:263). The Church is "the wombe where my soule must be mellowed for this first resurrection" [Donne here refers to a spiritual resurrection from sin] (D VI:72). Breasts and the womb, symbolic of redemptive powers, are countered by the belly, symbolizing those forces which would hinder our reconciliation. It is "the seat and scene of Carnal Desires, and inordinate Affections" (D IV:94); it is the ignoble part of the body on which the serpent must creep out his days; it constitutes "the bowels of sin" (D X:184).

Most of Donne's many vivid and dramatic sketches of man sinning are marked by the might of concupiscence. The lust of the body, that desecrating surrender of the Temple of the Holy Ghost to something less than holy and righteous purposes, underlies and motivates most acts of sin. Thus Donne views the male organ as the great symbol of war against God's purpose. The most extended disquisition on the penis appears in a sermon on the text of Genesis 17:24: "Abraham himselfe was ninety nine yeares old, when the foreskin of his flesh was circumcised." Abraham might well have asked, Donne points out, why God commanded him "so base and uncleane a thing, so scornfull and mis-interpretable a thing, as Circumcision, and Circumcision in that part." The primary answer is that such a mark could always serve as a concrete reminder against intemperance and incontinency. Donne stresses the power of the penis to work evil: it is the most rebellious part of the body; it was the only part which Adam covered, because it was the only part beyond his control; it is the one organ which God suffers to rebel against him, "for though the seeds of this rebellion be dispersed through all the body, yet, *In illa parte magis regnat additamentum Leviathan*, sayes Saint *Bernard*, the spawns of *Leviathan*, the seed of sinne, the leven of the Devil, abounds and reignes most in that part of the body; it is *sentina peccati*, saies the same Father, the *Sewar* of all sinne. . . ." This is true not only because we inherit original sin through our generation, but because the sins of gluttony, pride, excess, anger, malice, and murder are all woven into the same fabric which displays the mark of lust. Yet, though Abraham may indeed have questioned the rite of circumcision, he must soon have realized that it signified more than the trimming of man's most contentious organ; it was also "a signe of the *Covenant* between *God* and *Abraham*; the *Covenant* was the *Messias*, who being to come, by a carnall continuance of *Abrahams* race, the signe and seale was conveniently placed in that part." Circumcision had other significances as well: it represented or typified baptism; it dissuaded the Jews from idolatry, from falling prey to the customs and fellowship of the uncircumcised barbarians; most importantly, it prefigured the circumcision of the heart, the new life in Christ to which the faithful could look forward. (D vi:190-193) It is seldom that Donne does not see some promise and hope in a condition which may at first glance seem baneful or evil. Here we find that the penis, which uncontrolled can become an instrument to our damnation, is related to the heart, the cleansing of which is a sign of our union with God.

Another characteristic of Donne's imagery is that he will occasionally organize an entire sermon around one central metaphor. A fine example of such a practice is his discourse on the text of Matthew 21:44: "Whosoever shall fall on this stone, shall be broken; but on whomsoever it shall fall, it will grinde him to powder." The stone, of course, is Christ, and it is many-charactered. In the first place, it is the foundation stone of all good and lasting buildings; it remains firm to the end, just as Christ's love, which impels him to call men, to accompany them, and to reward them at the Last Judgment, is enduring. Secondly, it is, like Christ, the cornerstone which unites all Christians, however diverse they may be; as a cornerstone Christ unites God and man in his Person, unites God and mankind in his Office, and reconciles man to man in a world become divisive through the fall of Adam. "As wee consider him [Christ] in the foundation," Donne writes, "there he is the root of faith, As we consider him in the Corner, there hee is the root of charity. . . ." Christ is also *Lapis Jacob*, the stone of peace and security upon which Jacob rested his head. Fourthly, he is the stone which David shot from his sling to conquer the hostile and wicked Goliath, and he in like manner "enables the weakest man to over-throw the strongest sinne. . . ." Fifthly, he is *Lapis Petra*, a stone which is a rock, the same rock from which the Israelites drew water, honey, and oil, the same rock which is our defense in all manner of adversities. "As Christ is our foundation," Donne concludes Part One of his ser-mon, "we beleeve in him, and as he is our corner-stone, we are at peace with the world in him; as he is *Jacobs* stone, giving us peace in our selves, and *Davids* stone, giving us victory over our enemies, so he is a Rock of stone, (no affliction, no tribulation shal shake us.)" (D II:180-188)

Part Two of the sermon, already discussed in the section on Donne's doctrine of the Church, names the dangers attendant upon our disregard of the beneficent and life-giving qualities of the stone. The man whose sinful actions lead him to fall upon the stone is, paradoxically, fortunate. For to fall *upon* the stone is to be convicted of our sins, to know ourselves as we really are, and to realize for the first time our desperate need for the redemptive power of this stone: ". . . onely he which is fallen, and fallen upon this stone, can say, *Susceptor meus es tu*, only he which hath been overcome by a temptation, and is re-stored, can say, Lord thou hast supported me, thou hast recollected my shivers, and reunited me; onely to him hath this *stone* expressed, both abilities of stone; first to breake him with a sense of his sin, and then to give him peace and rest upon it." And it is the Church which cushions this fall, enabling the sinner to fall upon the stone instead of having the stone fall upon him; the con-victed and contrite sinner is "brought to a neerenesse of being pieced againe, by the Word, by the Sacraments, and other medicinall institutions of Christ in his Church." But woe to the man whose fall is not broken, who remains outside the institution ordained by God to save the sinner, for on him the stone will fall with the force of eternal damnation, grinding him to powder beneath its awful weight. For such persons there are no means "to recompact them againe, no voice of Gods word to draw them, no threatnings of Gods judgements shall drive them, no censures of Gods Church shall fit them, no Sacrament shall cement and glue them to Christs body againe; In temporall blessings, he shall be unthankfull, in temporall afflictions, he shall be obdurate: And these two shall serve, as the upper and nether stone of a mill, to grinde this reprobate sinner to powder." This grinding will be effected at the Last Judgment, when the stone will act not as a supporting foundation, but as a crushing and fatal weight. (D 11:188-196)

In another sermon Donne makes use not of a material and symbolic object as a central image, but of a process, the process of being clothed. The text—"For, all yee that are baptized into Christ, have put on Christ" (Galatians 3:27)—instructs us that the Sacrament of Baptism is an appareling ourselves with the Lord. All other appareling is but partial, usually serving to conceal some defect or evil; thus a hat may symbolize any effort to hide intellectual shallowness, and a glove any effort to cloak the wicked deeds of which our hands may be guilty. Man's sartorial inadequacies have a long history: Adam and Eve, motivated by a desire to cover only those parts of which they were ashamed, limited themselves to fig leaves; but God, seeing their need for a fuller appareling, one which would protect them from the violence of nature and the diseases of this world, gave them durable skins to replace their inadequate foliage. The garment which is Jesus Christ is also a coverall, covering not only the generative organs which are the channels of original sin, but all the actual and habitual sins which deform our daily lives. This process of appareling is not one which man can accomplish in his own strength, but neither is it one which God thrusts upon him: God enables man to put on Christ, but man's heart must be responsively willing to do so. When man does apparel himself with Christ, he finds that not merely certain of his human failings are covered, but rather his whole self, so that even God may see in him only the white of Christ's innocence and the red of his blood. (D v:153-155)

The garment of a Christian is a double one, consisting of the inner clothing of faith, the outer of good works. The latter, the mark of our sanctification, must be worn not occasionally, but throughout each day of our life. This garment, which is Jesus Christ, is all that is needed for salvation, yet all of it is needed and it is needed on the whole of man: "He that puts on Christ, must put him on *all*; and not onely find, that Christ hath dyed, nor onely that he hath died for *him*, but that he also hath died *in* Christ, and that whatsoever Christ suffered, *he* suffered *in* Christ." The Lord's redemptive act in itself makes us his servants, but our application of the redemption—our putting on Christ—makes us sons. Even beyond this, our appareling ourselves in the garment of Christ enables us to share his very nature, to "be of the same nature and substance as he." Thus we put on not only a garment but a person. And we must take care not to be hypocrites, taking on only the semblance of Christ that we may delude others into believing us righteous. The Lord will not acknowledge us if we "put *him* on, (that is, take his profession upon . . . [us]) either in a *courser stuffe*, (*Traditions* of Men, in stead of his word) or in *scantier measure*, (not to be always a Christian, but then, when . . . [we have] *use* of being one) or in a *different fashion*, (to be singular and *Schismaticall* in . . . [our] opinion) for this is one, but an ill manner of putting on of Christ as a garment." Instead we must conform ourselves to Christ, presenting ourselves naked before God, putting on the Lord's garments, and thus coming to our transfiguration. Then God "shall use us in all things, as his sonne; and we shall find restored in us, the Image of the whole Trinity, imprinted at our creation; for by this Regeneration, we are adopted by the Father in the bloud of the Sonne by the sanctification of the holy Ghost." Relating the clothing image to the Sacrament of Baptism, Donne affirms that the appareling implies both our election and our sanctification, and that baptism "comes *between both*, as a seale of the first, (of Election) and as an instrument, and conduit of the second, Sanctification." (D v:156-160)

We have seen many of the ways in which Donne turns to metaphor in order to enrich his sermons: how he draws comparisons between religious and secular experiences, makes analogical and symbolic use of various parts of the human body, and occasionally builds a sermon around one central image. The two images or symbols used most frequently and extensively throughout the sermons are those of light and water, a fact which should occasion little surprise in view of the prominence of these words in Scripture. I shall confine my discussion of Donne's use of light symbolism to three sermons, one delivered on Easter, one on Christmas, one on Easter Monday.

On Easter Day, 1628, Donne preached to his St. Paul's congregation on the familiar text of 1 *Corinthians* 13:12: "For now we see through a glasse darkly, but then face to face; now I know in part, but then I shall know, even as also I am knowne." The sermon, carried out with a fine mathematical precision, is a model of organization and clarity. It is an exposition of the four steps, in ascending order, of God's self-revelation, with each step symbolized by a certain kind of light. The four stages or lights through which God reveals himself are the light of natural reason, the light of faith, the light of glory, and the light which is God. Two of these lights bring to us a revelation of God while we are still on earth; two bring that clearer revelation which we will receive after our ascension into heaven. Two of them bring to us the sight of God; two bring something greater than the sight of him, namely, the knowledge of him.

The first step in the process of revelation is the sight of God which we gain while in this world. The place in which we see God under these circumstances is the physical universe; the medium or glass through which God's being is reflected is "the Booke of Creatures," the whole of creation; the faculty which enables us to see God in his works, the light which is turned upon the scene, is our natural reason. If our reason functions properly, it will behold God in all that is, an argument which, like St. Paul's statement in Romans 1:20, gives no comfort to the atheist, who can thus not excuse himself for his ignorance of God. Yet man's rational perceptions, clouded by his fall, can see only darkly, and reason is in fact not sufficient for a saving vision of God. (D VIII:219-225)

Since the light of natural reason is blurred, we are given another light, that of faith, to help us in our search for God while we are on earth. This second light, stronger than the first since it is a source of knowledge rather than of sight, emanates not from the whole universe, but from the Church; the medium through which God is here reflected is "the Ordinance and Institution of Christ in his Church"; the faculty which enables us to make "application of those Ordinances in that Church" is the light of faith. 'Scripture is the most powerful means possessed by the Church to bring us to a knowledge of God, a knowledge sealed in us through participation in the sacraments. But even the light of faith, which enables us to understand Scripture and which is more powerful than our natural reason, enables us to know God only in part and not with the completeness that will be man's blessing in the next world: "that sight of God which we have *In sepeculo, in the Glasse*, that is, in nature, is but *Cunabula fidei*, but the infancy, but the cradle of that knowledge which we have in faith, and yet that knowledge which we have in faith, is but *Cunabula visionis*, the infancy and cradle of that knowledge which we shall have when we come to see God *face to face*." (D VIII:225-230)

The sphere in which the man of persevering faith will eventually see God is Heaven, and our medium is God's more direct laying open of himself to us there. The light which will become ours when we pass from mortality into immortality is the light of glory, difficult to define, though we may say that, compared to it, "The Cherubims and Seraphims are but Candles; and that Gospel it self, which the Apostle calls the glorious Gospel, but a Star of the least magnitude." But even the light of glory, which enables us to see God face to face, is not the greatest light, for to *see* him so is not to *know* him in the same way that we are known by him. It is in this final stage and most perfect light, Donne writes, that "God alone is all; in all the former there was a place, and a meanes, and a light; here, for this perfect knowledge of God, God is all those." God will not then work through instruments, through the created world or through the Church, but directly through himself. (D VIII:231-236) As Donne affirmed earlier in his sermon, this ultimate revelation is "not a light which is His, but a light which is He" (D VIII:220). And so man is brought to the greatest joy for which he yearns, progressing step by step through those lights which God has ordained for his creature's salvation and eternal peace. The sermon is finely appropriate for that day on which Christ's resurrection served as a promise for those who would follow the way of the Cross.

The first of three sermons on the text of John 1:8—
"He was not that light, but was sent to bear witnesse of
that light"—was preached at St. Paul's on Christmas Day,
1621. Of Donne's many disquisitions on the symbol of
light, this discourse is the most complex. He begins simply
enough, stating that the *light* of the text denotes Christ's
divine nature, and that the sermon will be concerned primarily with *who* the light is, namely Jesus Christ, and
with *what* the light signifies—the supernatural light of
faith and grace. In the first chapter of the Fourth Gospel
the word is not to be understood metaphorically: "Christ
is not so called *Light*, as he is called a *Rock*, or a *Corner-
stone*; not by a metaphore, but truly, and properly." And
when other persons—John the Baptist or the apostles or
the faithful—are said to be the light, we are to understand
that they are but weak lights in comparison with the perfect
light which is Christ. The first part of the sermon is in
large part an intended corrective to those who view the
light of the text as the light of natural reason. Donne,
insisting that the power of reasoning is limited, urges his
congregation not to reduce the light of Christ to the light
of natural reason and not to accept only those affirmations
by and about the Lord which can be understood by reason. Good use of a modest degree of rational aptitude,
leading one to seek the light of faith in prayer and reading
of Scripture, is more beneficial than a purely worldly employment of a powerful faculty of reasoning. It is with
comforting words that Donne addresses the man who has
wisely directed his humble intellectual capacities: ". . . thou
by thy small light hast gathered *Pearle* and *Amber*, and
they by their great lights nothing but shels and pebles;
they have determined the light of nature, upon the booke
of nature, this world, and thou hast carried the light of
nature higher, thy naturall reason, and even *humane arguments*, have brought thee to reade the Scriptures, and to

that *love*, God hath set to the seale of *faith*." (D iii:351-362)

The second half of the sermon, in which Donne defines those diverse lights which "admit an application to this light in our Text, the *essentiall* light, *Christ Jesus*; and the *supernaturall* light, *faith* and *grace*," is of considerable complexity. The lights are presented in pairs and in order of descending power. The first pair consists of the essential light of God, which awaits us in Heaven and yet in which we may enjoy some participation on earth; and the light of glory, which will burst into fullness on the Judgment Day but of which we receive some adumbration as we confess our sins on earth. Below these are the light of faith, our conviction that Christ is Saviour, and the light of nature, which may lead us to faith. The third pair are *Lux æternorum Corporum* and *Lux incensionum*. The former includes the sun, moon, and fixed stars of Heaven, but excludes such transitory bodies as meteors and comets; the doctrines of the Christian Church, like the fixed bodies of Heaven, are unchangeable and not subject to increase, as the Council of Trent might wrongly suggest. *Lux incensionum* refers to earthy and combustible objects, or to those persons kindled through devotion and zeal to a love of God and neighbor; Paul, for example, was set on fire by the vision beheld on the Damascan road. The fourth and final pair are *Lux Depuratarum Mixtionum* and *Lux Repercussionum*. The former is called *the light of precious stones* because of the similarity between the origin and fruition of a precious stone and of a righteous action. Precious stones, Donne tells us, originate as drops of dew from Heaven and are then so refined by the sun that they gain esteem in the eyes of men; and "so those *actions* of ours, that shall be precious or acceptable in the eye of God, must at first have been conceived from *heaven*, from the *word* of God, and then receive *another concoction*, by a holy *deliberation*, before we bring those actions to *execution*, lest we may have mistaken the roote thereof." *Lux Repercussionum*, the light of reflection, involves the use of man as God's instrument to help lead others to his glory; the light of God shines so in the faithful that others, looking upon him, may see the reflection of God's goodness and love. Donne brings his sermon to an end by reminding his congregation that no man possesses light in and from himself, but that all light is of divine origin. (D III:362-375) Whether this sermon brought more enlightenment than confusion to the congregation is difficult to say; certainly it called for an exceptionally attentive ear.

The sermon which Donne preached on Easter Monday, 1622, on the text of II Corinthians 4:6—"For, God who commanded light to shine out of darkness, hath shined in our hearts, to give the light of the knowledge of the glory of God, in the face of Jesus Christ"—is beautifully organized around the three main divisions of the text. The first light is the light of our creation; the second, of our vocation; the third, of our glorification. Each light brings us from one condition or status to another—from nothing to being, from Gentile to Christian, from man to saint; the first enables man to see the created world, the second to see himself, and the third to see God. (D IV:92-93) As Donne moves through his exposition, he turns to other symbolic treatments of the word *light*, working out still another hierarchy and showing how each succeeding light outshines the one before it: man's light of reason is more noble than the light of creation; the light of the Law and the prophets exceeds that of the stars; and the light of the Son is greater than that of the sun (D IV:104).

Donne carefully traces man's progress from his creation to his sanctification. Created by the light of God and called by God through his light shining in our hearts, we are finally brought to our glorification through the light of

Jesus Christ. Turning to a discussion of the nature of our glorification, Donne writes that, "Till Christ all was night; there was a beginning of day, in the beginning of the Gospel, and there was a full noon in the light and glory thereof; but such a day, as shall be always day, and over-taken with no night, no cloud, is onely the day of Judgement, the Resurrection: And this hath brought us to our last step, to the consideration of these three terms; 1. *knowledge*; 2. *glory*; 3. *the face of Christ Jesus in that everlasting Kingdom*." When we are taken into God's kingdom, our knowledge will be as the knowledge of angels, and our glory will be the sitting down at the right hand of God the Father; on that last day God "will perfect, consummate, accomplish all, and give. . .[us] *the light of the glory of God, in the face of Christ Jesus* there." (D iv:118-130) Thus we may understand, through a symbolic discussion of the three great light-giving acts of God, our full voyage from our creation, to the time of our being called by God into his Church, to that final day when we shall be raised to his full glory.

Donne makes even more frequent and manifold use of *water* as a symbol than of *light*. Whereas the latter is found in Scripture only with the most favorable connotations, the former has a much wider range of meaning. It is both the *sine qua non* of life and the harbinger of death, the element of life-giving baptism and of the life-destroying flood.

We might first examine Donne's frequent recourse to the word *sea*. The gathering together of all the means necessary for the attaining of salvation is compared to the gathering together of all the waters under the heavens on the third day of creation. As God established a sea at the beginning, so did he establish a Church, which, Donne writes, "is that Sea. . ." (D i:290). The Bible also is a sea; Donne, in illustration of his Protestant conviction that God's Word is to be read not simply by a few but by all those who will come to it in humility, affirms that "the Scriptures are a Sea, in which a *Lambe* may wade, and an *Elephant* may swimme" (D ix:124). And one of his sermons begins with a striking analogy between the blood of Christ and a sea:

"As when a Merchant hath a faire and large, a deep and open Sea, into that Harbour to which hee is bound with his Merchandize, it were an impertinent thing for him, to sound, and search for lands, and rocks, and clifts, which threaten irreparable shipwrack; so we being bound to the heavenly City, the new Jerusalem, by the spacious and bottomelesse Sea, the blood of Christ Jesus, having that large Sea opened unto us, in the beginning of this Text, *All manner of sin, and blasphemy shall be forgiven unto men,* It may seeme an impertinent diversion, to turne into that little Creek, nay upon that desperate, and irrecoverable rock, *The blasphemy against the Holy Ghost shall not be forgiven to men*" (D v:77).

A more extended analogy, in which the sea is compared to the world, is found in one of the two sermons on the text of Christ's calling Peter and Andrew to him and bidding them become "fishers of men." The world, like the sea, is subject to storms, and yet man may drown in a calm sea as well as in a turbulent one: he may also be destroyed in a world of prosperity as well as of adversity. The immensity and ways of both the sea and the world exceed our comprehension, yet the sea has a bottom and shores, just as the world of man has limitations imposed on it by God. Like the floods and ebbs of the sea are the worldly vicissitudes which beset men's bodies, fortunes, and minds. As the sea furnishes the world with all its waters, but not with truly thirst-quenching water, so does the world supply man's natural needs, though not his spiritual ones. The stronger fish of the sea, in their destruction of the weaker, are like the stronger men of this world. And as muddy fish, having no means to clean themselves, must depend on the currents, "So have the men of this world no means to cleanse themselves from those sinnes which they have contracted in the world, of themselves, till a new flood, waters of repentance, drawne up, and sanctified by the Holy Ghost, worke that blessed effect in them." The detailed comparison continues as Donne notes that the sea is not a place of habitation, but a way to habitation, and the world not a continuing city but a passage to our eternal home. Though a part of every sailing ship must be under water and a part of every man's life be bent upon the activities beneath Heaven, yet the sails which give the ship its power are above the water, and the devout meditations of man, those aids to his heavenly voyage, are directed above this world to God. Thus with considerable ingenuity Donne describes the sea and the world in which Peter and Andrew were "fishers of men." (D ii:306-307)

There are also many cases in which the word *sea* (or a variation thereof) is used with unfavorable connotation, as when Donne speaks of a person's being raised out of a sea of ignorance, or being raised out of the Mediterranean Sea, "the sea of *Rome*, the sea of Superstition" (D iii:219). In another sermon the man of faith is told that he may view from the ark that violent flood which is the anger of God, as it devours the wanton man, the ambitious man, and the voluptuous man (D vii:224). And as a swelling river will in time flow into various channels and then cover a whole field, so do our concupiscences swell, overflowing throughout our body and finding issue through our ears and eyes and hands: ". . .sin overflowes all, *Omnia pontus*, all our wayes are sea, all our works are sin. This is our fulnesse, originall sin filled us, actuall sin presses down the measure, and habituall sins heap it up" (D iv:286). There is also an interesting reversal of this image, in which concupiscences are compared to dry, combustible powder, which may be dampened and assuaged by tears of contrition (D VIII:200).

In a sermon on the text of Genesis 1:2—"And the Spirit of God moved upon the face of the waters"—Donne affirms that *"Baptisme,* and *Sin,* and *Tribulation,* and *Death,* are called in the Scripture, by that name, *Waters,"* and then elaborates on his statement. Tertullian, St. Jerome, St. John of Damascus, and the "Divine *Basil"* all viewed the *waters* of this text as a figure of baptism. On the other hand, waters may refer to sins, as when we are told in Revelation 17:1 that the great whore of Babylon sits upon waters, which in turn are hatched into numerous sins. And Donne goes on to cite Scriptural passages in which tribulation and death are metaphorically referred to as water. (D IX:104-108)

Donne is at his paradoxical best when he shows how closely related are two forms of water which seem so diametrically opposed—baptism and the flood. Life-giving baptism is like the death-bringing flood in that it destroys the sin within us and enables the truly repentant man later in life to drown the actual sins which he daily commits. Equally paradoxical is the fact that baptism delivers us over to tribulations, to the crosses which we must bear in the name of Christ, and yet to crosses which lead us to the eternal waters of life. (D V:110) Many are the variations played upon the theme of water.

Finally I should like to discuss two sermons whose structures are determined by a central water analogy. One of them, preached appropriately on the first Friday in Lent, 1623, is on the text of John 11:35: "Iesus wept." There is a threefold division, based on the three times in his life when the Lord wept. At the death of Lazarus he shed human tears, called forth by "a humane and naturall calamity fallen upon one family." As he approached Jerusalem and foresaw its destruction he wept again, this time prophetic tears occasioned by a national calamity. At his passion, as he contemplated sin and its punishment, he shed pontifical tears, brought on by his grief for all mankind. His first tears, shed for a family, are comparable to a spring or a well; the tears shed for a nation are like a river; and the "teares upon the Crosse, are as the Sea belonging to all the world." The waters of the spring flow into the river, thence into the sea. (D IV:325-326)

In Part Three of the sermon, Donne discusses the nature, the use, and the benefit of the tears shed on the Cross. "These teares, the teares of his Crosse," Donne writes, "were expressed by that inestimable waight, the sinnes of all the world. . . . In these third teares, his pontificall teares, teares for sin, for all sins (those we call a Sea) here is *Mare liberum*, a Sea free and open to all; Every man may saile home, home to himselfe, and lament his own sins there." And what is the nature of these tears? They are both the sweat produced by the blood of Christ, shed as a cure for our sickness in sin, and the blood itself, which unites us with God. And their use? They are shed to lament, not the loss of a worldly object, but the sin of the world, and from them we must learn to weep for our sins. The benefit of Christ's tears, and of those wept by men in imitation of his, is incalculable. They torment the devil more than hell-fire itself; even the Jesuit Mendoza confessed that a contrite tear does a man as much good as all the purifying flames of purgatory. "We have said more than once," Donne writes, "that man is a spunge; And *in Codice scripta*, all our sins are written in Gods Booke, saies S. *Chrysostome*: If there I can fill my spunge with teares, and so wipe out all my sins out of that Book, it is a blessed use of the Spunge." Such are the tears that lead to joy, and in them are the meeting of mourning and rejoicing. Donne dismisses his Lenten congregation with fitting words to guide them through a season which is simultaneously a time of lamentation and of joyful hope: "Weep these teares truly, and God shall performe to thee, first that promise which he makes in *Esay* [Isaiah], *The Lord shall wipe all teares from thy face,* all that are fallen by any occasion of calamity here, in the militant Church; and he shall performe that promise which he makes in the Revelation, *The Lord shall wipe all teares from thine eyes,* that is, dry up the fountaine of teares; remove all occasion of teares hereafter, in the triumphant Church." (D ⅳ:338-344)

The organization of the first of three sermons on the text of Psalms 38:4—"For mine iniquities are gone over my head, as a heavy burden, they are too heavy for mee" —is also determined by a water analogy. This discourse may well be read in conjunction with Donne's later statement that "the Holy Ghost. . .abounds in no Metaphor more, then in calling Tribulations, *Waters.* . ." (D ⅸ:328). The man encompassed by sins resembles a man under water: the former finds it as difficult to recover from his spiritual sickness as the latter to rise above the destructive waters. The man under water is in serious condition because he "hath no aire to see by, no aire to hear by, he hath nothing to reach to, he touches not ground, to push him up, he feels no bough to pull him up. . ." (D ⅱ:96).

Donne carries out a fourfold analogy between sins and floodwaters. In the first place our sins separate us from God: just as the man under water is cut off from life-giving air, so is the sinful man cut off from God by the arch, the roof, of sins over his head. Secondly, our sins over our head sound a clamor, like the roar of waters, which ascend to God himself. Thirdly, our sins resemble covering waters, especially in the fact that they stupefy us. Thus our eyes, to which God reveals himself in the creation, and our ears, to which he reveals himself in his Word, have no more power or sensitivity when they are covered by sin than when they are covered by water:

"The habituall, and manifold sinner, sees nothing aright; Hee sees a *judgement*, and cals it an *accident*. He hears nothing aright; He hears the Ordinance of *Preaching* for salvation in the next world, and he cals it an invention of the State, for subjection in this world. And as under water, every thing seems distorted and crooked, to man, so does man himself to God, who sees not his own Image in that man, in that form as he made it. When *man hath drunk iniquity like water*, then, *The flouds of wickednesse shall make him afraid*; The water that he hath swum in, the sin that he hath delighted in, shall appear with horrour unto him. As God threatens the pride of *Tyrus*, *I shall bring the deep upon thee, and great waters shall cover thee*, That, God will execute upon this sinner; And then, upon every drop of that water, upon every affliction, every tribulation, he shall come to that fearfulnesse, *Waters flowed over my head*; then said I, *I am cut off*; Either he shall see nothing, or see no remedy, no deliverance from desperation."

Finally, a man in bondage to sin finds his master as much a tyrant over him as surging water is to a drowning person. (D II:110-118) The sustained image is a powerfully effective one.

TONE

Perhaps the quality in which Donne's sermons fall stylistically most short of his poems is in the range of tone. This is not to suggest that the sermons are in any way deficient in their power to draw vividly the terrors of damnation or the bliss of salvation, or to move the congregation with their exhortations to the godly life. But it is to say that such tonal qualities as irony or satire or sarcasm find little proper place in the pulpit, and the reader of Donne's poetry knows what effective and devastating use he could make of such weapons. There are some exceptions. In a passage warning his hearers against placing themselves in the way of temptation, he suggests amusingly that they can well do without that "little *sociablenesse*, and *conversation*" which led Lot's wife to her permanent immobility, that they must not feel honor-bound to live up to certain commitments to the Devil, and that they must not be led by "a little of the *compassion* and *charity* of Hell" to join others in sin lest they wax miserable and lonely (D ii:57). He inveighs against a double standard in marriage by saying that "the wife is not as the Chancell, reserv'd and shut up, and the man as the walks below, indifferent and at liberty for every passenger" (D iii:248). In commenting to married couples on the verse, "Submit your selves to one another, in the feare of God" (Ephesians 5:21), he remarks that he need not elaborate on the submission of wives "because husbands at home, are likely enough to remember them of it" (D v:115). His rebuke to those who behave improperly in church is marked by sarcasm: "And you come to God in his House, as though you came to keepe him company, to sit downe, and talke with him halfe an houre; or you come as Ambassadors, covered in his presence, as though ye came from as great a Prince as he" (D vii:317-318).

The most frequent target of Donne's wit is the Roman Church. In one of· his marriage sermons he ridicules the celibacy of the priesthood by asserting that, "When God had made *Adam* and *Eve* in Paradise, though there were foure rivers in Paradise, God did not place *Adam* in a Monastery on one side, and *Eve* in a Nunnery on the other, and so a River between them" (D iii:242). In his first sermon preached to King Charles, Donne directs his remarks against the proliferation of Roman doctrine. Rome has made salvation costly: "Threescore yeares agoe, a man might have beene sav'd at halfe the price hee can now:

Threescore yeares ago, he might have beene saved for beleeving the *Apostles Creed*; now it will cost him the *Trent Creed* too" (D VI:249). The Roman Church, Donne preached at another time, has imprisoned the Holy Ghost within the bosom of the pope: "And so, the Holy Ghost is no longer a Dove, a Dove in the Ark, a Dove with an Olive-Branch, a Messenger of peace, but now the Holy Ghost is in a Bull, in Buls worse then *Phalaris* his Bull, Buls of Excommunication, Buls of Rebellion, and Deposition, and Assassinates of Christian Princes" (D VIII:265). Perhaps the most effective barbs of all are hurled against the Roman custom of indulgences. Working up to one such attack, Donne mentions that some contemporary philosophers have called into question the element of fire, arguing that of the four elements fire alone produces nothing and that the existence of a nonproductive element is improbable. Donne then moves to his point:

"Here is a fire that recompences that defect; The fire of the Roman Purgatory hath produced Indulgences, and Indulgences are multiplied to such a number, as that no heards of Cattell upon earth can equall them, when they meet by millions at a Jubile, no shoales, no spawne of fish at Sea, can equall them, when they are transported in whole Tuns to the West Indies, where of late yeares their best Market hath beene; No flocks, no flights of birds in the Ayre can equall them, when as they say of S. *Francis*, at every prayer that he made, a man might have seene the Ayre as full of soules flying out of Purgatory, as sparkles from a Smiths Anvill, beating a hot Iron." (D VII:184-185)

The few gibes which Donne does make in his sermons are well executed, but the literary genre of the sermon, calling as it does for the breath of charity, affords little opportunity for rapier thrusts.

CHAPTER FOUR

Interpreter of God's Ways to Men

VIA MEDIA

FROM his ordination in 1615 until his death in 1631, John Donne spent virtually all his time responding to his vocation as preacher, a man sent by God to call other men to Christ through an expounding of the means to salvation, Holy Scripture. Not a systematic theologian, not a writer of an *Institutes of the Christian Religion*, he was yet a man whose training and reading had so grounded him in the Bible, as well as in the writings of the Church Fathers and of the Roman and Protestant theologians, controversialists, and Biblical commentators, that he had a well-defined theology of his own even though he never reduced it to systematic statement. My own reading of the sermons leads me to believe that Donne's theological position, his beliefs about the nature of God and of man's relationship to God, was virtually the same when he preached his first sermon at Paddington in 1615 as when he preached his last under vastly different conditions and to a totally different congregation at Whitehall in 1631. A man so devoted as Donne was to theological studies in his earlier years is unlikely to undergo any significant changes in his religious beliefs after his fortieth year. It is true that Donne became a more effective preacher with years in the pulpit, and that the varying conditions both of his mind and spirit and of his nation led him to different emphases in his sermons from one time to another during his sixteen years as minister; but his best sermons and his weakest, his sermons on sin and redemption, on marriage and death, on State and Church are all informed by the same basic and pervasive theological understanding.

John Donne was an early seventeenth-century Anglican to the core. If the *Divine Comedy* is a literary monument to Thomism and *The Pilgrim's Progress* the dramatic embodiment of Puritanism, then the Sermons of Donne are the most compelling presentation of that *Summa* of Anglicanism: Richard Hooker's *Of the Laws of Ecclesiastical Polity*. The genius of Anglicanism, and one of its provoking qualities as well, is that it knows not only what to say but what to leave unsaid. It consequently allows for a flexibility, away from which the Roman Church had been moving for centuries and for which the Council of Trent offered little quarter, and in which Calvinism was lacking even in its inception. It was a flexibility which Elizabeth encouraged and for the lack of which the Church later received a near-fatal blow, as King Charles and Archbishop Laud learned too late. The Anglican position has accurately been designated as the *via media*,[1] the middle way between Rome and Geneva, the way in which, it was hoped, the less extreme Romans and Reformers might be beckoned into the communion of a church of peace, a truly catholic church at whose breasts (to use Donne's own figure) all faithful and sensible followers of Christ might gain salvation. And one of the greatest tributes that can be paid Donne as Anglican is that he seldom lost his balance in walking a doctrinal tightrope between Rome and Geneva. If he turned more often to the differences between Roman Catholicism and Anglicanism than to those between the Reformed churches and Anglicanism, it was not because he was further from Rome than from Geneva, but because the Anglican Church seemed in his lifetime to be more endangered by the Roman Communion than by the Puritans and Separatists. The Spanish Armada and the Gunpowder Plot, referred to several times by Donne, were

[1] See H. J. C. Grierson, "John Donne and the 'Via Media,'" *Modern Language Review*, XLIII (July 1948), 305-314.

symbolic to Englishmen of hostilities that might lie as much in the future as in the past, and the Thirty Years' War was a present reality. That the Puritans would soon claim the lives of the head of the Anglican Church and its Archbishop would probably have struck Donne as fantastic.

The beauty of Anglicanism, Donne affirmed, was that it knew both the necessity of and the proper limits of reformation; it knew how to reform without destroying; it knew how to effect a circumcision without moving on to a concision. In a sermon preached at St. Paul's Donne took from Philippians, an epistle urging the necessity of unity within the Christian body, his text: "Beware of the concision" (3:2). Circumcision, he writes, "is an orderly, a usefull, a medicinall, a beneficiall pruning and paring off, that which is superfluous." Concision, on the other hand, "is a hasty and a rash plucking up, or cutting downe, and an unprofitable tearing, and renting into shreds and fragments . . ." (D x:112). The disease of Romanism was superfluity; that of Separatism, deficiency. One of the central tasks of the Church was to affirm the foundations of Christian belief, distinguishing between those beliefs which are absolutely fundamental to the Christian faith and those traditions and customs which, hardly worth fighting over, should be left to the discretion of the particular faith or denomination, whether it be the Church of Rome or of England, of Luther or of Calvin. The various classical creeds had, of course, sought to define the necessary foundations of belief, and Donne was willing to take his stand with the Apostles' Creed and with the somewhat more extended Thirty-nine Articles of his own Church.

In essence, Donne would view the Anglican Church as the church of the circumcision, the church which had with greatest care sought to prune away the superfluities accrued by the Roman Church, superfluities leading it further and further away from the primitive church of

New Testament times. The many Separatist sects, feelingly defined by Donne as "rotten boughes, gangrened limmes, fragmentary chips, blowne off by their owne spirit of turbulency, fallen off by the waight of their owne pride, or hewen off by the Excommunications and censures of the Church" (D III:87-88)—these sects went beyond a proper circumcision with an irresponsible wielding of the knife of concision. Readers of Donne's poetry are familiar with the distinctions he draws between Rome and Geneva. In "Satire III," Mirreus seeks true religion at Rome, "because hee doth know/That shee was there a thousand yeares agoe,/He loves her ragges so," the rags being those unhappy additions to Rome's once primitive purity; Crantz in reaction goes to the other extreme, following what "at Geneva is call'd/Religion, plaine, simple, sullen, yong,/Contempuous, yet unhansome." A somewhat similar sentiment is expressed in a later sonnet:

> Show me deare Christ, thy spouse, so bright and clear.
> What! is it She, which on the other shore
> Goes richly painted? or which rob'd and tore
> Laments and mournes in Germany and here?

The same thrusts at Rome and Geneva are found in the sermons. True religion, Donne argues, is not to be found "either in a *painted Church*, on one side, or in a *naked Church*, on another; a Church in a *Dropsie*, overflowne with *Ceremonies*, or a Church in a *Consumption*, for want of such Ceremonies, as the primitive Church found usefull, and beneficiall for the advancing of the glory of God, and the devotion of the Congregation" (D VI:284). The golden mean is to be found in the Church of England: ". . .we stript not the Church into a nakedness, nor into rags; we divested her not of her possessions, nor of her Ceremonies, but received such a Reformation at home, by their hands whom God enlightned, as left her neither in a Dropsie, nor in a Consumption; neither in a superfluous and cumbersome fatness, nor in an uncomely and faint leanness and attenuation." (D iv:106; see also D i:246)

It would be difficult to overemphasize the importance which Donne places on the Church's responsibility to distinguish between the fundamentals and the nonfundamentals of belief, and he finds one of the great triumphs of the Anglican Church to lie in its ability to make such an all-important discrimination. Furthermore, we discover that his remarks about virtually all aspects of the religious life, whether they are matters of doctrine or ecclesiastical government or ritual and ceremony, are guided by his consideration of whether they are foundation stones or interior decorating, useful perhaps but not indispensable. The first extended reference to the problem appears in a sermon on Easter Day of 1619:

". . .nothing becomes a Christian better than sobriety; to make a true difference betweene problematicall, and dogmaticall points, betweene upper buildings, and foundations, betweene collaterall doctrines, and Doctrines in the right line: for fundamentall things, *Sine hæsitatione credantur*, They must be beleeved without disputing; there is no more to be done for them, but beleeving; for things that are not so, we are to weigh them in two balances, in the balance of Analogy, and in the balance of scandall: we must hold them so, as may be analogall, proportionable, agreeable to the Articles of our Faith, and we must hold them so, as our brother be not justly offended, nor scandalized by them; wee must weigh them with faith, for our own strength, and we must weigh them with charity, for others weaknesse. Certainly nothing endangers a Church more, then to draw indifferent things to be necessary; I meane of a primary necessity, of a necessity to be beleeved *De fide*, not a secondary necessity, a necessity to be performed and practised for obedience: Without doubt, the Roman Church repents now, and sees now that she should better have preserved her selfe, if they had not defined so many particular things, which were indifferently and problematically disputed before, to bee had necessarily *De fide*, in the Councell of Trent" (D ii:203-204).

This passage is an explicit statement of what was perhaps Donne's greatest objection to the practice and procedure of the Roman Catholic Church, to their insistence upon "draw[ing] indifferent things to be necessary." The disease, Donne believed, had been gaining momentum for centuries, reaching a climax in the Council of Trent, convened by the Pope in an attempt to marshal his forces against the growing power of the Reformation. The areas in which Donne felt the Roman Church to be dogmatic in indifferent matters were many.

At the root of the trouble, Donne thought, was Rome's misconception of the function of the Church, its overvaluing of the Church and undervaluing of Scripture. Rome seemed bent on usurping the function of God's voice speaking through Scripture; she forgot that the Church does not make articles of faith, but merely declares them: "In the Gospell, the way is, *Fecit, & dicta sunt*, God makes articles of faith, and the Church utters them, presents them" (D iii:94-95). It is consequently of great importance, Donne tells King Charles and a congregation at Whitehall on April 1, 1627, to "Take heed what you heare" (Mark 4:24). When Christ so addressed his apostles, he was urging them to "Preach all that, preach nothing but that, which you have received from me" (D vii:-395). As Donne points out in a later sermon, the Roman Church does not say that the Anglican Church does not preach the truth, but rather that it does not preach all the truth; Anglicanism is true as far as it goes, but it does not go far enough. On the other hand, Canterbury does not say that Rome does not teach all the truth, but rather that not all that she teaches is true. Rome accuses England of defectiveness; England accuses Rome of superfluity. (D VIII:262-263) The superfluity, Donne asserts, takes many forms. Most importantly, the Church of Rome does not rest content with the Scriptural Canon; they are not satisfied to "preach nothing but that" which they find in God's inspired Word: ". . .they deliver *more* then the Scriptures doe, and make other Rules and Canons equall to Scriptures. In which excesse, they doe not onely make the *Apocryphall* Books, (Books that have alwaies had a favourable aspect, and benigne countenance from the Church of God) equall to Canonicall Scriptures, But they make their decretall Epistles of their Popes and of their *Extravagants*, (as they call them) and their occasionall *Bulls*, nay their *Bull-baitings*, their Buls fighting, and crossing and contradicting one another, equall to Canonicall Scripture." (D VII:402)

One of the most fatal and unhappy results of Roman multiplication and proliferation of doctrine is that the distinction between the fundamental Scriptural teachings and the accrued traditions of the Church is lost; and thus Rome utters the cry of heresy and damnation as quickly and as vehemently at those who challenge collateral doctrines as at those who deny the fundamental teachings of Christ. The Church of Rome

"will apply all the capital and bloody penalties of the Imperial Laws (made against *Arrians*, *Manicheans*, *Pelagians*, and *Nestorians*, Hereticks in the fundamental points of Religion, and with which Christ could not consist) to every man that denys any collateral and subdivided Tradition of theirs; that if a man conceive any doubt of the dream of Purgatory, of the validity of indulgence, of the Latitude of a work of Supererogation, he is as deep in the fagot here, and shall be as deep in Hell hereafter, as if he denyed the Trinity, or the Incarnation and Passion of Christ Jesus; when in a days warning, and by the roaring of one Bull, it grows to be damnation to day, to beleeve so as a man might have beleeved yesterday, and have bin saved, when they will afford no Salvation, but in that Church which is discernable by certain and inseparable marks, which our Country-man *Saunders* makes to be six, and *Michael Medina* extends to eleven, and *Bellarmine* declares to be fifteen, and *Bodius* stretches to a hundred, when they make every thing Heresie . . ." (D IV:141).

The teachings of Scripture alone are sufficient for salvation, and to seek to go beyond Scripture is to be impertinently curious. Rest firmly in the foundations of belief, Donne urges, and do not endanger the foundations by overburdening them with the "enormous super-edifications," with the "incommodious upper-buildings" which are part and parcel of the Roman Church (D VII:129). Remember above all that "nothing endangers a Church more, then to draw indifferent things to be necessary."

But having made this point clear in his offensive against the right wing of Christianity in Rome, Donne must defend himself against the left wing, the offspring of Geneva then making some headway in England. For the sectarians, Donne points out, "have gone away from us, and vainly said, that they have as good cause to separate from us, as we from *Rome*" (D X:174). If Rome had too many "super-edifications" for Canterbury, then Canterbury had too many for Geneva. The Puritans and Separatists would admit that Anglicanism had moved in the proper direction but would insist that it had not gone far enough. The Anglican view was that if the Romanists overvalued the Church and its traditions, the Separatists undervalued the

Church; and that if Rome was too hasty in exalting the indifferent in matters of doctrine and ceremony, the Separatists were too hasty in indiscriminate rejection of the indifferent.

Hooker's *Of the Laws of Ecclesiastical Polity* reflects the storm raised by the Puritans about matters which Donne would classify as indifferent, matters which were not essentially and directly related to a man's salvation, matters such as liturgical worship, church music, clerical garb, kneeling at prayer. At the center of the Puritan argument was the contention that they would do nothing that was not specifically called for in Scripture. In their view of nonfundamental matters, they were as rigid in their own way as the Roman Catholics were in theirs. But whereas the Roman Catholics insisted on the absolute necessity of maintaining those traditions and customs born of the Church, the Puritans insisted on the absolute necessity of discarding them. Take, for example, the practice of kneeling. Roman Catholics kneel at the Sacrament, Donne tells us, as indeed they should; but they kneel for the wrong reason, not in obeisance to the incalculable benefit which they are receiving at God's hand and not because the priest is praying in their behalf, but because it is an act of "adoration of that *bread*, which they take to be God" (D x:151). In its relation to the Eucharist and to the belief in the transubstantiation of the bread into the flesh of the Lord, kneeling becomes to Papists a necessity for salvation. Certain of the sectarians, on the other hand, finding no Scriptural authority for the practice and eschewing anything that savors of Rome, refuse to kneel at all, thus attaching as much importance to the practice as the Catholics do. Donne takes the customary middle road. He does not attribute to kneeling any inherent quality which will lead to salvation, but he does view it as that humble and reverend posture in which God is to be worshiped (D ix:59). As

Justin Martyr said, "*Genuflexio est peccatorum*, kneeling is the sinners posture" (D ix:152-153), and Donne makes the reasonable assumption that all men are sinners.

Donne speaks as a true servant of his Archbishop and King when he reminds the English Separatists that they are to bend an ear not only to the authority of Christ but also to that of the Anglican Church: there are rules and laws in the Church Militant as well as in the Church Triumphant. In one sermon, after cautioning Roman Catholics not to confuse the collateral with the fundamental, he turns his attention to the Separatists: "Call not *Ceremoniall*, and *Rituall* things, *Essentiall* parts of Religion, and of the worship of God, otherwise then as they imply *Disobedience*; for *Obedience* to lawfull Authoritie, is alwayes an *Essentiall* part of Religion" (D vi:258). The first part of the statement frees Anglicans from the demands of Roman ceremony and would seem to free Separatists from the demands of Anglican ceremony; the second keeps the Anglicans free, for they recognize no lawful authority in the Pope, but it at the same time puts the clamp on the Separatists, for they are lawful citizens of King Charles, head of both State and Church. And Donne also addresses himself to English sectarians or would-be sectarians when he states that, "Except there be errour in *fundamentall* points, such as make that Church no Church, let no man depart from that Church, and that religion, in which he delivered himself to the service of God at first" (D iii:129).[2]

The Separatists, Donne argues, are contentious, far too willfully and proudly assured of their own opinions, and utterly lacking in respect for lawful authority. They would rather desert the Church than go along with it in nonfun-

[2] See the relevant and interesting note by E. G. Lewis: "The Question of Toleration in the Works of John Donne," *Modern Language Review*, XXXIII (April 1938), 255-258.

damental matters. They think that God can be worshiped only in a garret, and when they do attend an Anglican service, they "wink at the ornaments, and stop their ears at the musique of the Church" (D x:222). Donne makes his point most forcefully in his sermon on the text, "Beware of the concision":

"To a *Circumcision* of the *garment*, that is, to a paring, and taking away such *Ceremonies*, as were superstitious, or superfluous, of an ill use, or of no use, our *Church* came in the beginning of the *Reformation*. To a *Circumcision* we came; but those *Churches* that came to a *Concision* of the *garment*, to an absolute taking away of *all ceremonies*, neither provided so safely for the *Church* it self in the substance thereof, nor for the exaltation of *Devotion in the Church*. . . . Ceremonies are *nothing*; but where there are no Ceremonies, order, and uniformity, and obedience, and at last, (and quickely) Religion it selfe will vanish." (D x:116)

The Anglicans had carried the paring far enough—in their own judgment; to the Roman Catholics the paring had almost effected the vanishing of religion; but to the Separatists the paring had just begun.

Despite Donne's occasionally vitriolic remarks, despite the possibility of a certain arbitrariness as to where the line between fundamentals and nonfundamentals should be drawn, and despite the fact that Canterbury's offense against Rome and defense against Separatism might seem at times colored by inconsistency and expediency, in Donne and the Anglican position is found a great measure of reasonableness and charitableness. It was not merely a burst of partisan passion that led Donne to believe that the Church of England was the true catholic Church. He knew well the Roman Communion in which he had been born and bred, and he was intellectually convinced that the Roman Church of his time had strayed many steps away from the primitive Christian Church which should serve as the pattern for the Christianity of any century. For Donne, the trouble with the Roman Church was that it was, in fact, not catholic, that it did not possess that universal character which was the mark of Anglicanism. "The Church loves the name of Catholique," Donne once wrote, "and it is a glorious, and an harmonious name; Love thou those things wherein she is Catholique, and wherein she is harmonious, that is, *Quod ubique, quod semper,* Those universall, and fundamentall doctrines, which in all Christian ages, and in all Christian Churches, have beene agreed by all to be necessary to salvation; and then thou art a true Catholique" (D II:280). This statement is the basis of Donne's essentially tolerant position. His tolerance is not the kind that reduces all to a dull gray, but it does allow a latitude, a flexibility that is the mark of a devout and charitable heart. "Where two contrary opinions are both probable," he writes, "they may be embraced, and beleeved by two men, and those two be both learned, and discreet, and pious, and zealous men." And he goes on to say that this fact should keep men from reviling and condemning those of different persuasions in problematical matters. In matters that are not fundamental, it is better to be wrong than to be uncharitable, and the man who is uncharitably right may have less chance of entering heaven than the one who is charitably wrong, "for, in such cases, humility, and love of peace, may, in the sight of God, excuse and recompence many errours, and mistakings." (D VII:97)

Such a disposition to charity occasions Donne's lament that religious controversy so frequently turns to name calling. "Who would not tremble," he writes with his own fellow churchmen in mind, "to heare those *Infernall* words, spoken by men, to men, of one and the same Religion fundamentally, as *Indiabolificata, Perdiabolificata,* and *Superdiabolificata*. . .wee see more Bookes written by these men against one another, then by them both, for *Christ*." Such a torrent of abuse is grievous. "But the uncharitablenesse of the *Church* of *Rome* towards us all, is not a *Torrent*, nor it is not a *Sea*, but a *generall Flood*, an universall Deluge. . . ." (D vi:246) The Puritans have their own particular kind of perversity. Instead of weighing a matter on its own merits, they will eschew it simply because Rome has embraced it. The Puritans "refuse to doe such things as conduce to the exaltation of Devotion, or to the order, and peace of the Church, not for any harme in the things, but onely therefore because the Papists doe them. . . ." Because Papists kneel in idolatrous worship of the bread in the Sacrament, Puritans will not kneel in thanksgiving for God's grace therein; because Papists pray to saints, Puritans reproach or ignore saints; because Papists abuse the Cross, Puritans abhor the Cross. (D iii:175)

It is a mark of Donne's reasonableness that he judges religious matters in terms of their intrinsic merit, not of whether they have been labeled Papist or Puritan. And it is a mark of his tolerance that he recognizes certain virtues in practices of churches which in many respects are distant from Anglicanism. Donne would above all be recognized as a Christian, and he has no objection to being called Papist or Puritan if the epithet results from his following a Christian practice which happens to be associated in particular with persons not fully sympathetic with the truly catholic Church of which he is a priest:

"Beloved, there are some things in which all Religions agree; The worship of God, The holinesse of life; And therefore, if when I study this holinesse of life, and fast, and pray, and submit my selfe to discreet, and medicinall mortifications, for the subduing of my body, any man will say, this is Papisticall, Papists doe this, it is a blessed Protestation, and no man is the lesse a Protestant, nor the worse a Protestant for making it, Men and brethren, I am a Papist, that is, I will fast and pray as much as any Papist, and enable my selfe for the service of my God, as seriously, as sedulously, as laboriously as any Papist. So, if when I startle and am affected at a blasphemous oath, as at a wound upon my Saviour, if when I avoyd the conversation of those men, that prophane the Lords day, any other will say to me, This is Puritanicall, Puritans do this, It is a blessed Protestation, and no man is the lesse a Protestant, nor the worse a Protestant for making it, Men and Brethren, I am a Puritan, that is, I wil endeavour to be pure, as my Father in heaven is pure, as far as any Puritan." (D ix:166)

In the foregoing rather extended introductory remarks to this chapter on Donne's theology, I have tried to make clear some of the basic premises of his theological thought. Emphasis has been placed on his supporting the Anglican and middle way between the claims of Roman Catholics on the right and Puritans and Separatists on the left; on his insistence that a Church must above all be able to distinguish between the essential and absolute foundations of Christianity, the *sine qua non* of the faith, and the problematical and collateral matters which do not directly affect a man's eternal destiny; on his conviction that the Roman Church had a superfluity of doctrine, exalting nonessential matters to a position of equal importance with truly fundamental matters, and his conviction that England's left-wing Protestants were deficient in the areas of ceremony and ritual, as eager to divest themselves of all nonessential beliefs and practices as the Romanists were to exalt them; and on his basically reasonable and charitable disposition to judge all doctrinal and ceremonial questions on their own merits, looking to Scripture as the source of all doctrine and looking to the Sovereign of the English State and Church as the final arbiter for all Englishmen on the discipline and order of the Church.

I should now like to turn somewhat more specifically to Donne's theology, to his beliefs about the nature of God and the nature of man under God. Since Donne's views underwent no appreciable change during his preaching years, no chronological problem is involved. Though he preached more specifically on the nature of sin during his earlier years in the pulpit than in later years, his doctrine of sin remained unchanged; though he directed himself toward expounding the evils of Rome with greater frequency and emphasis during the years 1626-1628 than at any other time, his attitude toward the Roman Catholic Church was essentially the same throughout his priesthood; though he had spells of depression and spells of elation and consequently might tend at one time to emphasize that there is no health in us and at another to remind us joyfully of the immensity of God's mercy to the most notorious of sinners, his views on depravity and redemption and their relationship were fairly well fixed by the time of his ordination. I have chosen to speak of Donne's theology through a discussion of remarks of his which fall within three major areas of religious thought: sin and redemption, grace and free will (or faith and works), and death and resurrection. Admittedly there are many other areas of theological thought—the creation, the Trinity, Christology, to mention a few about which Donne preaches many times and at great length. But to discuss thoroughly the three areas which I have chosen is to say a great deal about other theological problems which are closely related to them. If one wished to sum up Donne's central beliefs in most compact form, he could conveniently turn to one of the St. Paul's sermons and hear Donne tell his congregation that "The simplest man, as well as the greatest Doctor, is bound to know, that there is one God in three persons, That the second of those, the Sonne of God, tooke our nature, and dyed for mankinde; And that there is a Holy Ghost, which in the Communion of Saints, the Church established by Christ, applies to every particular soule the benefit of Christs universall redemption" (D v:276). The Father, the Son, the Holy Ghost, the Communion of Saints which comprise that Body of Christ known as the Church—of these loving powers and redeemed people the reader of Donne's sermons does not lose sight for a moment. And if Donne would on the one hand urge a unity within the Christian body—a forgetting of the names of Lutheran and Calvinist, of Papist and Anabaptist, and a remembering of the name of Christian— he would on the other hand remind us that *Christian* is set off from all other names. Jesus Christ, the one person in whom are found the nature of man and the nature of God, the one person anointed to be man's Saviour, the one person who combines the offices of prophet, priest, and king—to him the Christian must look for his name. The Christian must, moreover, know Christ as he is a member of the Trinity which makes up the Godhead. Simply to believe in God the Father, Donne contends, is not enough. All men believe in such a power, but what distinguishes the Christian from other men is the grace to be able "to conceive aright of the Power of the Father, of the Wisdome of the Son, of the Goodnesse of the Holy Ghost; Of the Mercie of the Father, of the Merits of the Son, of the Application of the Holy Ghost; Of the Creation of the Father, of the Redemption of the Son, of the Sanctification of the Holy Ghost. Without this, all notions of God are but confused, all worship of God is but Idolatry, all confession of God is but Atheisme; For so the Apostle argues, *When you were without Christ, you were without God.*" (D viii:59)

[163]

SIN AND REDEMPTION

The fact of sin presents a considerable problem to the theologian who would call God both all-powerful and all-loving. If God were omnipotent but not all-loving, sin could be attributed to the fact that though he is powerful enough to prevent it, he derives a certain pleasure from seeing his creatures encompassed by evil; if God were all-loving but not omnipotent, it could be said that though his loving heart wills that there be no sin, he simply is not mighty enough to prevent it. But the Biblical God is affirmed to be both all-powerful and all-loving, and yet there are manifold evidences of sin and evil in the world of man. One of the central problems to confront Donne—and theologians before and after him—was that of accounting for the origin, presence, and nature of sin in a universe created, governed, and sustained by the God who reveals himself in Scripture.

An attempt to discover the origin of sin must begin with an examination of the creation of the world. Donne many times refers to the creation, emphasizing that it was a creation out of nothing and that it was a good creation. He will have nothing to do with the Manichaean heresy that the God of the Old Testament was a blundering, incompetent maker to be carefully distinguished from the Father of the Lord Jesus Christ; such dualism was abruptly discountenanced by the early Church Fathers and by Donne himself, though it would provide an explanation of a kind for the presence of sin. Donne calls attention to the divine refrain which climaxes most of the days of creation in the first chapter of Genesis: "it was good." And he elaborates on the meaning of the word *good* through a reference to the medieval theologians: ". . .when it is ordinarily inquired in the Schoole, whether any thing be essentially good, it is safely answered there, that if by essentially we mean independantly, so good as that it can subsist of it self, without dependance upon, or relation to any other thing, so there is nothing essentially good: But if by essentially good, we mean that whose essence, and beeing is good, so every thing is essentially good." (D vɪ:237) The same point was put more poetically by John Milton, whose Raphael warned Adam that his creaturely goodness was perfect, but not immutable:

> "Son of Heaven and Earth,
> Attend! That thou art happy, owe to God;
> That thou continuest such, owe to thyself,
> That is, to thy obedience; therein stand.
> This was that caution given thee; be advised.
> God made thee perfect, not immutable;
> And good he made thee; but to persevere
> He left it in thy power—ordained thy will
> By nature free, not over-ruled by fate
> Inextricable, or strict necessity."
>
> (*Paradise Lost*, v, 520-528)

Donne's careful reading of Scripture is evidenced by his noting that God did not conclude the sixth day of creation with his customary "it was good," a fact which leads Donne to suggest that, "of Man, it seemes, God was distrustfull from the beginning; He did not pronounce upon Mans Creation, (as he did upon the other Creatures) that *He was good*; because his goodnesse was a contingent thing, and consisted in the future use of his free will" (D ɪx:373). A distinction must be made, however, between God's judicious distrust of man's future behavior and God's responsibility for such behavior, which responsibility, Donne thought, was at least implied by Calvin's doctrine of double predestination, the view that God not only elected some to salvation but also relegated others to damnation. To accept such a view was to make God responsible for sin. "There are men that will say and sweare," Donne once told the students at Lincoln's Inn, "they do not meane to make God the Author of sin; but yet when they say, That God made man therefore, that he might have something to damne, and that he made him sin therefore, that he might have something to damne him for, truly they come too neare making God the Author of sin, for all their modest protestation of abstaining" (D III:262-263).

The authors of sin were our first parents, Adam and Eve, who out of their God-given free will chose to disobey their Creator. It would be accurate to say also that all men are authors of that first sin of disobedience. Donne summons the authority of St. Augustine to insist that "to the guiltinesse of originall sin, our own wills concurre as well as to any actuall sin," that is, to any sin committed by us in our day-to-day lives. Since every man was in Adam, "so every *faculty* of every man, and consequently the will of every man concurred to that sin, which therefore lies upon every man now." (D II:106) Donne treats fascinatingly the question of precisely how every human being inherits at his conception that venomous quality which all men share. In the first place, the very action through which our parents conceive us is sinful; thus we are conceived in their sin and become the subjects of original sin through their sinfully generative action. But this makes for a complex problem. For in the substance or flesh of which we were made, there could be no sin, since substance in itself, devoid of will and of the possibility of choosing, is incapable of sinful action. Neither could the soul which God creates to enter that substance be sinful, since God does not create anything infected with sin. Thus both the body and the soul are created innocent. Whence then comes sin? It comes instantaneously in the union of body and soul, as Donne proceeds to explain in a fantastic passage:

". . . the *union* of this soul and body is so accompanied
with Gods *malediction* for our first transgression, that in
the instant of that *union* of life, as certainly as that *body
must die*, so certainly *the whole Man* must be guilty of
Originall sin. . . . in the very first minute of our life, in
our quickning in our mothers womb, wee become guilty
of *Adams* sin done 6000 years before. . . . In the first
minute that my soul is infus'd, the Image of God is imprinted in my soul; so forward is God in my behalf, and
so early does he visit me. But yet *Originall sin* is there, as
soon as that Image of God is there. My soul is capable of
God, as soon as it is capable of *sin*; and though sin doe
not get the start of God, God does not get the start of
sin neither. Powers, that dwell so far asunder, as *Heaven*,
and *Hell*, *God* and the *Devill*, meet in an instant in my
soul, in the minute of my quickning, and the Image of
God, and the Image of *Adam*, Originall sin, enter into me
at once, in one, and the same act. So swift is this arrow,
Originall sin, from which, all arrows of subsequent tenta-
tions, are shot, as that God, who comes to my first minute
of life, cannot come before death." (D 11:58-59; see also
D v:171-172)

Original sin, that unhappy legacy of every man, "that
snake in my bosome . . . that poyson in my blood . . .
that leaven and tartar in all my actions," inclines and
disposes man to those manifold sins which he commits in
his daily life (D 11:120). Donne makes careful and dramatic distinction among the various kinds of sins which
may issue from the fount of man's first disobedience. There
are sinful thoughts, which mature into sinful actions, which
in turn mold themselves into sinful habits. Such actions
are designated as speaking sins, such habits as crying sins.
But prior to all these is a speechless or whispering sin
heard only by our own conscience. With what tenderness

[167]

we nurture this bud of sin Donne tells us in fine prose: ". . . when a sinful thought or purpose is born in our hearts," he writes, "first we rock it, by tossing, and tumbling it in our fancies, and imaginations, and by entertaining it with delight and consent, and with remembring, with how much pleasure we did the like sin before, and how much we should have, if we could bring this to pass; And as we rock it, so we swathe it, we cover it, with some pretences, some excuses, some hopes of coveraling it. . . ." (D 1:224)

Though both Walton and Gosse make too much, I think, of the conversion experience in Donne's life, of the black and white distinction between Donne's wild youth and his saintly manhood, it is nevertheless true that Donne's intensive concern with and analysis of sin, so markedly evident in his early preaching years, would seem to argue a fairly sudden and penetrating awareness of personal sin. I can hardly concur with Walton's judgment that Donne was a second Augustine in terms of the conversion experience; and Gosse's autobiographical approach to Donne's love poetry, a critical method which leads Gosse to attribute to Donne sexual liaisons which are then contrasted with the Dean's later purity—this I view with skepticism. Both Walton and Gosse, I believe, are too eager to preach the beauty and the miracle of conversion. Yet, even if Donne was never either the irresponsible libertine or the devout saint, his preoccupation with sin is indeed the mark of a converted man. Only a man who feels an intensely personal conviction of sin has the power to anatomize it with the consuming perception which Donne exhibits, and, though he may have nothing quite to equal Augustine's recital of his youthful pear-stealing expedition or Bunyan's vignette about his profane boyhood ringing of the church bells, Donne certainly convinces his readers that a new faith had opened up to his heart and imagination a very real sense of the meaning of sin.

Donne does not absolutely deny the Augustinian paradox that sin is essentially nothing. He agrees that it is a deprivation, a missing of the mark of righteousness. But he takes little comfort in this position. One might argue, he asserts, that sickness and death are nothings or deprivations too. Sickness is a deprivation of health; death, of life; and damnation, of the sight and presence of God. It would be more realistic, if less philosophic, to affirm that "Sin is so far from being nothing, as that there is nothing else but sin in us"; there is no human action, however righteous it may seem in the eyes of this world, that is not vitiated by the inherited and accrued corruption of its doer. (D II:99-100) If sin is at once nothing and everything, it is also a stupidity (D V:209), a view that would find favor in Greek thought.

If one prerequisite of great preaching is that the preacher have a conviction of sin, another is that he be able to bring his more complacent parishioners to a like conviction. This Donne sought to do in a variety of ways. In two of his earliest extant sermons he directs himself specifically to the task of warning those people who, not having felt the wrath of God, persist in their sins under the assumption that they will go unpunished. The appropriately chosen texts are Ecclesiastes 8:11—"Because sentence against an evil work, is not executed speedily, therefore the heart of the children of men, is fully set in them, to do evil"—and Psalm 55:19—"Because they have no changes, therefore they fear not God." The most dangerous condition in which a sinner may find himself is happiness, a condition which suggests his unawareness of his sin or of its damning consequences; satisfied with things as they are, thoughtless of the terrible destiny which awaits him unless he repents, he becomes hardened in sin. Perhaps worst of all, the sinner is led by God's very patience, by God's indisposition to strike quickly—the sinner is led by these merciful qualities to continue in sin. This particular kind of sinner proceeds rationally and logically; he works, as both Biblical texts suggest, from a "because" to a "therefore"; he thus perverts the gift of which he is of all creatures the exclusive possessor, his reason, to the service of sin. (D 1:168-169) The reason of such a man misleads him not only in its urging a freedom to sin in general; it misleads him also to assign false causes to his individual sins. A man will comfort himself by assigning his sin to his youth or to his constitution, to his station in life or to his calling, to powers which lie outside himself, to the fact that he does not wish to cut himself off from sinning mankind. But man is without excuse and is only putting his reason to perverse use when he does so try to excuse himself. (D 1:226)

Somewhat later in his preaching career and again with the hope of leading his hearers to a knowledge of their true condition and to a conviction of sin, Donne reminds them that a person does not have to commit an outward sin to be sinful—intention or desire is enough. A man may "die under an everlasting condemnation of fornication with that *woman*, that lives, and dies a Virgin, and be damn'd for a murderer of that man, that outlives. . .[him], and for a robbery, and oppression, where no man is damnified, nor any penny lost" (D 11:102). Nor (to give a final example of Donne's seeking to make clear the universality, variety, and fatality of sin) should a man feel that he is safe if he limits himself to what he may feel to be *"smaller sins."* For the crafty Devil "keeps thy reckoning exactly, and will produce against thee at last as many lascivious glaunces as shall make up an Adultery, as many covetous wishes as shall make up a Robery, as many angry words as shall make up a Murder; and thou shalt have dropt and crumbled away thy soul, with as much irrecoverableness, as if thou hadst poured it out all at once; and thy merry sins, thy laughing sins, shall grow up to be crying sins, even in the ears of God; and though thou drown thy soul here, drop after drop, it shall not burn spark after spark, but have all the fire, and all at once, and all eternally, in one intire and intense torment." (D 1:195) In short, man is without excuse for sin, and he is without hope unless he surrenders himself to the redemptive power of God.

The burden of sin sinks a man, wearies him, slows him down, and causes him to stumble (D 11:132-136); of all God's creatures sinful man is most miserable: "Miserable man! a Toad is a bag of Poyson, and a Spider is a blister of Poyson, and yet a Toad and a Spider cannot poyson themselves; Man hath a dram of poyson, originall-Sin, in an invisible corner, we know not where, and he cannot choose but poyson himselfe and all his actions with that" (D 1:293). And how does a man know when the poison has won its victory and placed him beyond cure? It is not simply when man dwells pleasurably on the titillating memory of his sins; it is not when he succumbs for a time to temptation; it is not when the devil works successfully to lead man astray. Rather it is when man has made sin so habitual, when his heart is so wholly set upon evil, that sin is self-generating, no longer needing the devil's crafty motivation, no longer needing any outer temptation. A man so conquered by sin, so independent of the stimulation of temptation, would be ambitious in a hospital, licentious in a wilderness, voluptuous in a famine! (D 1:178-179)

It would require an obdurate heart and a closed ear to remain unmoved by Donne's discourses on sin. If a man were, without benefit of sermon, too insensitive or too obtuse to recognize himself as one of the fallen, certainly Donne's analysis of sin should enable him to recognize its presence within himself, and certainly Donne's description of the status and destiny of the sinner should lead him to recognize his frightful predicament. A preacher is called, however, not only to bring fallen man to a conviction of his sin, for this alone might lead only to desperation. He is called also to proclaim God's power to redeem the penitent man. And John Donne could never be charged with leaving man in the Slough of Despond; his sense of man's depravity is more than balanced by his sense of God's redemptive love. It is true that he warns us that a persistent misuse of God's grace, a determined and stubborn insistence on pursuing evil ways, will carry man outside the bounds of salvation, not because God cannot save him but because God will save no man against his own will. It is true that he speaks of "sinnes, which in their nature preclude repentance, and batter the *Conscience*, devastate, depopulate, exterminate, annihilate the *Conscience*, and leave no sense at all, or but a sense of *Desperation*" (D VI:256). It is true that he will not go so far as Origen and proclaim a universal salvation, to include even the Devil himself. And it is true that he thinks Papists too lenient in their view of the consequences of sin: he questions their conception of venial sin and accuses them of treating too lightly the deeds which are so characterized (D II:100); he speaks contemptuously, and hardly accurately, of the ease with which sins are forgiven within the Roman Church: "Our new *Romane Chymists*. . .they that can *transubstantiate bread into God*, they can change any foulness into cleanness easily. They require no more after sin, but *quendam tenuem dolorem internum*, A little slight inward sorrow, and that's enough" (D I:203). But for all this, Donne is loath to point to any man and say that he is clearly beyond salvation.

Donne's reticence in this respect is most clearly shown in a sermon on the text of Matthew 12:31: "Wherefore I say unto you, All manner of sin and blasphemy shall be forgiven unto men; but the blasphemy against the Holy

Ghost shall not be forgiven unto men." Treating almost apologetically Christ's words that there is a sin beyond forgiveness, Donne asserts that the first part of the text is "the sentence, the proposition, and the sense is perfect in that"; the second part, the part following the semicolon, is "but a *Parenthesis*, which Christ had rather might have been left out, but the Pharisees [to whom Jesus is addressing himself], and their perversenesse inserted" (D v:78). And what is this blasphemy against the Holy Ghost? It is " 'a totall falling away from the Gospell of Christ Jesus formerly acknowledged and professed, into a verball calumniating, and a reall persecuting of that Gospel, with a deliberate purpose to continue so to the end, and actually to do so, to persevere till then, and then to passe away in that disposition.' " So heinous does Donne make the sin, so elaborately does he state its absoluteness and finality, that one can understand his emphasis on its "parenthetic" character. He concludes his paragraph of definition with the most comforting of sentences: "Here we have that sin, but, by Gods grace, that sinner no where." (D v:88) Donne would seem to be suggesting that this utterly damning sin is present only potentially.

All men are, nonetheless, mired in sin and must become convinced of that fact. Such a conviction is the first step in the journey toward redemption, is "our quickning in our regeneration, and second birth" (D ix:299). Donne at one time speaks of the redemptive process as threefold: first, man, who threw himself away to the Devil, is restored to himself by God; second, God sends the Holy Ghost to serve as man's guide; third, God improves man, making him better than he was in his original innocence (D 1:162-163). Man is restored to himself through the Sacrament of Baptism, which cleanses him of his original sin. Yet the cleansing is not complete, is not enough to effect a moral purity throughout the rest of our lives; for when we fell

with Adam, "we fell upon a *heape of sharpe stones. . .*and
we feel those wounds, and those bruises, all our lives after;
Impingimus meridie, we *stumble at noone day*; In the
brightest light of the *Gospell*, in the brightest light of
grace, in the best strength of *Repentance*, and our resolu-
tions to the contrary, yet we stumble, and fall againe." To
protect us from the continued presence of these sharp
stones, God both sends the Holy Ghost to guide and protect us and provides us with a second sacrament, the blood
of our Saviour. (D v:172-173) Once we have been restored
by God through the washing away of original sin by baptism; once we have received the Holy Ghost as guardian
and been cleansed of our actual sins through the Sacrament
of the Holy Communion; then we are further blessed by
being brought to a condition superior to that of the pre-
lapsarian Adam. Actually we have good reason to rejoice in
our sins. Viewed retrospectively, the fall of Adam was a
fortunate one for the generations of man, if not for Adam.
In the first place, man's inheritance from Adam possesses
a kind of inoculative virtue. The greatest sins are committed by those who are without former sin: "The first
Angels sin, and the sin of *Adam* are noted to be the most
desperate and the most irrecoverable sins, and they were
committed, when they had no former sin in them." Our
lesser sins serve as warnings to us and prevent our going
on to the excess of Adam's first sin. And our sins and the
temptations thereto work to our good in still another way:
"If man had been made *impeccable*, that he could not
have sinned, he had not been so happy; for then, he could
onely have enjoyed that state, in which he was created, and
not have risen to any *better*; because that *better* estate, is
a reward of our willing obedience to God, in such things,
as we might have disobeyed him in." (D ii:122-123) One
is reminded of *Paradise Lost*, and of Adam's joyous words
to Michael after the archangel had unfolded to him in

[174]

apocalyptic fashion the coming of Christ and the future ages of the world:

"O Goodness infinite, Goodness immense,
That all this good of evil shall produce,
And evil turn to good—more wonderful
Than that which by creation first brought forth
Light out of darkness! Full of doubt I stand,
Whether I should repent me now of sin
By me done and occasioned, or rejoice
Much more that much more good thereof shall spring—
To God more glory, more good-will to men
From God—and over wrath grace shall abound."

(XII, 469-478)

One mark of Donne's preaching is his reiteration of this same theme, that apparent evil is sometimes actual good, that good frequently comes out of evil. God's hand is a medicinal one, and, whatever his actions may be, his purpose is always to correct and recover us, not to destroy us. The temptations which come to us and occasion such pain if we resist them may be the very disciplines which prepare us for salvation (D VI:111). Tribulations, which seem so evil at the time of their striking, may actually purge us of our sin: violent illness may purge man of his licentiousness, poverty of his usuriousness, disgrace of his ambition, eviction of his oppression (D VI:198). Death itself, the product of our sin, is used by God as a means to resurrection, to a glorifying of the very body whose sin brought death (D VI:72). Thus, all that we call sin and evil and suffering may well be the means of our salvation. Donne quotes St. Augustine: "*Novit Dominus vulnerare ad amorem*; The Lord, and onely the Lord knowes how to wound us, out of love; more then that, how to wound us into love; more then all that, to wound us into love, not onely with him that wounds us, but into love with the wound it selfe,

[175]

with the very affliction that he inflicts upon us; The Lord knowes how to strike us so, as that we shall lay hold upon that hand that strikes us, and kisse that hand that wounds us" (D vi:212). Suffering indeed may be the surest way to salvation, a fact which Donne makes clear in his "Hymne to God my God, in my sicknesse":

> We thinke that *Paradise* and *Calvarie,*
>> *Christs* Crosse, and *Adams* tree, stood in one place;
> Looke Lord, and finde both *Adams* met in me;
>> As the first *Adams* sweat surrounds my face,
>> May the last *Adams* blood my soule embrace.
>
> So, in his purple wrapp'd receive mee Lord,
>> By these his thornes give me his other Crowne;
> And as to others soules I preach'd thy word,
>> Be this my Text, my Sermon to mine owne,
>> Therfore that he may raise the Lord throws down.

Adam's fall, it would seem, is by no means an unmitigated evil.

God works for man through his Church, through the sacraments of water and blood, and through the sending of the Holy Ghost. Man too has his part to play, both in the resisting of temptations and in the repentant confession of sins, which, Donne insists, must be confessed, even though the meditation of a priest may not be necessary. To think that we can hide our sinful actions from God is sheer folly; humbly and penitently to confess them is great wisdom (D v:174). If the two sacraments of water and blood are purifying, so is that washing which comes through those contrite tears accompanying our confession of our sins to God (D v:176). And Donne calls our attention to the paradox that "if I say my sins are mine own, they are none of mine, but, by that confessing and appropriating of those sins to my selfe, they are made the sins of him, who hath suffered enough for all, my blessed Lord and Saviour, *Christ Jesus*" (D ii:102).

Donne is following his calling as preacher by simultaneously establishing in his hearers a conviction of their sin and assuring them of God's redemptive power over the worst of sinners. In his effort to lead them to their salvation Donne also makes clear that vast difference between the state of the damned and the Kingdom to which the truly repentant can look forward. Discussing some of the conceptions of Hell he affirms that, "when all is done, the hell of hels, the torment of torments is the everlasting absence of God, and the everlasting impossibility of returning to his presence." It is a fearful thing to fall into the hands of the living God, "but to fall out of the hands of the living God, is a horror beyond our expression, beyond our imagination." (D v:266) And to what can the redeemed look forward? "We shall see him [Christ] in a transfiguration, all clouds of sadness remov'd; and a transubstantiation, all his tears changed to Pearls, all his Blood-drops into Rubies, all the Thorns of his Crown into Diamonds: for, where we shall see the Walls of his Palace to be Saphyr, and Emerald, and Amethist, and all Stones that are precious, what shall we not see in the face of Christ Jesus? and whatsoever we do see, by that very sight becomes ours" (D iv:129).

Most appropriate as a conclusion to this section on sin and redemption is Donne's statement of the relationship between man's sin and God's mercy; in it we find the Christian's ultimate assurance and hope of salvation:

"Reprove thy selfe; but doe it by convincing, not by a downe-right stupefaction of the conscience; but by a consideration of the nature of thy sin, and a contemplation of the infinite proportion between God and thee, and so between that sin and the mercy of God; for, thou canst not be so absolutely, so intirely, so essentially sinfull, as God

[177]

is absolutely, and intirely, and essentially mercifull. Doe what thou canst, there is still some goodnesse in thee; that nature that God made, is good still; Doe God what hee will, hee cannot strip himselfe, not devest himselfe of mercy." (D vi:329-330)

GRACE AND FREE WILL

In no respect does Anglicanism more thoroughly fulfill its claim to the middle way than in its view of the relationship between God and man in the redemptive process. Christians have always agreed that man is fallen, that Paradise has been lost, but they have held divergent views regarding how Paradise is to be regained. One of Martin Luther's principal indictments of the Roman Church was that it underestimated the role of God and overestimated the role of man in its concept of salvation, that it overassessed man's freedom and, in so doing, called into question God's omnipotence. His position is well reflected in both the title and content of his treatise *On the Bound Will*, written in 1525 in response to Erasmus's *On The Free Will*, an essay expressing essentially the Roman conception of the relationship between God's grace and man's will. To Erasmus the justice of God demands that man possess a rational liberty and that man not be punished for sins he cannot avoid. To Luther God's sense of justice need not conform to man's; God's every action is by definition just.

The problem involved is that of judging precisely where to draw the line between God's work and man's in the latter's journey from his lost condition to redemption. One of the central problems of Christian theology has always been to effect a statement on the relationship between God's grace and man's will which would sustain both the omnipotence of God and the freedom of man. When the balance has been tipped to one side, so that either God's power or man's freedom seems endangered, a theologian, seeking to right the balance, will step in and frequently tip the balance too far the other way. Even the same theologian may seem to vacillate in his own position, as he seeks first to combat one extreme position and then the other. Donne was aware that the heat of controversy occasionally led a person to go beyond his real position—the Church Fathers themselves succumbed to this human failing: "In heat of disputation, and argument, and to make things straight, they bent them too much on the other hand, and to oppose one Heresie, they endangered the inducing of another, as in S. *Augustines* disputations against the Pelagians, who over-advanced the free will of man, and the Manicheans, who by admitting *Duo principia*, two Causes, an extrinsique cause of our evill actions, as well as of our good, annihilated the free will of man, we shall find sometimes occasions to doubt whether S. *Augustine* were constant in his owne opinion, and not transported sometimes with vehemency against his present adversary, whether Pelagian, or Manichean" (D vii:203).

John Donne and the Anglican Church tread with great deliberation the narrow path between the position of Rome and the positions of Luther and Calvin on the matter of grace and free will. Donne would preserve both God's omnipotence and man's freedom, and, in so doing, he directs his criticisms against both the Roman Catholics and the Reformers. Nor is he ever so "transported . . . with vehemency" against one adversary that he slips over into the camp of the other. On the one hand he attacks the whole Roman apparatus of belief which to him accords man too much freedom in the determination of his salvation: belief in the efficacy of prayers for the dead, the concept of Purgatory, the theory of indulgences, the value of pilgrimages and relics. And on the other he speaks out against the Calvinist view of the irresistibility of God's grace and of double predestination.

The Roman and Reformed traditions are in agreement that Adam's disobedience, man's voluntary severing of himself from God's kingship, has reduced man to a weakness from which he cannot recover on his own initiative. It was within Adam's grasp to resist sin—he was able not to sin, as Augustine put it—but the man who has fallen and has not yet been quickened by the rays of God's grace is not able not to sin. "We have lost our possession, and our possibility of recovering, by *Adams* sin," writes Donne in agreement. "*Adam* at his best had but a possibility of standing; we are fallen from that, and from all possibility of rising by any power derived from him: We have not only by this fall broke our armes, or our legs, but our necks; not our selves, not any other man can raise us" (D VI:116). Adam is like the prodigal son who was given freedom by his father and then abused it, thus losing it; but Adam lost not only his own free will, but ours as well (D I:162). All Christendom is in agreement, not only that man lost in Adam's fall all possibility of standing righteous in God's eyes but also that God must take the initiative in man's recovery. This return, this reconciliation, of man to God, God has made possible through the sacrificial death of Jesus Christ. "Such a renewing it is," Donne writes of God's merciful recovery of man, "as could not be done without God; no man can renew himselfe, regenerate himselfe; no man can prepare that worke, no man can begin it, no man can proceed in it of himselfe. The desire and the actuall beginning is from the preventing grace of God . . . ." (D II:305)

It is important to note that, up to this point, Donne is not in a controversial area; it is true that the Pelagians, who would have claimed the name of Christian, had a different view of Everyman's relation to Adam's fall, but the Pelagians had been pronounced heretical by the central Christian tradition. The Roman Church, the Reformed

Churches, and the Anglican Church were fundamentally at one in the conviction that man had, through Adam, voluntarily surrendered his free will and could not regain it without God's prevenient grace. Disagreements began when the various churches turned to a consideration of man's role in the God-man relationship after God had shed the first rays of his grace. As I said before, Luther—and Calvin after him—felt that the Roman Church attributed to man more than was his due in the gaining of salvation, that Roman doctrine and practice implicitly called into question God's omnipotence. With this central contention Donne agreed, but, true to Anglicanism, he felt that the Reformers had gone too far in the other direction, and he took up a halfway position between what he believed to be the two extremes. I should like to examine his arguments —first against the Roman Communion into which he had been born, and then against the principal Reformers of the sixteenth century and their adherents in seventeenth-century England.

Evidence of Rome's disposition to accord man too much freedom is found, Donne believes, primarily in their view of the efficacy of prayers for the dead, in their conception of Purgatory, and in their practice of indulgences. Donne's most extended treatment of these matters is contained in a sermon preached at St. Paul's on May 21, 1626, on the text of 1 Corinthians 15:29: "Else, what shall they doe which are baptized for the dead? If the dead rise not at all, why are they then baptized for the dead?" In this resurrection text the Roman Church sees its authority for the practice of prayers for the dead, which Donne classifies as the "Grand-mother Error"; from the grandmother error is derived the mother error, Purgatory itself; and from the mother spring the children—indulgences. Donne traces in some detail the genesis of the practice of prayer for the dead, insisting that it has no Scriptural authority.

He by no means views it as altogether evil, pointing out
as he does that it testifies to "a good, and tender, and pious
affection." Indeed, so long as it remained a practice which
one could take or leave according to his own disposition, it
was not a matter to challenge. But when the Roman
Church made of it a dogmatic matter, a fundamental condition of man's faith, then it became an evil, an example of
the Roman confusion between the fundamental and the
problematical. (D VII:168-176) Nor did the evil end there,
for the view that prayer for the dead might help them is
to imply that there is a Purgatory, a place to which the
dead might go for that cleansing which would prepare
them for entrance into Heaven. And there is no Scriptural
authority for Purgatory. Donne does not deny that there
is a kind of Purgatory, that there is a purging which man
must undergo before he is acceptable in God's Kingdom,
but it is a purging effected by Christ alone. Christ dies that
we may be purged, and even after his death, "*still our own
clothes defile us*, our own evill habits, our owne flesh pol-
lutes us, therefore God sends us a Purgatory too in this life,
Crosses, Afflictions, and Tribulations, and to burne out
these infectious staines and impressions in our flesh, *Ipse
sedet tanquam ignis conflans, God sits as a fire, and with
fullers soape*, to wash us, and to burne us cleane with afflictions from his own hand." What is of particular importance to note here is that the purging of sin is brought
about by Christ's initial action and by the sinner's following
him in the way of the Cross; man is not purged after death
by the prayers of the living. (D VII:176-184)

More dangerous than the custom of praying for the
dead or than the belief in Purgatory is the practice of indulgences, with all the implications of that practice. Indulgences are called by Donne the children of Purgatory and
are validated by the Roman Church on a false interpretation of the text of this sermon; according to Donne, Rome

argues that, "if there be no such Indulgences, If the works of Supererogation done by other men, may not be applied to the soules that are in Purgatory, If there be no such use of Indulgences, *why are then these men baptized for the dead?*" To the abuse of indulgences by the Roman Church Donne attributes the Reformation itself, and he finishes his sermon with a survey of the growth of the practice of indulgences and a castigation thereof. (D vii:184-189)

Donne turns frequently throughout his sermons to the theological beliefs which lay behind the Roman theory of indulgences, beliefs which show more strikingly than anything else that exalted view of man so repugnant to Luther and other Reformers. Donne attributes to Rome the extreme view that some men "are not onely without sin in themselves, but that they can save others from sin, or the punishment of sin, by their works of Supererogation." Such men have gone beyond the call of Christian duty, have already gained their own salvation, and may thenceforth have all their good deeds accredited to the accounts of others, to those more desperately in need of them for their own salvation. These sanctified men outdo the saints, who can only pray for others, whereas these men can "work out the salvation of others." In fact, they can even go beyond Christ, "for Christ did save no man here, but by dying for him; These men save other men, with living well for them, and working out their salvation." (D ix: 170) This view that the Roman Church possessed a treasury of the good deeds of sanctified men from which living and dead sinners could draw for the advancing of their own salvation is attacked in the following passage:

"Other mens crosses are not my crosses; no man hath suffered more then himselfe needed. That is a poore treasure which they boast of in the Romane Church, that they have in their Exchequer, all the works of supererogation, of the Martyrs in the Primitive Church, that suffered so much more then was necessary for their owne salvation, and those superabundant crosses and merits they can apply to me. If the treasure of the blood of Christ Jesus be not sufficient, Lord what addition can I find, to match them, to piece out them! And if it be sufficient of it selfe, what addition need I seek? Other mens crosses are not mine, other mens merits cannot save me." (D ii:300-301)

At the heart of the Roman error is the belief that man can merit something in the sight of God. So vast is the distinction between the righteousness of God and the best of man's actions, so merciful and forgiving has God been to man, that it would be impossible for man to square his own account, much less make God his debtor. And even if man does live what may seem in the eyes of this world to be an exceedingly virtuous life, even if he does seem to be a fountain of good works, his actions will be truly righteous only if they are done with the right intent, are directed to the right ends. Here again the Papists labor under the greatest of misconceptions, accomplishing their outwardly good deeds in order to place God in their debt:

"One of the Ancients hath given us this caution, *Vt nemo bonus dicatur qui malum bono permiscuerit*, That we call no man *good*, that is good to *ill ends*, nor beleeve any man to speak truth, that speaks truth at some times, to make his future lies the more credible. And much this way does the *Romane Church* proceed with us, in this behalf. They magnifie *sanctification*, and *holinesse of life* well; well doe they propose many good means, for the advancement, and exaltation thereof; *fasting*, and *prayer*, and *almes*, and other Medicinall Disciplines, and *Mortifications*. But all this to a wrong end; Not to make them the more acceptable to God, but to make God the more beholden to them; To *merit*, and over-merit; To *satisfie*, and super-satisfie the justice of God for their own, and for others sins. Now, God will be served with *all our power*; But, say they, wee may serve God, with more then all our power. . . . All that my Saviour hath taught me, in this, to pray for, is but this, *Dimitte debita*, Lord forgive mee the not-endevouring to keep thy Commandements: But for *not doing more* then thy Commandements, I ask no forgiveness, by any prayer, or precept recommended to mee by him." (D ix:120-121)

Rome shows its tendency to overvalue man's works in other ways as well, particularly in its admission of the efficacy of pilgrimages and of relics. Donne presents a cursory sketch of the history of "meritorious Pilgrimages." Innocent the Third pardoned of all their sins those men who, as soldiers, went to the Holy Land or contributed to its recovery. Later, indulgences were granted to those who went to Jerusalem as pilgrims, as well as to those who went as soldiers. Boniface the Eighth granted indulgences for pilgrimages to Rome, and Clement the Sixth granted to every man who went on a pilgrimage the power "to deliver foure soules out of Purgatory, which he would," and commanded the Angels of Heaven "to carry their soules that dyed in that Pilgrimage, immediately to Heaven, without touching upon Purgatory." Donne seriously doubts that the mere going to Jerusalem will make of a man a better Christian. (D ix:209-211) And he believes that if a power which rests in God's hands alone is mistakenly attributed to popes and pilgrims, a false power is also attributed to man-pronounced relics. It is wicked and absurd, Donne suggests, "when any ragge of their [saints'] skin, or chip of their bones, or lock of their haire, is kept for a Relique, and made an Universall balme, and Amulet, and Antidote, against all temporall, and all spirituall diseases, and calamities, not onely against the rage of a Feaver, but of hell it selfe." There is only one relic, Donne continues, which is granted us for our salvation: "What their counterfait Reliques may doe, against their counterfait hell, against their Purgatory, I know not: That powerfull, and precious, and onely Relique, which is given to us, against hell it selfe, is onely the Communion of the body, and blood of Christ Jesus, left to us by him, and preserved for us, in his Church, though his body be removed out of our sight." (D vi:270-271)

The common denominator of these various Roman Catholic practices about which Donne complains is their implied overestimation of the power and role of man in his relationship to God. He is following the Reformed tradition and saying nothing of significance which Luther had not said before him. But Donne and his Church were convinced that the Reformers, particularly the Calvinists, had, in their zealous opposition to Rome, been carried away into a counterposition equally false to the true God-man relationship. If the Roman Church would attribute too much power to man, the Calvinists would seem to deprive him of all power, reducing him to the status of a puppet. Paul's attacks on the Pharisees for their self-righteousness and Augustine's treatises against the Pelagians for their exaltation of man's freedom of will are earlier evidences of the same basic disputation, with the Calvinists carrying to its logical extreme the tradition of Paul and Augustine. One of the difficulties is that the carrying of the doctrine of God's omnipotence to its logical conclusion may lead one to view God as an arbitrary tyrant, one whose mercy is severely limited and whose disposition shows as great a readiness to damn as to save. Furthermore, an extreme view of God's omnipotence may logically lead to the conclusion that, from the beginning of time, God had predestined some to salvation, and others to damnation, a doctrine of double predestination which would mean that some men were destined to eternal damnation before their conception and could do absolutely nothing to escape God's damning decree. Donne, in a sermon on the text of Ezekiel 33:32, strongly rebukes those who preach such doctrine. The text reads, "And lo, thou art unto them as a very lovely song, of one that hath a pleasant voyce, and can play well on an instrument; for they hear thy words, but they doe them not." But the song that Calvinists preach, Donne affirms, is hardly a lovely one; and their instrument, with its message of God's reprobation, is inharmonious: "If we shall say, that Gods first string in this instrument, was Reprobation, that Gods first intention, was, for his glory to damn man; and that then he put in another string, of creating Man, that so he might have some body to damn; and then another of enforcing him to sin, that so he might have a just cause to damne him; and then another, of disabling him to lay hold upon any means of recovery: there's no musick in all this, no harmony, no peace in such preaching." (D ii:170) Even worse perhaps, those who would thus make God the author of sin and those who would cast such doubts upon the scope of God's mercy are confident of their own election: Donne speaks of "The over-pure despisers of others; Men that will abridge, and contract the large mercies of God in Christ, and elude, and frustrate, in a great part, the generall promises of God. Men that are loth, that God should speak so loud, as to say, *He would have all men saved*, And loth that Christ should spread his armes, or shed his bloud in such a compasse, as might fall upon *all*. Men that think no sinne can hurt them, because they are *elect*, and that every sin makes every other man a *Reprobate*." (D ix:119)

Donne is suggesting that the Calvinist doctrine of reprobation would make of man a puppet powerless to respond to God's grace, and that their doctrine of the elect would make him equally powerless to resist God's grace. Admitting that God's grace is stronger than the resistance of any man or the Devil, Donne yet fears that there is danger of a man's taking undue confidence in the doctrine of irresistible grace and feeling that he can idly sit back and leave the whole matter of his salvation to God alone (D vii:156). He speaks scathingly of the Calvinist emphasis on resistibility and irresistibility: "New fashions in men, make us doubt new manners; and new terms in Divinity were ever suspicious in the Church of God, that new Doctrines were hid under them. *Resistibility*, and *Irresistibility* of grace, which is every Artificers wearing now, was a stuff that our Fathers wore not, a language that pure antiquity spake not." (D 1:255) Warning his congregation that no man should feel "so secure in his election, as to forbear to work out his salvation with fear and trembling," and assuring them that "God saves no man against his will," Donne goes on to distinguish between power and force: "There is a name of force, of violence, of necessity attributed to a God, which is *Mauzzim*: but it is the name of an Idol, not of a true God. The name of the true God is *Dominus tzebaoth*, the *Lord of Hosts*; a name of power, but not of force." (D 1:261)

At the basis of all these remarks is Donne's conviction that the Calvinists have gone too far and that their views may lead some to a damning despair and others to a smug and equally damning overconfidence. No man should feel that he is beyond either God's grace or his damnation; no man should for a moment relax his own vigilant working out of his salvation with fear and trembling; no man should rest confident in the fact that he at the moment is graced with faith and righteousness. Far from being a will-less puppet, man plays an active role in his relationship to God. All men should humbly know their own power; and those members of Donne's Church, of the Body of Christ, should preserve this gift with all care. They must not thoughtlessly drift into the unhappy state of the person who, fallen from grace, is described in the following passage:

". . . when thou hast had Christ offered to thee, by the motions of his grace, and seal'd to thee by his Sacraments, and yet wilt cast him so far from thee, that thou knowest not where to find him, when thou hast poured him out at thine eyes in prophane and counterfeit tears, which should be thy souls rebaptization for thy sins, when thou hast blown him away in corrupt and ill intended sighs, which should be *gemitus columbæ*, the voice of the Turtle, to sound thy peace and reconciliation with thy God; yea when thou hast spit him out of thy mouth in execrable and blasphemous oathes; when thou hast not only cast him so far, as that thou knowest not where to find him, but hast made so ordinary and so indifferent a thing of sin, as thou knowest not when thou didst lose him, no nor dost not remember that ever thou hadst him; no, nor dost not know that there is any such man, as *Dominus tuus*, a Jesus, that is, *thy Lord*; The *Tulerunt* is dangerous, when others hide Christ from thee; but the *Abjecerunt* is desperate, when thou thy self doest cast him away" (D 1:245).

If both the Roman Catholics and the Reformers missed the mark in their view of the relationship between God's grace and man's freedom, what was the middle way of the Anglicans? The various churches, as we have seen, were in agreement at their starting point, and neither Rome nor Geneva would dispute Donne's description of unregenerate man as one who "lay smothered up in *massa damnata*, in that leavened lump of *Adam*" (D 1:273), or would deny Donne's statement that we who have sinned and not yet been reconciled "have lost all possibility of

doing, or receiving any good of our selves" (D 1:276).
From this point on Donne threads his way carefully between the two positions he is combating. One of the sermons in which his own position is stated most clearly is on
the text of Genesis 32:10: "I am not worthy of the least
of all thy mercies, and of all the truth which thou hast
shewed unto thy servant; for with my staff I passed over
this Jordan and now I am become two bands." Donne points
out that these words of Jacob to God, spoken as the powerful Esau draws toward his brother, express both man's
unworthiness and his capacity to receive God's grace. This
capacity distinguishes man from all other creatures. "It is
but little, that man is, proportioned to the working of
God," writes Donne, "but yet man is that creature, who
onely of all other creatures can answer the inspiration of
God, when his grace comes, and exhibit acceptable service to
him, and cooperate with him. No other creature is capable
of grace, if it could be offered to them." From that time
when God first bestows his grace upon a man, a twofold
activity is necessary. In the first place man must respond
to God's prevenient grace if he wishes God to continue
to pour forth his grace; secondly, God must continue to
pour forth his grace if man is to retain the capacity to do
righteous deeds. (D 1:271-272)

Donne returns to this problem in many of his sermons,
and his general position shows that he has a more favorable judgment of the natural, unregenerate man than the
Reformers do. Mass of corruption that man is, his natural
faculties still possess an inherent power of response. God
bestows his grace only "where there is a sweet, and souple,
and tractable, and ductile disposition wrought in that
soule." This statement Donne immediately qualifies by
saying that such a disposition is no cause of the gift of
grace; the cause lies purely in God's goodness. "But yet,"
Donne continues, "*without* such a disposition, God would

not give that; and therefore *let us cleanse our selves from all filthinesse*, says the Apostle; There is something, which *we ourselves* may doe." (D v:177) We must not make the Pelagian mistake of "making Naturall faculties joynt-Commissioners with Grace," but neither must we go to the other extreme of denying that these faculties can be the servants and instruments of grace. If man is in need of God's grace for the power of righteous action, so is God in need of man's will in order that righteous action may be accomplished in this world: ". . . Grace could not worke upon man to Salvation, if man had not a faculty of will to worke upon, because without that will man were not man." (D v:316-317) Some of Donne's loveliest passages are those in which he preaches that continuous flow of God's grace which enables the responsive man to continue in righteous ways:

". . . as his mercy is new every morning, so his grace is renewed to me every minute, That it is not by yesterdaies grace that I live now, but that I have *Panem quotidianum*, and *Panem horarium*, My daily bread, my hourely bread, in a continuall succession of his grace, That the eye of God is open upon me, though I winke at his light, and watches over me, though I sleep, That God makes these returnes to my soule, and so studies me in every change, this consideration, infuses a sweeter verdure, and imprints a more cheerefull tincture upon my soule, then any taste of any one Act, done at once, can minister unto me. God made the Angels all of one naturall condition, in nature all alike; and God gave them all such grace, as that thereby they might have stood; and to them that used that grace aright, he gave a farther, a continuall succession of grace, and that is their Confirmation; Not that they cannot, but that they shall not fall; not that they are safe in themselves, but by Gods preservation safe." (D viii:368)

[191]

Directly related to the problem of grace and free will is that of faith and works. Faith is a product of grace and persuades a man to bend his will to good works. Both faith and works are prerequisites to the Kingdom, yet the two are to be distinguished from each other in a number of ways. Faith is the evidence of our election, and good works are the seal of it (D v:195); a man stands on his faith in the sight of God, on his good works in the sight of other men (D v:197); our love of God is expressed through our faith, our love of neighbor through our good works (D II:256); faith comes before good works, yet faith is nursed by good works: *"Per ea augescit fidei, & pinguescit*, saies *Luther*, Our faith grows into a better state, and into a better liking, by our good works" (D vi:190). Faith without works and works without faith would be equally ineffective. To show the foolishness of placing one's trust in works which are not rooted in faith, Donne turns to Augustine for illustrative material: if you saw a man rowing until his eyestrings, sinews, and muscles broke, and asked him whither he rowed; if you saw a man run until fatigued, and asked him whither he ran; if you saw a man dig until his back broke, and asked him what he sought—and if any one of them said he did not know, you would consider him mad. "So," Donne writes with a glance at Roman Catholics, "are all Disciplines, all Mortifications, all whippings, all starvings, all works of Piety, and of Charity madnesse, if they have any other root then faith, any other title or dignity, then effects and fruits of a preceding reconciliation to God." (D ix:383-384)

In his discussion of faith, Donne also attacks the Roman Catholics for their blind faith, for what he calls their blind obedience to the Church of Rome (D viii:49). He insists that true faith must always be grounded in reason: "As faith without *fruit*, without *works*, is no faith; so faith without a *root*, without *reason*, is no faith, but an *opinion*"

(D v:102). In one sermon Donne proclaims that the image of God within man is reason itself, and that grace grows in this reason (D x:46-47). In another he preaches that "*Knowledge* cannot save us, but we cannot be saved without Knowledge; Faith is not on this side Knowledge, but beyond it; we must necessarily come to *Knowledge* first, though we must not stay at it, when we are come thither. For, a regenerate Christian, being now a *new Creature*, hath also *a new facultie of Reason*: and so believeth the Mysteries of Religion, out of another Reason, then as a meere naturall Man, he believed naturall and morall things" (D iii:359). Neither faith alone, nor good works alone, nor reason alone will save man. But the man who responds to God's grace with the new life of an intelligent faith pouring forth the fruits of good works will reach the Kingdom.

The whole problem of the relation between grace and free will, between faith and works, between God and man is manifestly an exceedingly complex and mysterious one. It is evident that Donne followed, and indeed helped to form, the Anglican position, the middle way between the Roman and the Reformed theologians. He shared with Luther and Calvin and their followers the fear that much of the apparatus of Roman belief and practice detracted from the glory of God. The thought that a man might go beyond the line of duty to God, that he might satisfy the necessary terms for his own salvation and then place his works of supererogation in a treasury from which they might, through indulgences, be sold to the less meritorious, was anathema to the entire Protestant tradition. And the belief that the going on a pilgrimage might in itself help one to reach Heaven or that a good man's relics might have redemptive value was almost equally as unpalatable. But like many good things, the Reformed movement had, Donne felt, gone too far. In an effort to preserve the truth of God's omnipotence they had sacrificed God's best creation, man, depriving him of virtually all activity in the redemptive process. If Rome had seemed to overassess man's role, Geneva had seemed to reduce it by a ruthless logic to zero, saying that God destined some to be damned from the beginning of time and others to be equally powerless, though considerably more fortunate, before the force of his irresistible grace. The Anglican position, Donne's position, might not stand the full test of logical argument. But the total Scripture message and man's day-to-day experience would seem to give some authority to the paradox that, on the one hand, man is absolutely governed in his every action by God and, on the other, that man is nonetheless a responsible moral agent, called upon to choose between life and death and empowered to do so through God's grace. The final answer to such problems is shrouded in mystery, never to become perfectly clear to man's reason, enfeebled as it has become through Adam's sin.

DEATH AND RESURRECTION

In his Easter sermon of 1623 John Donne told his St. Paul's congregation that both the first stone and the last of the Christian faith lay in the "article of the Resurrection." The first stone Donne defines as God's promise in Genesis that the seed of Adam and Eve, whom Christian commentators interpreted to be Christ, would bruise the serpent's head—that is, would destroy sin and its attendant death. The last stone is God's promise of a final Judgment Day. It is through Christ's resurrection that both promises are fulfilled, for his rising is a victory over sin and death and is necessarily prior to the Last Judgment. Thus at the very center of the Christian faith is the doctrine of the resurrection, and to it all preaching should ultimately bear witness. (D iv:355)

Donne implies that God's first plans for the universe included no resurrection. "God intended life and immortality for man," he writes; and had Adam never fallen, no resurrection would have been necessary. For resurrection grows out of death, and Adam in innocence knew no death. Adam and his more immediate generations, though condemned by their sin to death, received what Donne calls a long reprieve from death, living on to seven and eight hundred years; but so miserable did man's life become through the increasing burden of sin that the Lord mercifully decimated his years on earth. Whether death comes late or soon, however, it comes to all, an enemy wrought by man and growing out of his first disobedience. (D vi:349)

Death is not only man's enemy; it is his last enemy, the one which will indefatigably outlast all other hostile forces which were given life by man's sin. Its longevity is celebrated in a sermon preached at Whitehall on March 8, 1622, on the text of 1 Corinthians 15:26: "The last enemie that shall be destroyed, is death." Death, Donne asserts, is an enemy not only to man but to Heaven itself, for the Kingdom of Christ will be lacking in perfection as long as the bodies of men, which should properly belong to Christ, lie under the dominion of death. There can be no true peace in Heaven until death is destroyed and until those angels which Heaven lost through Satan's revolt are replaced by the creatures of the sixth day whom God made to be with him. On earth death is the cleverest of enemies, reserving its awful power against every man until he is in his weakest and most vulnerable condition. Death waits until his sure victim is so drained of energy that his only motion is the shaking engendered by his fever and palsy; death waits until the dimness of his prey's eyes gives the bitter foretaste of eternal darkness, the chattering of his teeth the foretaste of everlasting gnashing, the agonies of his body the foretaste of the waiting and everlastingly gnawing worm. And when death has taken his fill of this engaging spectacle, he casts the body from bed to grave, where he stands triumphant sentinel. (D IV:45-56) Here the power of death carries on beyond man's three-score years and ten, joining forces with the worms of the earth to visit upon that man created in the image of God the most ignoble and humiliating of fates. Commenting on Job 17:14—"I have said to corruption, Thou art my father: to the worm, Thou art my mother, and my sister"—Donne proceeds in his most macabre fashion: "*Miserable riddle*, when the *same worme* must bee *my mother*, and *my sister*, and *my selfe*. *Miserable incest*, when I must bee *maried* to my *mother* and my *sister*, and bee both *father* and *mother* to my *owne mother* and *sister*, *beget*, and *beare* that *worme* which is all that *miserable penury*; when my *mouth* shall be *filled* with *dust*, and the *worme* shall *feed*, and *feed sweetely* upon me. . . ." (D x:238)

Yet, for all its power, for its dominion over every man that lives and over the worm-infested, dust-dissolving body of every man that dies, for its delaying the perfect peace of Heaven itself—in spite of all these things, death must ultimately die. This death of death is the final and happy irony proclaimed by Christian doctrine. All men, even Christ himself, are subjected to what Donne calls the first death, the last breath of the human body. But to the faithful this first death is to be not only patiently endured but joyfully welcomed, for it is, paradoxically, the gate and the only gate to life. The time of its striking we must leave to God, neither courting it nor fleeing it of ourselves. Our shunning that which makes of our bodies food for worms is understandable; yet we must know death not only as a force that casts us out of this world and into the grave but as the anteroom to Heaven. As Donne approaches his own death, he writes in his "Hymne to God my God, in my sicknesse," that he stands at the door to "that Holy roome,/Where, with thy Quire of Saints for evermore,/I shall be made thy Musique." And he preaches that, though he would decline death in so far as it is "a sordid *Postern*, by which I must be thrown out of this world," yet he would embrace it as it is "the gate, by which I must enter into Heaven" (D vii:359). A better known statement of his joy in the face of death is found in the aforementioned "Hymne":

> I joy, that in these straits, I see my West;
>   For, though theire currants yeeld returne to none,
> What shall my West hurt me? As West and East
>   In all flatt Maps (and I am one) are one,
> So death doth touch the Resurrection.

Death, enemy that it is in so many ways, is to be feared only by the unrepentant, for that man must face not only the last heartbeat, not only the first death which is the portion of all mankind; he must suffer also the second death, the death which does not touch upon the resurrection but which delivers its victim to eternal damnation. The penitent man, however, has nothing to fear, for he may look well beyond the grave. Donne makes much of the glory that lies beyond, and though he is said to dwell on death and to play a morbid tune upon it, the fact is that the note of joy and hope is much more frequently heard in his sermons. He does go to great ends to impress upon man his mortality and the frailty of all earthly things, but he does so in an effort to persuade man not to place his trust in the ephemeral and untrustworthy. God is man's only sure stay and the only conqueror of death, and the man who remembers this will move toward death as a weary traveler nears some great city which is his destination. When the faithful man approaches his own sunset, when all his treasures and his loved ones are to make their final departure from him, when his own eyes grow faint and his family's tearful, then he will behold the new light of his Saviour; and though in the eyes of men he will appear but a motionless statue lying on his bed, in the eyes of God he will stand "as a Colossus, one foot in one, another in another land; one foot in the grave, but the other in heaven; one hand in the womb of the earth, and the other in *Abrahams* bosome: And then *vere prope*, Salvation is truly neer. . ." (D II:267).

This man may look toward the resurrection, an event seldom far from the center of Donne's preaching and upon which he plays many variations. Of the resurrection of the soul he preaches relatively little, probably because he feels that the soul's immortality is self-evident; as he says, "There are so many evidences of the immortality of the soule, even to a naturall mans *reason*, that it required not an Article of the Creed, to fix this notion of the Immortality of the soule" (D VIII:97-98). But the doctrine of the body's resurrection, not so self-evident, calls for an Article in the Creed and an act of faith. Donne eloquently suggests some of the problems entailed in this resurrection:

"Where be all the splinters of that Bone, which a shot hath shivered and scattered in the Ayre? Where be all the Atoms of that flesh, which a *Corrasive* hath eat away, or a *Consumption* hath breath'd, and exhal'd away from our arms, and other Limbs? In what wrinkle, in what furrow, in what bowel of the earth, ly all the graines of the ashes of a body burnt a thousand years since? In what corner, in what ventricle of the sea, lies all the jelly of a Body drowned in the *generall flood*? What cohærence, what sympathy, what dependence maintaines any relation, any correspondence, between that arm that was lost in Europe, and that legge that was lost in Afrique or Asia, scores of yeers between? One humour of our dead body produces

worms, and those worms suck and exhaust all other humour, and then all dies, and all dries, and molders into
dust, and that dust is blowen into the River, and that
puddled water tumbled into the sea, and that ebs and flows
in infinite revolutions, and still, still God knows in what
Cabinet every *seed-Pearle* lies, in what part of the world
every graine of every mans dust lies; and, *sibilat populum
suum,* (as his Prophet speaks in another case) he whispers,
he hisses, he beckens for the bodies of his Saints, and in the
twinckling of an eye, that body that was scattered over all
the elements, is sate down at the right hand of God, in a
glorious resurrection." (D vIII:98)

In another sermon Donne presents what he terms
rational arguments even for the resurrection of the body.
Certainly God could accomplish this act; it must have
been harder to create man's body out of nothing than it
would be to mend or restore that body through a resurrection. And it is reasonable to think that God would do
this for the creature whom he loves. To see the bodies of
men rising out of the grave would be no stranger than to
see an oak rise out of an acorn, were we not already so
familiar with the latter. And is the resurrection of the body
really any more incredible than the annual springtime
resurrection of the natural world? Since the very preservation of the natural world depends on its dying, may we
not believe, Donne continues, that the same holds true of
God's human creatures? (D III:96-98)

In a sermon on the text of 1 Corinthians 15:50—"Now
this I say brethren, that flesh and blood cannot inherit the
Kingdome of God"—a text which some Biblical scholars
had cited as a denial of the resurrection of the body,
Donne turns to some of the more interesting heresies on
the subject. Simon Magus affirmed that there was no resurrection of any kind, body or soul. The Gnostics limited the

resurrection to the soul alone. The Armenians acknowledged a resurrection of the body, but insisted that all
bodies "should rise in the perfecter sex, and none, as
women." Origen limited the duration of the body's resurrected state to a thousand years, during which time it
would enjoy many pleasures, but after which it would be
absorbed into God's own essence. (D III:114-116) Donne
devotes his sermon in great part to the argument that
though sinful and corrupt flesh and blood cannot inherit
the Kingdom, sanctified and glorified flesh and blood can.
And we find elsewhere that he goes to great lengths in
his exaltation of the body: "The Father was pleased to
breathe into this body, at first, in the Creation; The Son
was pleased to assume this body himself, after, in the Redemption; The Holy Ghost is pleased to consecrate this
body, and make it his Temple, by his sanctification; In
that *Faciamus hominem, Let us*, all us, *make man*, that
consultation of the whole Trinity in making man, is exercised even upon this lower part of man, the dignifying
of his body" (D VI:266). It is only fitting that a work on
which so much love has been bestowed should be finally
raised to its glory.

On more than one occasion Donne speaks of a threefold
resurrection. The first phase, limited to this world and consequently temporary in nature, is a resurrection from the
calamities of our earthly existence—it might, for example,
encompass the deliverance of the Church from persecution
and the escape of an individual from ill fortune. Donne
states that the principal intention of Ezekiel's vision of the
coming to life of the dry bones was to assure the Israelites
of their resurrection from present troubles. The second
phase is a spiritual resurrection from sin, accomplished
through repentance and through a daily triumph over be-
setting temptations. This spiritual resurrection prepares
man for the final resurrection, in which the sanctified body

rises from the grave into eternal glory, that last rising which marks the death of death itself. (D iv:56-62; D vi:-62-80)

There is also a threefold process involved in the last resurrection, taking place between man's physical death and his arrival, body and soul, in Heaven. In physical death there is a threefold fall: first, death occasions a divorce between body and soul, with the former repairing to the grave and the latter to Heaven; second, the body is dissolved into atoms and grains of dust; third, the dust is scattered about the four imagined corners of the earth. The threefold fall is matched by a threefold resurrection, as at the last day the grains of dust are re-collected, and the re-collected grains are recompacted into that body whence they came, and the body is reunited with that soul which had dwelt therein. (D vii:103) Speaking of this reuniting of body and soul, Donne remarks that the first marriage was that of the body and soul in creation and the first divorce that of the body and soul by death through sin; and he insists, against the doctrine of transmigration, that the soul never remarries another body, that the immortal man will find the marriage of his body and soul ultimately indissoluble (D vii:257).

One of Donne's most fascinating speculations concerns the way in which God will, on the Last Day, enable the soul to return to the physical world to reassemble all those parts, those atoms, of the body in which it once dwelt. In one of his sonnets he calls upon those souls which have been divorced from their bodies by death to "arise, arise/From death, you numberlesse infinities/Of soules, and to your scattred bodies goe." And, in his poem "The Relique," Donne remarks on the bracelet of his love's hair which he has wound about his bone, and asks if he who later breaks up the grave will not "thinke that there a loving couple lies,/Who thought that this device might be some way/To make their soules, at the last busie day,/Meet at this grave, and make a little stay?" Donne also returns in his sermons to this miraculous process of reassembling. Those who are elected to arise on the Judgment Day will be able to say that they arise as the same persons, compounded of the same bodies and same souls possessed in this life: "Shall I imagine a difficulty in my body, because I have lost an Arme in the East, and a leg in the West? because I have left some bloud in the North, and some bones in the South? Doe but remember, with what ease you have sate in the chaire, casting an account, and made a shilling on one hand, a pound on the other, or five shillings below, ten above, because all these lay easily within your reach. Consider how much lesse, all this earth is to him, that sits in heaven, and spans all this world, and reunites in an instant armes, and legs, bloud, and bones, in what corners so ever they be scattered." (D III:109)

No one, not even Christ, knows the time of the Last Judgment, but we can be assured that all men from Abel to those who are alive at the Lord's second coming will rise into Heaven at the same moment: "As between two men of equal age, if one sleep, and the other wake all night, yet they rise both of an equal age in the morning; so they who shall have slept out a long night of many ages in the grave, and they who shall be caught up in the clouds, to meet the Lord Jesus in the aire, at the last day, shall enter all at once in their bodies into Heaven" (D VI:363). Donne explicitly rejects the Chiliast or Millenarian assertion that after Christ's second coming the righteous will be resurrected to enjoy one thousand years of a kind of material bliss as recompense for their former sufferings, to be followed by a resurrection of the wicked and a subsequent assigning of the righteous and the wicked to their due places in the eternal scheme of things (D IV:77-78).

The faithful man's assurance of resurrection rests, of

course, in the resurrection of Christ. Christ alone arose
from the dead, whereas the faithful man must be raised
from the dead, yet there would be a certain incomplete-
ness about Christ's resurrection were it not followed by the
resurrection of his subjects. What kind of Lord would he
be, Donne asks, if he had no subjects? *"Cum videmus caput
super aquas,* when the head is above water, will any
imagine the body to be drowned? What a perverse consideration were it, to imagine a live head, and dead members? Or, consider our bodies in our selves, and *Our bodies
are Temples of the Holy Ghost;* and shall the Temples
of the holy Ghost lye for ever, for ever, buried in their
rubbidge?" (D IV:356)

The resurrection, of course, works great changes in the
body and soul which we now know. Donne gives us a rather
grim summary of the past, present, and future state of the
body: it was a totally unworthy substance in the parents'
loins; it is now "a Volume of diseases bound up together,
a dry cynder, if I look for naturall, for radicall moisture,
and yet a Spunge, a bottle of overflowing Rheumes, if I
consider accidentall"; it will be "but Putrifaction, and then,
not so much as putrification, I shall not be able to send
forth so much as an ill ayre, not any ayre at all, but shall
be all insipid, tastlesse, savourlesse dust; for a while, all
wormes, and after a while, not so much as wormes, sordid,
senslesse, namelesse dust" (D VII:390). And what will
be the nature of this body in its glorified state? Donne finds
no easy answer to this question, but he summons various
authorities who had something to say about it. Melancthon
had affirmed that the glorified body was the same body
which had dwelt on earth, but "yet not such a body."
Musculus had believed that the best key to the state of
man's resurrected body was the transfigured body of Christ,
witnessed by Peter, James, and John. St. Jerome had written that Christ in his Transfiguration retained the same

body with the same proportions, a body that was easily recognized by his disciples as his own, and yet a body over which a radiant and wonderful light had been cast. We should not be too curious about such mysteries, but we can rest assured that our bodies, defiled by the pitch of this earth, will be white as snow when they take their places in the heavenly society. (D III:118-121)

The soul too, so overburdened with sin and tribulation in this world, will be changed. Despite Donne's call to souls, in his sonnet "At the round earths imagin'd corners," to arise from death, he makes it clear in his sermons that the soul is not raised from death, from the grave, because the soul never dies; instead, the soul is restored to that state in which and for which it had been created. The soul finds its perfection only when it is reunited to the body which originally housed it, and so long as that body is dead the soul is widowed or divorced. Either the soul must die to join its dead body, or the body must be given life to join its living soul. Through the power and the love of the Lord, the body and soul come together in Heaven and assume that marriage for which they were created. (D VI:74-75; see also D IV:358) When the soul does attain this glorious marriage, Donne continues, ". . .her measure is enlarged, and filled at once; There she reads without spelling, and knowes without thinking, and concludes without arguing; she is at the end of her race, without running; In her triumph, without fighting; In her Haven, without sayling; A free-man, without any prentiship; at full yeares, without any wardship; and a Doctor, without any proceeding: She knowes truly, and easily, and immediately, and entirely, and everlastingly; Nothing left out at first, nothing worne out at last, that conduces to her happinesse" (D VI:76).

Not only are individual bodies and individual souls reunited in Heaven; old friends are also reunited. Through-

out Donne's sermons there is a constant emphasis on society, on the desire of both God and man to be with others.
The Trinity itself is one argument for God's love of company, and the fact that man was created so that he might
someday replace the fallen angels as the heavenly hosts is
another. The marriage of body and soul, of man and woman, of Christ and the Church, are other evidences of the
fundamental desirability of society. The fact that individual Christians are united as members of Christ's body, of
his Church, is still another testimony that no one is meant
to be alone. In one of his Easter sermons Donne persuades
his congregation not to mourn intemperately for the dead,
not to think that death forever sunders friends and lovers.
The dead have gone simply to "another room of the same
house," for the house of God includes both this world and
the next; they have gone simply into "another Pue of the
same Church," for the Church of God includes both the
Militant and the Triumphant. (D IV:63) In the Heavenly
Kingdom, the resurrected body will take on incorruption
and take to itself again its own soul, now invulnerable to
sin; and the new man will live in eternal joy with all those
faithful friends whom he had formerly known only under
the burden of sin. Clothed in white they will sing forth in
harmony the praises of the Saviour in whose presence they
are assembled.

Nor is this company so small and exclusive as the Calvinists would have us believe, for the mercy of God is immense. To those who might fall to the sin of despair which
a partial understanding of Calvin could induce, Donne
preached on the comforting text of Revelation 7:9: "After
this, I beheld, and loe, a great multitude, which no man
could number, of all nations, and kindreds, and people, and
tongues, stood before the throne, and before the lambe,
clothed with white robes, and palmes in their hands." The
sermon is divided into two parts: a proclamation of the

large number of persons who shall be saved, and a statement of the glorious qualities which they shall possess.
Donne early refers to God's sociableness and to his desire
"to have his kingdome well peopled." Though one God,
he desired the company of three persons, and he further
enlarged his society in the abundant creation of the natural
world, in the creation of angels, of beasts, and of men who,
unlike angels, could propagate their kind. In the ark,
which is the type of the Church, there was a proportion of
seven clean beasts to two unclean, an indication that in both
ark and Church more are destined for salvation than for
damnation. God set his image on our souls in the creation
and on our bodies and souls in the incarnation of Christ,
and he has further set his seal upon us in our baptism, and
in bestowing upon us a faith which is manifest in good
works. It is impossible to mistake God's intention to people
his Kingdom well. (D vi:151-161)

Donne turns to a number of Scriptural verses to substantiate his argument. Most interesting, I think, are his
comments on Matthew 7:13-14, in which Christ refers to
the strait gate and the narrow way. The gate, Donne affirms, is not in fact strait. Christ, whose every wound admits the whole world, is the gate; the Church, whose voice
has gone over the whole world, is the gate; the Word,
which reaches to every distress, is the gate. That Christ is
called the narrow gate is no indication "that the *greatest
man* may not come in, but called narrow, because he fits
himselfe to the *least child*, to the simplest soule, that will
come in: not so strait, as that all may not enter, but so
strait as that there can come in but *one at once*, for *he that
will not forsake Father and Mother, and wife, and children for him, cannot enter in.*" The Devil's way is called
broad because the man who walks in it goes burdened with
all his sinful gain; puffed up to the size of the camel which
cannot thread itself through the needle's eye, the sinful

man must shed his evil affections and ill-gotten gains in order to pass through the strait gate. At this gate Christ stands and knocks, ready to welcome "a great multitude, which no man could number." (D vi:161-165)

When the gate has been entered, the body of the resurrected one is clothed in a white robe, and into his hand is placed a palm, symbolic of those palm trees which welcomed the fleeing Israelites at Elim and signified their peace and redemption (Exodus 15:23-27). And having given his congregation some sense of God's infinite mercy, of his desire to have all men join in the heavenly choir, Donne brings his sermon to a close with this exhortation: "Go in, beloved, and raise your own contemplations, to a height worthy of this glory; and chide me for so lame an expressing of so perfect a state, and when the abundant spirit of God hath given you some measure, of conceiving that glory here, Almighty God give you, and me, and all, a reall expressing of it, by making us actuall possessors of that Kingdome, which his Sonne, our Saviour Christ Jesus hath purchased for us, with the inestimable price of his incorruptible blood. *Amen.*" (D vi:166-167)

"... but for All Time!"

The difference, and contrariety of mens judgements and opinions, is long since grown into a common saying, and become matter of every ones observation: But among all the subjects of various thoughts, there is scarce a greater diversity, than in the judgments Men make of *Preaching*; of which, besides the variety of Phancies, and the several degrees of understanding, this is a principal cause, *viz.* That men judge of Sermons by very *different measures*; and every one expects that the Preacher conform to *his* particular Rule of judging.[1]

JOSEPH GLANVILL's wise words serve well to introduce this final chapter, a general evaluation of Donne's sermons. Men are prone to disagree, he tells us, and seldom more variously than when passing judgment on sermons. Not only do "men judge of Sermons by very *different measures*" but it is also possible that the same man would be moved quite differently by the same sermon, according to whether he heard it preached or simply read it. Sermons, like plays, are almost always conceived to be delivered before the eyes and ears of a congregation or audience. And though some sermons, like some dramas, are better read than played, the fact remains that the primary function of a sermon is to teach and exhort to righteousness a seeing and listening congregation. A twentieth-century critic must, of course, depend on Donne's written sermons, and even then with the knowledge that the written discourse does not accord exactly with the sermon as it was preached over three hundred years ago. We know that Donne's usual practice was to write out a sermon after he preached it, sometimes soon after its delivery and sometimes from notes

---

[1] *An Essay Concerning Preaching*, p. 4.

or a partial manuscript long after its delivery. We know too, that since Donne usually confined himself to one hour in the pulpit and since most of his written sermons would take considerably more time than that to deliver, the latter must contain material, or elaboration upon material, not found in the former. It is, of course, extremely fortunate that Donne deliberately prepared his preached sermons for publication. We have his own word that he spent part of the plague year of 1625 revising his sermons (G 11:225); and we have Henry King's word that Donne, just before his death, entrusted into his hands a number of sermons, acknowledging that it was on King's insistence that he had prepared them for the press (W:14-15). As John Hayward has pointed out, Donne's sermons are "the only works which he designed for posterity, and which he left revised and corrected by his own hand with the wish that his son should print them after his death."[2] Whether Donne ultimately wished his son or Henry King to be responsible for the publication is not, in the context of this chapter, of particular importance; that we have the texts of most of the one hundred and sixty sermons as Donne would wish us to have them is of considerable importance.

Remarks by Donne's contemporaries attest to the fact that the sermons were impressively delivered. I have already quoted Walton's enraptured and dramatic account of the pulpit Donne, the earnest preacher who sometimes wept, who preached "like an Angel from a cloud," who carried some "to Heaven in holy raptures" and enticed others to amend their lives, who was adept at the concrete presentation of vice and virtue, and who did "all this with a most particular grace and an unexpressible addition of comeliness" (W:49). The various elegies written for the 1633 edition of his poems give further testimony that

[2] "A Note on Donne the Preacher," *A Garland for John Donne: 1631-1931*, p. 76.

Donne was not only a great writer of sermons, but a great preacher of them. Henry Valentine writes that Donne's preaching "to Extasie/Could charme the Soule. . . ."[3] Thomas Carew, admitting that the post-Donne pulpit was still useful in its dispensation of precept and doctrine, yet affirms that

> the flame
> Of thy brave Soule, that shot such heat and light,
> As burnt our earth, and made our darknesse bright,
> Committed holy Rapes upon our Will,
> Did through the eye the melting heart distill;
> And the deepe knowledge of darke truths so teach,
> As sense might judge, what phansie could not reach;
> Must be desir'd for ever.

Sir Lucius Carie writes of Donne's "heavenly Eloquence," asserting that "None was so marble, but whil'st him he heares,/His Soule so long dwelt only in his eares," and that "No Druggist of the Soule bestow'd on all/So Catholiquely a curing Cordiall." John Chudleigh speaks favorably of Donne's ability to move the affections. And Jasper Mayne refers in detail to specific characteristics of the pulpit manner of Donne, to whom he addresses these lines:

> Then should I praise thee. . .
> Who with thy words could charme thy audience,
> That at thy sermons, eare was all our sense;
> Yet have I seene thee in the pulpit stand,
> Where wee might take notes, from thy looke, and hand;
> And from thy speaking action beare away
> More Sermon, then some teachers use to say.
> Such was thy carriage, and thy gesture such,
> As could divide the heart, and conscience touch.

[3] All of the elegies here referred to may be found in H. J. C. Grierson's one-volume edition of *The Poems of John Donne* (London: Oxford University Press, 1933), pp. 339-366. John Chudleigh's elegy appeared first in the 1635 edition of the *Poems*, all the others in the 1633 edition.

Thy motion did confute, and wee might see
An errour vanquish'd by delivery.

We can hardly doubt Donne's ability to captivate a congregation: to what extent he used this skill as a means of
impressing the Word onto the heart of a parishioner to his
salvation, and to what extent he used it as a means of impressing his own talents upon a fascinated audience, would
be difficult to say. In any case, his awareness of the fact
that the pulpit was for the utterance of God's Word and
not of man's words he expresses in various sermons.

Donne's contemporary reputation as a preacher was tremendous; the only person of equal (and perhaps even
greater) stature was Lancelot Andrewes, who died in 1626.
From 1626 until his own death in 1631 Donne was clearly
in a class by himself, and the next person who is sometimes
thought worthy of comparison was Jeremy Taylor, who
was about eighteen at the time of Donne's death. As Dean
of St. Paul's Cathedral, Donne preached from one of the
most influential pulpits in England; and he also preached
to nobility at Whitehall and to groundlings at Paul's Cross.
Adverse criticism of Donne is hard to find, though lines
from Richard Busby's elegy suggest that some found
Donne's preaching a bit too intellectual to reach the heart
of the common man; some of his critics, writes Busby,

. . .humm'd against him; And with face most sowre
Call'd him a strong lin'd man, a Macaroon,
And no way fit to speake to clouted shoone,
As fine words [truly] as you would desire,
But [verily,] but a bad edifier.
Thus did these beetles slight in him that good,
They could not see, and much lesse understood.
But we may say, when we compare the stuffe
Both brought; He was a candle, they the snuffe.

There are many qualities in Donne's sermons which are for all time; his eloquence, his passionate exhortation, his incisive and perceptive interpretation of Scriptural texts, his moral and ethical persuasiveness—all of these qualities commend him to mid-twentieth-century readers much as they would to his own contemporaries. A preacher might today, with judicious use of a blue pencil and some vocabulary changes, make effective (and, I hope, acknowledged) use of Donne's text. On the other hand, some characteristics of his sermons mark Donne very much as a man of his own time. Perhaps the most evident of these characteristics, and one which may be particularly jarring to Americans who have been nurtured on the doctrine of separation of church and state, is the tremendously important place which Donne assigns to nation and monarch in ecclesiastical matters. Among the main tenets of Anglicanism are its beliefs that State and Church are inextricably wedded and that the king of England, in office by divine right, is also the head of the Church of England. Henry VIII's defection from Rome was caused in great part by his unwillingness to be subservient to the Pope, and the long struggle between England and the Roman Catholic powers was nourished in great part by the dispute over the matter of the Christian Englishman's first earthly allegiance, whether to the pope or to the king of England. And if the Anglicans of Donne's time had to assert themselves against the Papacy's claim to temporal power, they had also to stand guard against those Anabaptists and other separatist groups who would bow their knee to no earthly ruler or magistrate.

It is important that a reader of Donne understand the Anglican view of the relationship between State and Church, between king and clergy. A paragraph from the Thirty-seventh Article of Religion is in this respect enlightening:

"Where we attribute to the Queen's Majesty the chief government, by which Titles we understand the minds of some slanderous folks to be offended; we give not to our Princes the ministering either of God's Word, or of the Sacraments, the which thing the Injunctions also lately set forth by *Elizabeth* our Queen do most plainly testify; but that only prerogative, which we see to have been given always to all godly Princes in holy Scriptures by God himself; that is, that they should rule all estates and degrees committed to their charge by God, whether they be Ecclesiastical or Temporal, and restrain with the civil sword the stubborn and evildoers."

The Homilies of the Church of England, read with some frequency to Anglican congregations during the second half of the sixteenth century and on into the seventeenth, also stressed the necessity of obedience to the king and cited more than once the thirteenth chapter of the Epistle to the Romans as an authoritative text. Most explicit is the following statement:

"The holy Scriptures doe teach most expresly, that our Saviour Christ himselfe, and his Apostles Saint *Paul*, Saint *Peter*, with others, were vnto the Magistrates and higher powers, which ruled at their being vpon the earth, both obedient themselues, and did also diligently and earnestly exhort all other Christians to the like obedience vnto their Princes and Gouernours: whereby it is euident that men of the Cleargie, and Ecclesiasticall ministers, as their successours ought both themselues specially, and before other, to bee obedient vnto their Princes, and also to exhort all others vnto the same."[4]

The most extensive statement of the proper relationship between State and Church is found in the posthumously published Book Eight of Hooker's *Of the Laws of Ecclesi-*

[4] *The Second Tome of Homilies*, p. 308.

astical Polity, where he makes absolutely clear his position that the king, under Christ, is to have supreme power in all matters, civil and ecclesiastical. And one of the "Constitutions and Canons Ecclesiastical," published in 1640 in the reign of Charles, well summarizes the matter:

"The most High and Sacred Order of Kings, is of Divine Right, being the Ordinance of God Himself, founded in the prime Laws of Nature, and clearly established by express Texts both of the Old and New Testaments. A supreme Power is given to this most excellent Order by God Himself in the Scriptures, which is, That Kings should Rule and Command in their several Dominions all persons of what rank or estate soever, whether Ecclesiastical or Civil, and that they should restrain and punish with the Temporal Sword all stubborn and wicked doers."[5]

That neither the Roman Church nor the left-wing Protestant sects were in agreement with the Anglican position is patently clear.

From the quoted statements we may gather that the Church of England is, in one sense, a department of the State, and that the Archbishop of Canterbury carries a portfolio which might be labeled "Secretary of Religion." The Archbishop and the entire ecclesiastical hierarchy of Donne's time were, of course, called upon to answer to God for the spiritual direction and salvation of souls of the English citizenry, but they were also called upon to answer to the supreme earthly authority of their monarch. Donne draws an interesting comparison between State and Church in a sermon preached at Paul's Cross on May 6, 1627: "...though our *Religion* prepare us to our *Bene esse*, our

[5] *A Collection of Articles* [,] *Injunctions, Canons, Orders, Ordinances, And Constitutions Ecclesiastical; With other Publick Records of the Church of England* [,] *Chiefly in the Times of K. Edward VI.* [,] *Q. Elizabeth* [,] *K. James, & K. Charles I.*, London, 1675, p. 346.

well-being, our everlasting happinesse, yet it is the *State*, the civill and peaceable government, which preserves our very *Esse*, our very *Being*; and there cannot be a *Bene esse*, without an *Esse*, a well and a happy Being, except there be first a Being established." He goes on to point out that as the body came before the soul, and the vegetative and sensitive soul before the immortal and reasonable soul, so does a temporal government come before a church. (D vii:426)

Of all Donne's sermons, the one showing him most clearly as the King's spokesman and showing most clearly the kind of support expected from the Church by the State was preached at Paul's Cross on September 15, 1622. The sermon is Donne's defense of an order circulated by King James, entitled *Directions for Preachers* and designed to outlaw from Anglican pulpits the discussion of controversial matters. The *Directions* was neither the first nor the last of its kind. For example, a proclamation issued on December 27, 1558, early in the reign of Elizabeth, placed severe restraint on a priest's activities, seeking to put an end to certain violent sermons which marked the time.[6] And a decree of 1640 demanded that ecclesiastical officials take an oath "against all Innovation of Doctrine or Discipline."[7] James's order, motivated by the belief that "*divers young* Students, *by reading of late* Writers, *and ungrounded* Divines, *doe broach many times unprofitable, unsound seditious*, and *daugerous* Doctrines, *to the scandall of the* Church, *and disquiet of the* State, *and present* Governement," contained six directions. Among them are orders to follow more closely the Thirty-nine Articles, the Homilies, the Catechism, the Creed, the Ten Commandments, and the Lord's Prayer; to desist, if below

---

[6] Francis Procter and Walter Howard Frere, *A New History of the Book of Common Prayer* (London: Macmillan & Co. Ltd., 1955), p. 96.
[7] *A Collection of Articles, etc.*, p. 359.

the rank of bishop or dean, from preaching in any "Popular Auditory" on such mysterious matters as predestination, election, reprobation, the resistibility or irresistibility of God's grace; to desist from applying any limitation whatsoever to the authority of "Soveraigne Princes"; to desist from indecent maligning of Papists or Puritans; and—to archbishops and bishops—to be more careful in their licensing of preachers.[8] When Donne's sermon defending the *Directions* was published two months later, it was prefaced by a Dedicatory Epistle to the Marquis of Buckingham. The Epistle is an explicit statement of Donne's dual allegiance. He writes Buckingham that in the first part of the sermon, the explication of the text, he has spoken "*as the* Holy Ghost *intended*." In the second part, the application of the text, he has spoken "*as his Majestie intended*." (D iv:178-179) The text is Judges 5:20—"They fought from heaven; the stars in their courses fought against Sisera"—a part of the song of Deborah and Barak narrating the hammer murder of Sisera. About a third of the sermon is devoted to an explication of the text, after which Donne turns to its applicability to contemporary conditions in England.

The stars in the text represent ministers, and Sisera is the enemy against whom they preach. Just as the stars move in their regular courses, so are the ministers to proceed in an orderly fashion. If there is an order, there must be a head to declare what is orderly. Now God, of course, is the cause and sustainer of the world's order, but man sometimes strays from this divine governance and is in need of an auxiliary head or orderer. This "other *Order* is, not as man depends upon *God*, as upon his beginning, but as he is to be reduced and brought back to *God*, as to

[8] Arthur Wilson, *The History of Great Britain, Being the Life and Reign of King Iames the First, Relating To what passed from his first Accesse to the Crown, till his Death* (London, 1653), pp. 198-200.

his end: and that is done by meanes in this world. What is
that meanes? for those things which wee have now in
consideration, the *Church.* But *the body* speaks not, the
head does. It is the *Head of the Church* that declares to us
those things wherby we are to be ordered." The *Head* is
King James, whose recent *Directions* is evidence of his desire to restore an order which has been lost to the Church
of England. James took the action, Donne writes, only
after a request by clergymen high in the ecclesiastical hierarchy, a request motivated by the fact that some ministers
were preaching opinions of their own rather than hewing
to the established doctrines of the Church. James's intention has been to distinguish "between grave, and solid,
from light and humerous preaching." The end of preaching is to make known those things necessary to salvation,
and the *Directions* would put an end to sermons which
pronounce judgments on purely civil matters and which
indecently revile certain persons. Donne, turning to a
more positive argument, asserts that all relevant Anglican doctrine "is contained in the two *Catechismes,* in the
39. *Articles,* and in the 2. *Bookes of Homilies*"; it is to
these sources that James has directed his preachers. The
King's order, Donne states somewhat defensively, will
neither restrain nor abate preaching; it will simply restore
preaching to its proper order in the scheme of Church
and State. Thus ends a sermon which, Donne hopes, will
be acceptable to the Third Person of the Holy Trinity and
the Head of the English Church and State. (D iv:195-
209)

Donne's preaching on the relationship between Church
and State, on the excellence of monarchy as a form of
government, and on the advantages which the Church of
England enjoyed over all other churches, Roman and
Reformed, cannot be counted as that part of his preaching
which makes for its enduring reputation. One may today

read with considerable historical interest those portions of
his sermons, but a twentieth-century reader will hardly
find Donne's greatness to rest there. There is surely little
doubt, however, that such preaching contributed considerably to his contemporary stature. A volley against the
Pope or the unceremonious Puritans or the independent Anabaptists must have titillated the hearts of the
throngs who gathered to hear the eminent Dean of St.
Paul's. And there is no question that Donne's loyalty to
the essentially Erastian position of his Church helped gain
for him his deanship and helped sustain him in Stuart
favor during his incumbency. Such a position was no quirk
on the part of Donne; it was part and parcel of the foundation of Anglicanism. We can at least say that Donne
maintained this position without the scurrility to be found
in some Anglican pulpits, that he was in essence a preacher
of good and charitable taste.

In an attempt to discover something more about those
characteristics of Donne which may have been particularly
appealing to people of his own time, we might take a
brief look, first, at the six sermons published during his
lifetime and, second, at the sermons which appeared most
frequently in the seventeenth century, either in print or
in manuscript editions.

Donne's first published sermon—his defense of King
James's *Directions for Preachers* delivered on September
15, 1622—has already been sufficiently discussed. John
Chamberlain, voluminous letter writer in the late sixteenth and early seventeenth centuries, says of it that
Donne gave "no great satisfaction, or as some say spake
as yf himself were not so well satisfied,"[9] a statement leading one to question whether the sermon was published on
its intrinsic merit. But whether the discourse gave full
satisfaction and whether Donne was fully pleased with

[9] For the quotation I am indebted to D IV:34.

his effort, it is perfectly clear why James saw fit to command its publication.

On November 13, 1622, Donne preached at a meeting of the Virginia Company;[10] the sermon was published at the "Commandement" of the company shortly after its delivery. The sermon, at once a missionary one and a political one, is on the text of Acts 1:8—"But yee shall receive power, after that the Holy Ghost is come upon you, and yee shall be witnesses unto me both in Jerusalem, and in all Judea, and in Samaria, and unto the uttermost part of the earth." Donne admonishes his hearers not to limit their sights to the material gains which might accrue from a prosperous plantation, but rather to regard themselves as apostles of Christ, carrying the teachings of the Lord to the shores of Virginia: "O, if you could once bring a *Catechisme* to bee as good ware amongst them as a bugle, as a knife, as a hatchet: O, if you would be as ready to hearken at the returne of a *Ship*, how many Indians were converted to *Christ Iesus*, as what Trees, or druggs, or Dyes that Ship had brought, then you were in your right way, and not till then. . . ." (D IV:265-269)

But if the power of grace and the commandment of Christ must be followed, so must the power of nature and the law of nations, and in one fascinating paragraph Donne justifies colonialism. He argues that if the inhabitants of a piece of land do not make the most of its abundant potentialities, then it is the obligation of a responsible, advanced citizenry and nation to claim that land as its own and see that it brings forth its proper fruit: "*The whole world, all Mankinde must take care, that all places be emprov'd, as farre as may be, to the best advantage of Mankinde in generall.*" Furthermore, if a land is abundantly productive and yet

[10] For details of Donne's relationship to the Virginia Company, see Stanley Johnson, "John Donne and the Virginia Company," *ELH: A Journal of English Literary History*, XIV (June 1947), 127-138.

displays, to the impoverishment of friendly neighbors, an unwillingness to share its fruits, then it is justifiable to force the inhabitants to act more charitably. The Virginian Indians, one must infer, are guilty either of underproduction or selfishness, and the company to which Donne preaches has properly been commissioned and chartered by the King to instruct them in the error of their ways. But, continues Donne, turning from the law of nations to the law of Scripture, the company members must be certain that the Holy Ghost has also blessed their enterprise, has enabled their "Conscience to say, that ... [their] principall ende is not gaine, nor glory, but to gaine Soules to the glory of GOD. . . ." An upright conscience will be borne on the wings of their legal charter to fructify the earth, to see that the world's wealth is equitably distributed, and to bear Christ's witness to the savages of the New World. (D iv:274-275) It is to be hoped that the gentle motions of the Third Person of the Trinity could calm the strident ambitions of Mammon. In any case, the Virginia Company was happy with the suggestion that the Cross could be borne in one hand and the British flag in the other, happy enough to urge the sermon's publication.

Donne's third published sermon was preached on May 22, 1623, at the consecration of a new chapel at Lincoln's Inn, the institution which he had served as Reader in Divinity from October 1616 to February 1622. We learn from Chamberlain that the service was well attended and the sermon deemed excellent (D iv:40-41). It is entitled *Encænia. The Feast of Dedication*, and is on the text of John 10:22: "And it was at Ierusalem, the feast of the dedication; and it was winter; and Iesus walked in the temple in Salomons porch." The sermon, not one of Donne's most exciting or brilliant or moving, nevertheless fits the occasion admirably, speaking as it does of the propriety and benefit of festival days, of the Church as God's

principal dwelling place, and of the need for the dedication not only of the new chapel but of a Christian's own
self to the service of God. In his "Dedicatory Epistle"
Donne writes that, though his sermon is not a controversial
one, yet it is directed against the Roman calumny that
Anglicans "*have cast off all distinction of places, and of
dayes, and all outward meanes of assisting the devotion of
the Congregation*" (D IV:362).

The next two published sermons are of particular interest doctrinally. The first of these two was Donne's first
sermon before King Charles, preached on April 3, 1625,
one week after the death of James and just one day after
Charles had requested Donne to preach before him. It is
an impressive sermon, based on the text of Psalm 11:3—
"If the foundations be destroyed, what can the righteous
doe?"—and presents what is in many ways the essence of
Donne's religious position. Part One is a clear statement of
his insistence on distinguishing between fundamental and
collateral matters, his plea to hold firm in the former and
exercise charity in the latter; it also states his complaint
that the Roman Church views virtually every issue as
fundamental, rigidly claiming its infallibility and uncharitably demanding that everyone accept its doctrines
and decrees. Part Two is a discussion of the proper foundations of Church, State, family, and self. As Christ is
the foundation of the Church, so is law the foundation of
the State, a fact to which Rome is declared blind. Peace
is the foundation of the family, and conscience of the self.
When Church, State, family, and self enjoy these foundations, they must not quibble about nonessentials; and
if and when foundations have been destroyed, the righteous
must look to God for guidance in their difficulty. (D
VI:241-261) Charles found the sermon eminently acceptable, implying as it did the reasonableness of the Anglican
position on matters of doctrine and defending the English

claim that the State was the sole arbiter of temporal matters; it was published at the command of the King.

The second of these sermons was, of the six published during Donne's lifetime, the only one which was not prepared for some specific occasion. Like the former one, it was preached before Charles—on February 24, 1626—and was ordered by him to be published. Though it is implicitly a repudiation of the Calvinist doctrine of double predestination, it is not so much an attack on any theological position as it is an exhortation to the afflicted that they eschew despair and look forward joyfully to their redemption and salvation. It is a discourse on sin and redemption, in which there is a denial of God's tyranny, of the suggestion that he creates man that he may damn him, and a denial that any man is irrevocably doomed to perish. Man and not God is responsible for sin: "... how desperate soever our case be, how irremediable soever our state, we our selfes, and not *God*, are the cause of that desperate irremediablenesse"; and yet there is no man whom God places outside the bounds of his mercy: "There is no such matter, there is no such peremptory Divorce, there is no such absolute sale, there is no such desperate irremediablenes declard to any particular conscience, as is imagind, but you, any, may returne to ... [God], when you will, and ... [God] will receive you." (D vii:74) Of the six sermons preached before Donne's death this one, to a greater extent than any of the others, would seem to have been chosen because of its intrinsic homiletic merit, of its joyful statement that no man need despair of God's mercy and of his own salvation.

The last of Donne's sermons published during his lifetime is the moving, if somewhat too long, discourse in commemoration of his friend of twenty years, Magdalen Danvers. Unable to preach her funeral sermon, Donne, some three weeks later on July 1, 1627, spoke in commemoration of Lady Danvers at the Chelsea Parish Church, where she had been buried on June 8. He chose as his text II Peter 3:13—"Neverthelesse, we, according to his promises, looke for new heavens, and new earth, wherein dwelleth righteousnesse"—and divided his sermon into two parts, one *"To instruct the Living,"* and the other *"To commemorate the Dead."* He instructs the living not to be scornful of God's promises, to maintain a proper and holy terror of the Judgment Day, to know that all things can be accomplished only in Christ and not through oneself, and to await with great expectation the future Kingdom. (D VIII:63-80) Of the new heavens and the new earth we know little, except that they are the abode of angels, archangels, cherubim, and seraphim, that they are the dwelling places prepared for the saints of God. The new earth is a place where the waters are milk, and the milk is honey; where the grass is corn, and the corn is manna; where the earth is gold; where the minutes are ages, and the ages are eternity; "Where every thing, is every minute, in the highest exaltation, as good as it can be, and yet super-exalted, and infinitely multiplied, by every minutes addition; every minute, *infinitely* better, then ever it was before." The New Jerusalem is much more than a place of gold and precious stones, or a place in which to contemplate beauty and attend the harmonious music of the heavenly choirs, or a place to enjoy one's triumphant priesthood, or a place to partake of the marriage supper of the Lamb. Not simply a place in which the good things of this earth appear in their perfection it is a place where we will possess what we vainly yearn for in our mortal years—righteousness itself. Donne's instruction to the living is that they now surrender themselves to that power which alone can lead them to the righteousness promised to the faithful. (D VIII:80-85) Donne then turns to the second part of his sermon, to the commemoration of his dear friend, tracing the activities of her saintly life and her quiet, fearless, and holy passing into death. In death Lady Danvers patiently awaits the death of all others, that they together with her may be raised in triumph on the Last Day. Her godly past and her glorious future may serve as a model for all those who seek God's promise of those new heavens and that new earth where righteousness dwells; and we may know that, on the Last Day, "That *body*, which was the *Tabernacle* of a *holy Soule*, and a *Temple* of the *holy Ghost*, That *body* that was eyes to the blinde, and hands, and feet to the lame, whilst it liv'd, and being dead, is so still, by having beene so *lively* an example, to teach others, to be so, That *body* at last shall have her last expectation satisfied, and dwell *bodily*, with that *Righteousnesse*, in these *new Heavens*, and *new Earth*, for *ever*, and *ever*, and *ever*, and *infinite*, and *super-infinite evers*." (D VIII:85-92)

Interesting as it may be to peruse the content of the six sermons published during Donne's lifetime and to note that all of them were preached and published within a five-year period of his sixteen-year ministry, I doubt that they can serve as any real index of those qualities which most endeared him to his seventeenth-century congregations. With the exception of the fifth of these sermons, each one was preached for a special occasion, and their publication might suggest no more than that they were deemed to have served the occasion well. Three of them have definite political or temporal implications: James was eager to have his *Directions for Preachers* defended; the Virginia Company was pleased to have its colonial activities blessed from the pulpit; Charles was happy with the assurance that the English Church and State had greater regard for a charitable, tolerant religious position and greater respect for civil law than the Papacy did. Two of the sermons marked specific occasions—the consecration of the new chapel at Lincoln's Inn and the commemoration of Lady Danver's death. Only one, the sermon preached to Charles on February 24, 1626, would seem to have been published because it possessed some intrinsic merit unrelated to the glory of England or to an occasion in itself worthy of commemoration.

A conceivable measure of the nature of Donne's seventeenth-century popularity might be found in a study of those sermons appearing most frequently in extant texts, printed or in manuscript form, which date back to Donne's century. A very helpful table, headed "Occurrence of Sermons Extant in More than One Seventeenth-Century Text, in Printed Editions and in Manuscripts," appears in the Simpson and Potter edition (D 1:52).[11] The tabulation is based on the three folio editions—the *LXXX Sermons* of 1640, the *Fifty Sermons* of 1649, and the *XXVI Sermons* of 1661; the quarto edition of *Six Sermons* (1634); the *Sapientia Clamitans* (1638); separate printings; and the following six manuscripts: Merton, Dowden, Lothian, Dobell, St. Paul's Cathedral, and Ashmole. Those six manuscripts and the more recently discovered Ellesmere Manuscript all date from Donne's lifetime, are copied by various hands (not Donne's), and stem "from sources independent of any printed text" (D 1:33). To the aforementioned table, I have added the sermons found in the Ellesmere Manuscript (D 11:365-371). It is then discovered that, on the basis of extant sources, there are eight sermons for which we have five or more seventeenth-century texts, whether printed or in manuscript.

Before attributing too much significance to the value of the tabulation as an index of the nature of Donne's popularity in his own time (and Mrs. Simpson and the late Mr. Potter use the table for an entirely different purpose), it

[11] The table appears in D 1:52. For a detailed discussion of the bibliography of the sermons, of the various manuscripts, and of the text, see D 1:1-82. The more recently discovered Ellesmere Manuscript is discussed in D 11:365-371.

should be noted that the latest sermon to be found in manuscript form was preached on April 22, 1622, almost nine years before Donne preached his last sermon. So far as the dating of the manuscripts themselves is concerned, we know only that a part of the Lothian Manuscript was transcribed between August 3, 1624, and September 11, 1624 (D 1:39), and that the pen-and-ink title page of the St. Paul's Cathedral Library Manuscript is dated 1625 (D 1:41). Of the eight sermons appearing in five or more seventeenth-century texts, the seven which can be dated with some precision were preached between February 21, 1619, and May 30, 1621.

Of the eight sermons, four of them are primarily on the themes of judgment and repentance; one on temporal and spiritual blessedness; one on Christology, particularly the Incarnation; one on the joy of suffering; and one on marriage. They are, as a whole, far more directly concerned with the individual soul and the hope and way of salvation than were the six sermons printed during Donne's lifetime. The eight sermons do contain a few political and controversial references—the Spanish Armada and the Gunpowder Plot are mentioned, and there are warnings against the schismatical sects and the Calvinist doctrine of double predestination—but they have far less to do with the glory of English Church and State and the perfidy of English enemies than do the six sermons published during his lifetime. The eight sermons give the impression that Donne is speaking directly to and for the sinning, yet hopeful, congregation which sits before him, rather than for the benefit of English King or nation or ecclesiastical institution.

The sermon of which there are the most texts extant, two printed and six manuscript, was preached at Lincoln's Inn on April 18, 1619, on the text of Ecclesiastes 12:1: "Remember now thy Creator in the dayes of thy youth."

A part of its appeal may be attributed to its occasional character—it was Donne's farewell sermon before his German trip of 1619-1620, but the discourse must also have commended itself through its compellingly devotional character. Its central theme is that man may find his salvation through the use of his memory—memory, for example, of Old Testament promises of deliverance from sin and death through the coming Messiah (D 11:236); memory that it is never too late to repent (D 11:245)—memory, in short, which will lead man to praise his Creator and repent his sins.

Found in six texts is another summons to repentance, again with a reminder of God's goodness and a vivid portrayal of God's judgment. This sermon, already discussed at some length,[12] was preached on February 21, 1619, on the text of Matthew 21:44: "Whosoever shall fall on this stone, shall be broken; but on whomsoever it shall fall, it will grinde him to powder." The gifts of the Creator, the sin of man, the merciful judgment of God, the repentance and redemption of man—these are the great themes of this discourse which is, to me, one of the most impressive in the entire Donne canon.

Two other sermons, also found in six texts and always paired, though less moving than the two mentioned above, do suggest one particular aspect of seventeenth-century taste, a great fondness for paradox. On the morning and evening of January 30, 1620, Donne preached at Lincoln's Inn two sermons on apparently contradictory texts—"The Father judgeth no man, but hath committed all judgement to the Sonne" (John 5:22), and "I [the Son] judge no man" (John 8:15). In the evening sermon he resolves the seeming contradiction by affirming that "there was never any time when Christ was not Judge, but there were some

---

[12] See above, pp. 53-54, 129-131.

manner of Judgements which Christ did never exercise"
(D 11:326).

The other four of the eight sermons are found in five
seventeenth-century texts each. Two of these were preached
at Whitehall. On April 30, 1620, Donne spoke of temporal
and spiritual blessings in a well-organized sermon on the
text of Psalm 144:15: "Blessed are the people that be so;
yea blessed are the people, whose God is the Lord." (D
111:73-90) Donne preached again at Whitehall on February 16, 1621, this time before the King and on the text of
1 Timothy 3:16: "And without controversie, great is the
mystery of godliness: God was manifest in the flesh, justi-
fied in the Spirit, seen of angels, preached unto the Gentiles, believed on in the world, received up into glory." In
a straight expository discourse Donne moves clause by
clause through his text, presenting with simplicity a statement of the person and works of Christ, with particular
emphasis on the doctrine of Incarnation. (D 111:206-224)

A seventh of the eight sermons now under discussion was
preached at Lincoln's Inn on the text of Colossians 1:24:
"Who now rejoyce in my sufferings for you, and fill up
that which is behind of the afflictions of Christ in my flesh,
for his bodies sake which is the Church." Donne, for the
most part meditating on the joy of suffering, tells us that
joy "is the nearest representation of heaven it selfe to this
world" (D 111:334). He then proceeds to a word-by-word
exposition of the text, affirming that joy is the true mark
of the Christian, and that Paul found his joy through an
imitation of Christ in the Lord's sufferings for others, for
his Church.

The eighth of these sermons, preached at the marriage
of Robert Sandys and Margaret Washington on May 30,
1621, at the Church of St. Clement Danes, is to me one of
the most interesting of Donne's sermons. The text—"And
I will mary thee unto me for ever" (Hosea 2:19)—is di-

vided into three main parts: discussions of a secular marriage in Paradise, a spiritual marriage in the Church, and an eternal marriage in Heaven. Part One begins auspiciously with an enumeration of some of the more fascinating heresies formerly held about women and about marriage. The Nicolaitans were community-minded, believing in "a community of women, any might take any"; the Tatians went to the opposite extreme, forbidding marriage. The Manichaeans believed that women were created by the Devil; the Colliridians raised women to the stature of gods, sacrificing to them. St. Ambrose is charged with denying women souls; the Peputians thought so well of the souls of women that they accepted them into the priesthood. Donne cautions moderation, urging us "To make them [women] as God made them, wives...." (D III:241-242) Marriage was instituted for three sufficient reasons—for a remedy against burning, for propagation, and for mutual help. The first reason is the least noble, and a man of St. Paul's stature will quench or deflect his fire through vigorous and wholehearted participation in religious works. The second reason is a sufficient argument against any form of birth control. The third calls for a wise division of labor in which husband and wife both remember their proper places according to the seventeenth-century scheme of things. (D III:244-247)[13]

[13] In *Paradise Lost* Milton plays a number of variations on the same theme. For example, speaking of Adam and Eve he writes:

> ... though both
> Not equal, as their sex not equal seemed;
> For contemplation he and valour formed,
> For softness she and sweet attractive grace;
> He for God only, she for God in him. (IV, 295-299)

Milton's Adam also expresses his view:

> "... for nothing lovelier can be found
> In woman than to study household good,
> And good works in her husband to promote."
> (IX, 232-234)

[229]

From the persons who compromise the Paradisiacal marriage, Adam and Eve, and those who comprise the spiritual marriage, Christ and his Church, Donne goes on to those who comprise the eternal marriage in Heaven, the Lamb and the individual soul. One of the most effective prose passages in a sermon containing many brings this fine discourse to its close. Donne wishes to stress the eternal nature of this final marriage. Even the Angels were not so married, for they fell in a disobedience which incurred their divorce, their separation from God. But the faithful man will witness many divorces as he moves toward the heavenly place established for him, and Donne, making his peroration more dramatic by use of the first-person singular, speaks of the divorces which will punctuate his course to the only condition which knows no divorce:

"I shall see the Sunne black as sackcloth of hair, and the Moon become as blood, and the Starres fall as a Figge-tree casts her untimely Figges, and the heavens roll'd up together as a Scroll. I shall see a divorce between Princes and their Prerogatives, between nature and all her elements, between the spheres, and all their intelligences, between matter it self, and all her forms, and my mariage shall be, *in æternum*, for ever. I shall see an end of faith, nothing to be beleeved that I doe not know; and an end of hope, nothing to be wisht that I doe not enjoy, but no end of that love in which I am maried to the Lamb for ever. Yea, I shall see an end of some of the offices of the Lamb himself; Christ himself shall be no longer a Mediator, an Intercessor, an Advocate, and yet shall continue a Husband to my soul for ever. Where I shall be rich enough without Joynture, for my Husband cannot die; and wise enough without experience, for no new thing can happen there; and healthy enough without Physick, for no sicknesse can enter; and (which is by much the highest of all) safe

enough without grace, for no tentation that needs particular
grace, can attempt me. There, where the Angels, which
cannot die, could not live, this very body which cannot
choose but die, shall live, and live as long as that God of
life that made it. Lighten our darkness, we beseech thee, ô
Lord, that in thy light we may see light: Illustrate our
understandings, kindle our affections, pour oyle to our
zeale, that we may come to the mariage of this Lamb,
and that this Lamb may come quickly to this mariage: And
in the mean time bless these thy servants, with making this
secular mariage a type of the spirituall, and the spirituall
an earnest of that eternall, which they and we, by thy
mercy, shall have in the Kingdome which thy Son our
Saviour hath purchased with the inestimable price of his
incorruptible blood." (D iii:253-255)

That texts of this sermon are found in two printed editions
and three manuscripts of the seventeenth century should
occasion no surprise. It is a discourse which would move a
reader of any century, a discourse of witty observations, of
exciting prose, and of spiritual guidance in the meaning of
marriage, marriage in this life and in the one to come.

As I have already acknowledged, I am not certain just
how much we can conclude from a study of the six sermons
printed in Donne's lifetime and from those eight sermons
which appeared most frequently in seventeenth-century
texts. At the least, I think, we can see that most of the sermons summoned to a printer before Donne's death are of
an occasional nature and that half of them were used in the
service of the English nation, either to rebuke English dis-
senters, to justify colonial expansion when the Holy Ghost
would seem to encourage such activity, or to praise the
virtues of a State and Church which held to foundations in
contrast to the uncharitable and dangerous Roman brethren. And we can, I think, account for the popularity of the

other eight sermons primarily on the basis of their sound-
ing the goodness of God's creation, the falling of man
away from his original innocence, the necessity of the contrite and penitent heart in the face of one's conviction of
sin, the incredible mercy of God who condemns no man to
a black eternity as long as the heart beats, and the inexpress-
ible joys which face those who, faithful under the burden
of this miserable world, will ultimately come to dwell
eternally with the Lamb, who was conceived of the Holy
Ghost, born of a virgin, dwelled in suffering among us,
and willingly gave himself up to the death of the Cross.
With all their love of controversy, love of vitriolic remarks
at the expense of Rome's claim to authority and at the expense of the stubborn disobedience of the Separatists, and
love of clever and paradoxical argument, Donne's contemporaries, judging from the printer's ink and the pen's ink
which went into the reproductions of Donne's sermons,
still knew that the preacher's central function is to make
known God's Word and to sound forth those terms of and
promises of salvation, that condition without which Christianity would lose its joyful meaning.

It is perhaps a more interesting question to ask what significance and stature Donne's sermons might have for a
twentieth-century reader. About a century ago, Dr. Henry
Hart Milman, Dean of St. Paul's, confessed his astonish-
ment that the former Dean Donne had enjoyed such success as a preacher. He found it difficult to imagine how
Donne's Jacobean congregation could have listened "not
only with patience but with absorbed interest, with unflag-
ging attention, even with delight and rapture, to those in-
terminable disquisitions, to us teeming with laboured obscurity, false and misplaced wit, fatiguing antitheses."[14]
Present-day readers and critics of Donne—those who have

[14] Henry Hart Milman, *Annals of St. Paul's Cathedral* (London: John
Murray, 1868), p. 328.

committed themselves to print, at least—have not experienced Dean Milman's difficulty. They differ among themselves in their evaluation of Donne's sermons, but they express no amazement at Donne's fame in his own time. The greatest monument to Donne in recent years is, of course, the beautifully edited volumes of sermons prepared by Mrs. Simpson and the late Mr. Potter. These two devoted scholars would not have to record in words their own judgments of Donne's achievement; the many years of labor which they have given to their edition bear sufficient witness to their estimation of his work. One is reminded, in reading through this new edition, of some verses entitled *"Hexastichon ad Bibliopolam,"* prefixed to the 1635 edition of the *Poems*:

> *In thy Impression of* Donnes *Poems rare,*
> *For his Eternitie thou hast ta'ne care:*
> *'Twas well, and pious; And for ever may*
> *He live: Yet shew I thee a better way;*
> *Print but his Sermons, and if those we buy,*
> *He, We, and Thou shall live t'Eternity.*[15]

I shall mention but a few twentieth-century judgments on the sermons and then proceed to my own evaluation. Sir Arthur Quiller-Couch, somewhat scornful of Donne's poetry, utters an unqualified endorsement of the sermons. Therein one may seek for "the great Donne, the real Donne: not in his verse, into which posterity is constantly betrayed, but in his *Sermons*, which contain (as I hold) the most magnificent prose ever uttered from an English pulpit, if not the most magnificent prose ever spoken in our tongue." Two pages later he continues, in enthusiastic if somewhat purplish prose: "Thus in his *Sermons*, if you

[15] The verses were anonymously offered; Gosse attributes them to Isaak Walton (G II:307-308). The current asking price for "Eternity," by way of the Potter and Simpson edition, is $100.00, reasonable enough in our inflated economy.

seek, you will find the Donne I maintain to be the greater
Donne, master of well-knit argument, riding tumultuous
emotion as with a bridle, thundering out fugue upon fugue
of prose modulated with almost impeccable ear."[16] Austin
Warren is of much the same mind: "I venture to think,"
he writes, "[that Donne was] a greater preacher than poet,
able to express in that medium, and in that middle period
of life, a range and depth which the poems rarely reach."[17]
Certainly the most important dissenting voice is that of the
man who of all critics is most responsible for the great renaissance of Donne's poetry in our time, Mr. T. S. Eliot. Writing on the occasion of the three-hundredth anniversary of
Donne's death, Eliot shows little regard for the sermons:
"But actually (I for one have always been convinced) in
the history of English Theology it is not Donne, but
Cranmer and Latimer and Andrewes, who are the great
prose masters; and for the theologian even the high-sound-
ing Bramhall and the depressive Thorndike are more important names than Donne's. His sermons will disappear
as suddenly as they have appeared."[18] Two decades later
the Potter and Simpson edition began to make its appearance, certainly with the hope that Mr. Eliot's judgment is
mistaken, that one might say of Donne's sermons what
Ben Jonson said of Shakespeare, that they are "not of an
age, but for all time!"

What are the qualities of Donne's sermons which might
commend them to a twentieth-century reader? Certainly
one fruitful place to begin a discussion of this sort would
be to compare Donne with the only other preacher who
merits comparison in the first few decades of the seventeenth century, if not in the history of the English-speak-

[16] *Studies in Literature* (New York: G. P. Putnam's Sons, 1918-1930),
I, 107, 109.
[17] "The Very Reverend Dr. Donne," *Kenyon Review,* XVI (Spring,
1954), 276.
[18] "Donne in Our Time," *A Garland for John Donne: 1631-1931,*
p. 19.

ing pulpit. I refer, of course, to Lancelot Andrewes, who died in 1626 at the age of seventy-one, after having served as Master of Pembroke at Cambridge University, Dean of Westminster, and, successively, Bishop of Chichester, Ely, and Winchester; played an important role in the King James translation of the Bible and in the controversy with Cardinal Bellarmine; written some of the greatest devotional pieces in English; and preached before Queen Elizabeth and King James probably more often than any other man. To move, as I have moved in my own reading, from the one hundred and sixty sermons of John Donne to the *Ninety-Six Sermons* "by the Right Honourable and Reverend Father in God, Lancelot Andrewes, Sometime Lord Bishop of Winchester," is to encounter some very interesting differences.

If there is such a person as a preacher's preacher, I would say that Andrewes is the man. A poet's poet, a Spenser or a Keats, is one who, among other things, is a master of his craft; he is something more, of course, but he is certainly a writer who has control over his medium to a startling degree. The craft of a preacher is above all the exposition of a Scriptural text, the precise and comprehensive expounding of the Word of God. In the history of the English pulpit Andrewes has no equal as an expository preacher. The degree of his preoccupation with his text alone is almost beyond belief. Neither his own personal experience, nor his era, nor his congregation plays much of a role in discourses which seldom stray from the Biblical verses which preface them. No preacher is more absolutely dependent on the Bible than is Andrewes, and no one does it more justice. The kind of drama that is Donne's is definitely not Andrewes's; and if one might accuse Donne of overplaying his hand occasionally, of lapsing into melodrama, one might argue that Andrewes underplays his.

Andrewes's control over his subject matter, his absorption with his text, manifests itself in many ways. For one thing there is a perfection of organization, a step-by-step hewing to the text under consideration. We have already seen ample evidence of Donne's care in organizing his sermons, but there comes into them occasional extraneous material which may be of interest—gibes at Rome or Geneva, for example—and yet which somehow breaks the unity and perfection of the sermon itself. Of this practice Andrewes is not guilty, and when he preaches on, say, a Nativity or a Resurrection text, he does not digress from what is of immediate relevance. His Christmas sermon of 1610, preached before King James at Whitehall, is a good example of his method. He chooses as his text Luke 2:10-11—"The Angel said unto them, Be not afraid; for behold, I bring you good tidings of great joy, which shall be to all people. That there is born unto you this day a Saviour, Which is Christ the Lord, in the city of David." A reader, at first wondering if the divisions, subdivisions, and sub-subdivisions of the sermon will ever cease, bridles at the seeming complexity. But, in fact, there is an extreme simplicity, a deliberate and careful progression from word to word or phrase to phrase of the text. In the introductory paragraphs Andrewes calls attention to the significance of the choice of speaker—the Angel; to the significant choice of hearers—them, the shepherds; to the manner of delivery—*ecce enim evangelizo*, a "church-wise" activity; and to the purpose of the message—the spreading of great joy. To each of the two textual verses is devoted one of the main parts of the sermon: the first part discusses the hearkening to and the magnifying of the message—the beholding of the tidings of joy; the second, the message itself—the birth of a Saviour. And there is a sevenfold subdivision of the first part, and further subdivisions and sub-subdivisions of the second. A third and rather strikingly brief part summons the congregation to a proper response to the

good news of Christ's birth and saving power. (A 1:64-84)
A good companion piece to this Nativity celebration is an
Easter sermon on the Resurrection, again delivered at
Whitehall before King James, this time in the year 1608.
The text is Mark 16:1-7, the account of the Sunday morning visit by the three devoted women to the empty tomb of
Jesus. Again there is the minute division as Andrewes
moves step by step through an account of the three Marys,
of the risen Christ who speaks to them, and of the words
of his message. Once again the more personal reference,
the application of the text to those who hear Andrewes's
exposition, is brief. (A 11:221-237)

Andrewes, devout and learned Biblical scholar that he
was, focuses his attention on the redemptive Word, recalling to his congregation the events of history and the
convictions of faith which testify to the saving power of
Christ. His pulpit method is for the most part a relatively
objective exposition of the historical events as narrated in
the Bible and of doctrine. His own person does not enter
the drama which he unfolds; he does not, like Donne, bear
testimony to his own sins, his own difficulty in praying, or
his own hope of salvation. Nor are his words to his congregation so personal or direct as those of Donne. Nor is he
nearly so preoccupied in his sermons with a defense of
Anglicanism or with a castigation of enemies at home or
abroad. A Nativity sermon or a Resurrection sermon by
Donne might wander into various byways; Andrewes is
always more constantly true to his text. In his many Christmas sermons he occupies himself solely with the immense
and manifold significance of the birth of Jesus, of the Incarnation of God himself; and though it would be totally
inaccurate to say that Andrewes is not passionately concerned with the meaning of the Incarnation for sinners of
the Elizabethan and Jacobean eras, yet he spends far more
time speaking of the event itself and of the early years of

the Christian era than of sin and redemption through Christ in his own time. One mark of his method, then, is an exhaustive, painstakingly organized, word-by-word exposition of his text.

Of all Andrewes's sermons, one of those which stands in most interesting contrast to the Donne canon was preached before Queen Elizabeth on March 11, 1589, on the text of Psalm 75:3: "The earth and all the inhabitants thereof are dissolved; but I will establish the pillars of it." In a sermon preached before the head of the English State and Church, preached at the time of the Martin Marprelate pamphlets and just a year after the defeat of the Spanish Armada, and preached on a text which reflects the uncertain state of Israel during David's time, the temptation to sing the praises of England and Anglicanism and to fulminate against their enemies was one to which most Anglican preachers would surely have succumbed. We may well imagine in what specific detail Donne would have developed such a text against Puritans and Romans. Andrewes remains remarkably unperturbed. He points out early in his discourse that the text suggests, among other things, the method for preserving harmony in a commonwealth. He states the twofold danger to David's people: "1. The enemy or Egyptian smiting Israel from without; 2. The injurious Israelite wronging his brother, from within." What an opportunity would follow for enumerating the charges against the enemies of England. But Andrewes goes on to cite Balak as a wicked foreign prince and Balaam as a false and misleading prophet, and then calmly compares David's difficulties to those of Elizabeth: "The case is very like ours, and God grant us a thankful remembrance and meditation of it; of the long intelligence between Balak and Balaam for our overthrow, and how graciously and marvellously God hath delivered us!" (A II:9) The sermon is concluded with a reminder of the fact that David did repair Saul's ruins, principally because of his respect for religion and justice, the "pillars" referred to in the text; and with praise of and prayer for Elizabeth and England: "The Lord Who hath sent forth the like strength for our land, stablish the good things which He hath wrought in us! The Lord so fasten the pillars of our earth, that they never be shaken! The Lord mightily uphold the upholder of them long, and many years; that we may go forth rejoicing in His strength, and make our boast of His praise, all our life long!" (A 11:15) Thus we can see that, even when Andrewes is not preaching about so sacred and mysterious an occasion as the Incarnation or the Resurrection, even when he chooses a text which easily lends itself to the embroidery of contemporary controversy, he keeps remarkably close to a historical exposition of his text, with only the most general and muted references to his own time. He apparently feels that his congregation will need little assistance in drawing their own comparisons.

The styles of Andrewes and Donne are also quite distinct. On the whole, Andrewes's vocabulary is, I think, the more simple, and he uses few words which are not perfectly familiar to the twentieth century. A modern reader is likely to be less in need of a dictionary for Andrewes's sermons than for Donne's, which use words that may have been familiar in his time but have by now passed from even the learned vocabulary. I limit myself to a dozen examples: *anhelation, conculcation, contesseration, cribration, exhæredation, immarcessible, interpuncted, obcæcation, pre-increpation, re-efformation, reluctation, repullulation.* Both men shared the disposition of their age to play upon the words which they did use; and if Donne performed gymnastics with the words *Son* and *sun* and, in his poetry, with his own name, Andrewes too derived great pleasure in his play with the sounds and meanings of words. In one of his Nativity sermons, Andrewes plays witty variations on the prophesied name of Christ—*Immanuel*: "For if this Child be 'Immanuel, God with us,' then without this Child, this Immanuel, we be without God. 'Without Him in this world,' saith the Apostle; and if without Him in this, without Him in the next; and if without Him there—if it be not *Immanu-el*, it will be *Immanu-hell*; and that and no other place will fall, I fear me, to our share. Without Him this we are. What with Him? Why, if we have Him, and God by Him, we need no more; *Immanu-el* and *Immanu-all*." (A 1:145)

A sermon on Lot's wife gives Andrewes a welcome opportunity to play upon the idea of the preservative quality of salt. That the world might know and remember the seriousness of Lot's wife's relapse, "God hath not only marked it for a sin, but salted it too, that it might never be forgotten." In one sense, Andrewes informs us, Lot's wife's salt has not lost its savor. God might have sunk her into the earth or blown her up, "but for us and for our sakes He erecteth a pillar: and not a pillar only to point and gaze at, but a 'pillar or rock of salt,' whence we may and must fetch wherewith to season whatsoever is unsavoury in our lives." And a little later: "Now, from her story these considerations are yielded, each one as an handful of salt to keep us, and to make us keep." (A II:70-72)

The rhythm of Donne's prose seems to me more varied than that of Andrewes, who somewhat resembles Bacon in his pithiness and sparseness. In Andrewes there is usually a staccato and an elliptical quality, a minimum of connectives, an absence of the more mighty architecture and flow that is to be found in, say, Hooker's or Milton's prose, and occasionally in Donne's. A fine and moving example of Andrewes's prose at its best is found in a Nativity sermon on the theme of the Word made flesh. Its power comes from its wit, its directness, its dramatic dialogue, and its vivid re-creation of a scene; it follows immediately upon the statement that the Word was made flesh:

"I add yet farther; what flesh? The flesh of an infant. What, *Verbum infans*, the Word an infant? The Word, and not be able to speak a word? How evil agreeth this! This He put up. How born, how entertained? In a stately palace, cradle of ivory, robes of estate? No; but a stable for His palace, a manger for His cradle, poor clouts for His array. This was His beginning. Follow Him farther, if any better afterward; what flesh afterward? *Sudans et algens*, in cold and heat, hungry and thirsty, faint and weary. Is His end any better? that maketh up all: what flesh then? *Cujus livore sanati*, black and blue, bloody and swollen, rent and torn, the thorns and nails sticking in His flesh; and such flesh He was made. A great *factum* certainly, and much to be made of. To have been made *caput Angelorum* had been an abasement; to be *minoratus Angelis* is more; but, to be *novissimus virorum*, 'in worst case of all men,' nay, 'a worm and no man;' so to be born, so arrayed, and so housed, and so handled—there is not the meanest flesh but is better. So to be made, and so unmade; to take it on, and lay it off, with so great indignity: weigh it and wonder at it that ever He would endure to be made flesh, and to be made it on this manner. What was it made the Word thus to be made flesh? *Non est lex hominis ista*, 'flesh would never have been brought to it.' It was God, and in God nothing but love; *dilexit* with *sic*, *charitas* with an *ecce*; *fecit amor ut Verbum caro fierit*; *Zelus Domini exercituum fecit hoc*. Love only did it. *Quid sit, possit, debeat, non recipit jus amoris*, 'That only cares not for any *exinanivit*, any *humiliavit se*, any emptying, humbling, loss of reputation; love respects it not, cares not what flesh He be made, so the flesh be made by it.'" (A 1:92-93)

It is my impression that, on the whole, Andrewes's writing is not quite so vivid as that of Donne, that it does not turn so frequently to the concrete picture, to the delineation of some dramatic scene. But Andrewes is not lacking in ability to present a scene: note the long passage just quoted and the following sentences from a sermon on the Passion. Andrewes is speaking of those who derided Christ during his last hours: "Their shouting and outcries, their harrying of Him about from Annas to Caiaphas, from him to Pilate, from Pilate to Herod, and from him to Pilate again; one while in purple, Pilate's suit; another while in white, Herod's livery; nipping Him by the cheeks, and pulling off His hair; blindfolding Him and buffeting Him; bowing to Him in derision, and then spitting in His face. . . ." And a little later comes a description of those who gathered around the Cross, those who "stood staring and gaping upon Him, wagging their heads, writhing their mouths, yea blearing out their tongues; railing on Him and reviling Him, scoffing at Him and scorning Him; yea, in the very time of His prayers deriding Him, even in His most mournful complaint and cry for the very anguish of His Spirit." (A ii:173)

Andrewes does not compare with Donne in richness and variety of imagery. Donne carried into his sermons a literary habit which was the essence of his poetry, and his sermons wear their imagery well. Andrewes's most extensive use of analogy is found in some of his Gunpowder Treason sermons, those in which he pays more attention than usual to contemporary events and works out in detail the parallel between the events of the Gunpowder Plot and the events of Biblical history which are related to the text. There are two particularly fine examples of this kind of parallelism. One is a sermon preached on November 5, 1607, on the text of Psalm 126:1-4: "When the Lord brought again the captivity of Sion, we were like them that dream. Then was our mouth filled with laughter, and our tongue with joy; then said they among the heathen, The Lord hath done great things for them. The Lord hath done great things for us, whereof we rejoice. O Lord, bring again our captivity, as the rivers in the South." Andrewes begins by stating that the Psalm celebrates the joy felt by the Israelites upon their return from the Babylonian captivity, and states that though the freedom from Babylon is no perfect parallel to England's escape from the Gunpowder Plot, yet it is of all Scriptural history closest in nature to the escape. He suggests that only one word of the Biblical text need be changed to make it fully appropriate to the event of 1605: ". . . if we might but change that one word, and instead of reading, 'When the Lord turned away the captivity of Sion,' we might thus read, 'When the Lord turned away the blowing up of Sion;' all besides, every word else, would suit well, and keep perfect correspondency." (A IV:224) The sermon is an extended comparison of the two events separated by over two thousand years. The English were also "like them that dream," since their deliverance from destruction was so fortunate as to seem unreal. Many of them still slept at the time of the discovery of the perfidy just two years before this sermon. Their deliverance was dreamlike in that it came without their looking for it, came without any labor on their part, and came as an emancipation which would have seemed in their waking lives beyond hope. And, of course, it brought joy, coming as the work of the Lord upon a people over whom he watched. (A IV:229-230)

Another well-conceived analogy is found in a sermon which Andrewes delivered on November 5, 1612, on the text of Lamentations 3:22: "It is the Lord's mercies that we are not consumed, because His compassions fail not." Had the Roman Catholics succeeded in their plot, there would have been a day of lamentation in England, but the mercy of God delivered the nation from the awful plot that would, if carried out, have dealt such a catastrophic blow. The Chaldean attack on the gates of Jerusalem is compared in detail to the Roman Catholic plot on the very heart of England, on Westminster, the citadel which would have held King, Prince, Lords, and others who ministered most closely to the needs of their nation. And Andrewes goes on to point out in what respects the English were far more fortunate, far less harmed, than the Israelites in Jeremiah's time. November 5 is a day on which England should give thanks for the infinite mercy of God, a thanksgiving which might exceed that of Jeremiah. (A iv:261-276) Even in these sermons, which offer such opportunities for vitriolic attacks on the enemies of England, Andrewes exercises his usual control over his texts, never digressing or venturing into polemic which might have warmed the blood of his parishioners but which would not have directed their minds primarily to God's mercy. These two sermons on the Gunpowder Plot are good examples of Andrewes's skill in analogy, but his range is by no means comparable to Donne's.

The purpose of these paragraphs on Andrewes is, of course, to sharpen our sensibilities to the qualities of Donne's sermons, not to give a thorough treatment of Andrewes himself, and I shall refer back to the remarks on Andrewes upon coming to some final evaluation of the work of Donne. I should call attention at this time to a most stimulating and provoking essay by Mr. Eliot, entitled "Lancelot Andrewes" and appearing in a collection of essays, *For Lancelot Andrewes*, published in 1928. It is a brilliant essay, both for its analysis of Andrewes and for its comparison of him with Donne. Eliot does not predict the disappearance of Andrewes's sermons, even if he does feel that the Donne canon will fade into obscurity.

In fact, he ranks Andrewes's prose with the finest in the history of our language, for an audience fit though few. The comparison with Donne is all in Andrewes's favor, particularly because Andrewes possesses a quality which Eliot calls "relevant intensity," a virtue which Eliot seldom finds in the sermons of Donne:

"When Andrewes begins his sermon, from beginning to end you are sure that he is wholly in his subject, unaware of anything else, that his emotion grows as he penetrates more deeply into his subject, that he is finally 'alone with the Alone', with the mystery which he is seeking to grasp more and more firmly. . . . Andrewes's emotion is purely contemplative; it is not personal, it is wholly evoked by the object of contemplation, to which it is adequate; his emotion is wholly contained in and explained by its object. But with Donne there is always the something else. . . . Donne is a 'personality' in a sense in which Andrewes is not: his sermons, one feels, are a 'means of self-expression'. He is constantly finding an object which shall be adequate to his feelings; Andrewes is wholly absorbed in the object and therefore responds with the adequate emotion. Andrewes has the *goût pour la vie spirituelle*, which is not native to Donne. . . ."[19]

If I understand Mr. Eliot correctly, there is an implication that Andrewes surrenders himself to his calling, to the proclamation of the divine revelation, and that Donne sometimes surrenders his calling to himself, that he "uses" religion for purposes of self-fulfillment. Or one might interpret Mr. Eliot's remarks as suggesting that the proclamation of Scripture is for Andrewes an end in itself, for Donne a means of satisfying some emotional need. That Donne is more subjective, more personal, is indisputable; reflections upon his own person and upon his own con-

[19] *For Lancelot Andrews* (London: Faber & Gwyer, 1928), pp. 29-30.

gregation are prominent in his sermons. He is lacking in Andrewes's "relevant intensity" if by this we mean absorption in the text. But Donne has another kind of intensity, one which I would call an "existential intensity." It is an absorption in the relationship between Creator and created, in God's action for and toward man and man's response to this divine activity working through history. This passionate concern with the ways of man under God, along with the skill to express this relationship with a dramatic vividness, I would be inclined to call the most compelling aspect of Donne's preaching. I have said before that a preacher's craft is above all the exposition of a Scriptural text and that Andrewes has no peer in this respect; he comes as close as one can to an exhaustive interpretation of the text. But certainly the end of every preacher, the aim of every sermon, is to serve as an instrument for the salvation of every man who hears. The preacher must expound the text in such a way that his hearer may see the immediate relevance of the text to himself. Though not suggesting that Andrewes was deficient in this respect, and very far from suggesting that a tidy account can be kept of the souls which a particular minister has been instrumental in saving, I do feel that Andrewes falls short of Donne in the ability to bring a reader to an immediate sense of his own relationship to the Biblical pronouncement. It is, of course, obvious that different people are reached by different sermons; it should be equally obvious that many people are "reached" by preachers who do little more than exploit emotions, who stir people by moving proclamations, which, nevertheless, are not disciplined expositions of the Scriptural text. It is Mr. Eliot's contention that Donne's "success" is at times occasioned by a resorting to this kind of exploitation: "About Donne there hangs the shadow of the impure motive; and impure motives lend their aid to a facile success.

He is a little of the religious spellbinder, the Reverend Billy Sunday of his time, the flesh-creeper, the sorcerer of emotional orgy. We emphasize this aspect to the point of the grotesque. Donne had a trained mind; but without belittling the intensity or the profundity of his experience, we can suggest that this experience was not perfectly controlled, and that he lacked spiritual discipline."[20]

Such a charge is difficult either to refute or to sustain. It suggests, among other things, that Donne's heart was not always intent upon the glory of God, that he sometimes reveled in his own declamatory and literary powers, that he did not always practice what he preached in the following passage: ". . . It is not Many words, long Sermons, nor good words, witty and eloquent Sermons that induce the holy Ghost, for all these are words of men; and howsoever the whole Sermon is the Ordinance of God, the whole Sermon is not the word of God: But when all the good gifts of men are modestly employ'd, and humbly received, as *vehicula Spiritus*, as S. *Augustine* calls them, The chariots of the Holy Ghost, as meanes afforded by God, to convey the word of life into us, in Those words we heare The word, and there the word and the Spirit goe together, as in our case in the Text, *While Peter yet spake those words, the holy Ghost fell upon all them that heard The word*" (D v:36-37).

It is my contention that at least a part of that quality which Mr. Eliot defines as "emotional orgy" can be explained by Donne's existential view of God. Time and again Donne emphasizes that man in this world needs to dwell on God's existence, his relationship to man, more than on God's essence, his attributes; there is an emphasis more on God's immanence than on his transcendence. As early as 1617 Donne preached that "God calls not upon us, to be consider'd as God in himself, but as God towards

[20] *Ibid.*, p. 20.

us; not as he is in heaven, but as he works upon earth: And here, not in the School, but in the Pulpit; not in Disputation, but in Application" (D 1:234). In a sermon on the Trinity, delivered several years later, Donne writes:

"First then, the duty which God, by this Apostle, requires of man, is a duty arising out of that, which God hath wrought upon him: It is not a consideration, a contemplation of God sitting in heaven, but of God working upon the earth; not in the making of his eternall Decree there, but in the execution of those Decrees here; not in saying, God knowes who are his, and therefore they cannot faile, but in saying in a rectified conscience, God, by his ordinary marks, hath let me know that I am his, and therefore I look to my wayes, that I doe not fall. S. *Paul* out of a religious sense what God had done for him, comes to this duty, to blesse him." (D III:258) And, a few years later: ". . . we are to consider God, not as he is in himselfe, but as he works upon us: The first thing that we can consider in our way to God, is his Word" (D VI:216). In other words, Donne believes that his main aim must be to preach the nature of the divine-human relationship, so that man may see himself as a creature of God and learn how he may be borne on his way toward the Kingdom.

Obviously the proclamation of God's immanence and of his ways with man is not a call to emotional exploitation, though such proclamation does make way for a subjective element that might not be present in a sermon emphasizing God's transcendence. It makes way for the dramatic presentation of man's direct confrontation by God and of man's response to this terrible and ecstatic meeting. It is to my mind unfortunate that Donne presents some of his scenes in the first-person singular, and I gather from some of Mr. Eliot's references to Donne that he too is discomforted by the preacher's intrusion of himself. It could be argued that a first-person narrative heightens the dramatic effect and that Donne is simply using himself to refer to all mankind; but I shall cite two of those passages which, I think, would be far more moving and effective with a change of person, with less intrusion of the preacher's own person. The first is part of a long passage in which Donne is speaking of the necessity of a Christian's bearing his own Cross:

"And as *Elisha* in raysing the *Shunamits* dead child, put his mouth upon the childs mouth, his eyes, and his hands, upon the hands, and eyes of the child; so when my crosses have carried mee up to my Saviours Crosse, I put my hands into his hands, and hang upon his nailes, I put mine eyes upon his, and wash off all my former unchast looks, and receive a soveraigne tincture, and a lively verdure, and a new life into my dead teares, from his teares. I put my mouth upon his mouth, and it is I that say, *My God, my God, why hast thou forsaken me?* and it is I that recover againe, and say, *Into thy hands, O Lord, I commend my spirit.* Thus my afflictions are truly a crosse, when those afflictions doe truely crucifie me, and souple me, and mellow me, and knead me, and roll me out, to a conformity with Christ. It must be this *Crosse*, and then it must be *my crosse* that I must take up, *Tollat suam.*" (D 11:300)

In the second passage Donne is expressing a willingness to endure temporal and bodily affliction, so long as God's spiritual blessings remain with him:

"Let me wither and weare out mine age in a discomfortable, in an unwholesome, in a penurious prison, and so pay my debts with my bones, and recompence the wastfulnesse of my youth, with the beggery of mine age; Let me wither in a spittle under sharpe, and foule, and infamous diseases, and so recompence the wantonnesse of

my youth, with that loathsomnesse in mine age; yet, if
God with-draw not his spirituall blessings, his Grace, his
Patience, If I can call my suffering his Doing, my passion his Action, All this that is temporall, is but a cater-
piller got into one corner of my garden, but a mill-dew
fallen upon one acre of my Corne; The body of all, the
substance of all is safe, as long as the soule is safe" (D
VII:56).

In one sense these passages are examples of Donne's
style at its best. They possess a tremendously impressive
concreteness, a vivid pictorial quality which would certainly arrest the attention of the congregation. There is a
fine balance of clauses and phrases, with yet enough variation to obviate any possibility of monotony. And there is
in the second passage an effective alliterative quality. But,
unfortunately, the spotlight does not really fall upon the
divine-human meeting so much as it falls upon the person
of the narrator. For me, at least, Donne does not here so
much represent mankind as he represents himself. Such
passages savor just a bit too much of the sentimental, not
because of their sentiments or their statements or any in-
fidelity to the true relationship between God and his creatures, but because Donne intrudes himself.

When Donne's thoughts are truly centered upon the
state of his congregation under God, when the shepherd
is absorbed by the possible damnation or salvation of his
sheep, then he is at his best—that is, then he seems most
effective as an instrument of the Holy Ghost, as one who
leads his people toward the Kingdom. There is the nicest
balance between ethics and religion, between the entreaties
of the Sermon on the Mount and the insights of St. Paul.
In many ways, I think, Donne's preaching is a kind of
mean between that of Andrewes and Jeremy Taylor. For
if Andrewes is absorbed by his text and by doctrinal affir-

mations, Taylor is absorbed by ethical exhortation; if Andrewes comes close to theological lecture, Taylor comes close to ethical homily. One of Donne's great virtues as a preacher is that he always shows the relationship of doctrinal statements to the daily lives of the men and women who sit before him, and he always sees to it that his ethical statements are based on Biblical doctrines. He both teaches and exhorts, and his teaching and exhortation are seen in their relationship to each other. Again I will cite two examples, chosen from many. The first again has to do with the bearing of one's Cross; it has all the fine qualities of the passages most recently quoted, and it is not marred by infelicitous use of the first person. It is a passage which speaks of sin and redemption, of grace and free will, one which speaks persuasively of the relationship between every man and his Lord, between Christ's action and man's response to it. It is on this kind of prose that the greatness of Donne's preaching rests, for it is certainly this kind of persuasion which moves a man to set his heart on Christ's redemptive action and to surrender himself to it. It is more effective psychologically than most of Andrewes's preaching and more effective theologically than most of Taylor's. There is no impurity of motive here, as Donne is completely absorbed by the way of the Cross and by the redemptive power of Christ's blood:

"In our great work of crucifying our selves to the world too, it is not enough to bleed the drops of a Circumcision, that is, to cut off some excessive, and notorious practice of sin; nor to bleed the drops of an Agony, to enter into a conflict and colluctation of the flesh and the spirit, whether we were not better trust in Gods mercy, for our continuance in that sin, then lose all that pleasure and profit, which that sin brings us; nor enough to bleed the drops of scourging, to be lashed with viperous and venemous tongues by contumelies, and slanders; nor to bleed the drops of Thornes, to have Thornes and scruples enter into our consciences, with spirituall afflictions; but we must be content to bleed the streames of naylings to those Crosses, to continue in them all our lives, if God see that necessary for our confirmation ..." (D IV:297).

The passage is a call to the invitation of Christ, to follow him through his afflictions of circumcision, of the Garden of Gethsemane, of the crown of thorns, through to his sacrificial death on the Cross.

The second passage is one in which Donne urges his hearer to prepare devoutly and wisely for his death. It directs his attention to the relationship between a man's behavior in this life and his status in the next. It is a call to repentance and a reminder of God's mercy. Once again there is a fine balance between teaching and exhortation, between religious doctrine and the ethical life. Donne draws a compelling picture of a man's last moments before death and his prospect of salvation:

"... before the grinders cease, because they are few, and they wax dark, that look out at the windows, before thou go to the house of thine age, and the mourners go about in the streets, prepare thy self by casting off thy sins, and all that is gotten by thy sins: for, as the plague is got as soon in linings, as in the outside of a garment, salvation is lost, as far, by retaining ill gotten goods, as by ill getting; forgot not thy past sins so far, as not to repent them, but remember not thy repented sins so far, as to delight in remembring them, or to doubt that God hath not fully forgiven them; and whether God have brought this salvation near thee, by sickness, or by age, or by general dangers, put off the consideration of the incomodities of that age, or that sickness, and that danger, and fill thy self with the consideration of the nearness of thy salvation, which

that age, and sickness, and danger, minister to thee: that
so, when the best Instrument, and the best song shall meet
together, thy bell shall towl, and thy soul shall hear that
voice, *Ecce salvator*, behold thy Saviour cometh, thou maist
bear a part, and chearfully make up that musick, with a
veni Domine Jesu, Come Lord Jesu, come quickly, come
now" (D ii:268).

Still another important quality of Donne's preaching is
that he imbues his congregation with some sense of the joy
of a devout life. The almighty God whom he preaches is a
God who takes every conceivable care of, and who bears
every conceivable good relationship to, his children. I have
mentioned Donne's emphasis on God's existence rather than
on his essence, that is, on his activity in the world of man.
The various metaphors which Donne uses for God bear
out this acute and joyful sense of the divine-human relationship. In one passage he speaks of God as our Father,
potter, minter, statuary, tailor, steward, physician, neighbor,
Samaritan, gardener, architect, builder, sentinel, and shepherd (D ix:131-132). In another he affirms that, so long as
God is his potter, he is willing to be anything: that he
would as willingly be a sheep as a lion if God will be his
shepherd; a cottage as a castle if God will be his builder
(D ix:62-63). Time and again, particularly in the later
years of his ministry, Donne would seek to express the
fullness of that joy which flows from man's sense of his
bondage to God. Religion is no melancholy matter; it
bears no tincture of the sullen or the dour; it is an experience which brings with it true joy, a joy in this life which
is a foretaste of the fullness of joy which is yet to come.
It is true that the joy which the righteous man now experiences is not yet complete, mingled as it is with the
griefs which are an inevitable part of mortality. Yet this
present joy gives us some sense of that rejoicing which is

the mark of the Kingdom. In heaven joy has a "Fulnesse that needeth no addition; Fulnesse, that admitteth no leake." Our vision of God is as yet incomplete; we know of his working upon us, of his merciful and just activities throughout history from the time of the creation, but we must be content with a partial vision, with an experiencing of his existence rather than a seeing of his essence, a seeing of him face to face as he really is. "See him here in his Blessings, and you shall joy in those blessings here," Donne tells his congregation; "and when you come to see him *Sicuti est*, in his Essence, then you shall have this Joy in Essence, and in fulnesse...." (D x:228)

The way to this joy is through the Church of which John Donne is a priest, and it is with great power that Donne presents the efficacy of that Body of Christ which God ordained to be the means of salvation. The power of his expression derives from his conviction of the intensely personal and immediate relationship of every man to his Lord. Donne is neither aloof and academic nor sentimental and bathetic as he summons his congregation to an understanding of the meaning of the Church: "... we present an established Church, a Church endowed with a power, to open the wounds of Christ Jesus to receive every wounded soule, to spread the balme of his blood upon every bleeding heart; A Church that makes this generall Christ particular to every Christian, that makes the Saviour of the world, thy Saviour, and my Saviour; that offers the originall sinner Baptisme for that; and the actuall sinner, the body and blood of Christ Jesus for that; a Church that mollifies, and entenders, and shivers the presumptuous sinner with denouncing the judgements of God, and then, consolidates and establishes the diffident soule with the promises of his Gospell..." (D viii:308).

As Joseph Glanvill pointed out in the passage quoted at the beginning of this chapter, "men judge of Sermons by

[254]

very *different measures*." If there is any common denominator of judgment it would be, I should think, that the
aim of a sermon must be to bring the hearer to a deep
sense of repentance which would result in his turning to the
Lord and accepting the gift of salvation. The rub comes
when one is asked to enumerate the qualities of a sermon
which will succeed in this task. And the problem is made
more complex by the fact that a sermon which would
move one person to repent might not move the person
occupying the pew in front of him. A still further complica-
tion is that no one really knows the state of his neighbor's
soul, and that consequently no one can measure the only
kind of achievement which should be of any concern to a
minister.

Glanvill continues by saying that "every one expects
that the Preacher conform to *his* particular Rule of judging." It must by now be evident that Donne fares uncom-
monly well under my own rule of judging. As a first prin-
ciple I would say that most sermons should be detailed
expositions of the chosen text. It would seem to be frequently customary in our century for a preacher to use a
text as an afterthought, a convenient and buttressing ap-
pendage for some particular message which he wishes to
deliver to his congregation. That is to say, his starting
point is frequently not the Bible at all. To such a preacher
no physic would be more beneficial than a retreat with the
Ninety-Six Sermons of Lancelot Andrewes. For the pulpit
is, after all, the place from which the Word of God is to
be interpreted and proclaimed. Donne must indeed bow to
Andrewes as an expository preacher, though Donne himself enjoys a power and greatness in this respect, for his
expositions are thorough, orderly, and possessed of a scholarship which could derive only from a most careful study
of Scripture, of the writings of the Church Fathers, and
of the great commentaries. And though Donne may some-

times seem to stray perilously far from the Bible as he comments on contemporary affairs, the great bulk of his preaching is concerned with precise interpretation of text.

An exposition of text, however, must be accompanied by a moving demonstration of the relationship of God's Word to the lives of the hopeful sinners who sit beneath the preacher. And this relationship can be well drawn only by a man who understands the human heart and who has a keen sense of God's ways of working with man and of man's response, or lack of it, to this divine activity. Donne's sense of man's nature, of the depth of his sin and of his yearning for the grace to repent, is excessively acute. A reader of his poems and of his *Devotions upon Emergent Occasions* is fully aware of the profundity of Donne's understanding of the workings of man's mind and heart, and this perceptiveness is nowhere more fully manifested than in the sermons. Examples enough have already been given of Donne's keen and detailed analyses of sin, analyses which must certainly have led those who heard him to recognize their kinship to Adam. I know of no one who succeeds so well as Donne in making the Biblical text so relevant to the everyday lives of men. It is true that he may occasionally resort to the melodramatic in an effort to arrest the attention of his congregation and that he may occasionally show a distasteful preoccupation with himself. But there is far more drama in his sermons than melodrama, and he reflects much more frequently on his congregation than on himself. At the center of most of his sermons is the continuous interaction between God and man, between the God who has revealed himself and the individual men and women of the listening congregation. In the whole history of preaching there are few men who knew so much about the ways of mankind as Donne, and no minister of his own century was his equal in this respect.

The effectiveness of Donne's preaching was greatly increased by his ability to induce his congregation to feel so directly related to the sermon. It is not simply a matter of his knowing how a man feels and acts and thinks in a particular situation; it is also a matter of his being able to convince a hearer or a reader of the directness of the applicability of the sermon to himself. For the sermons are intensely personal; they are aimed at the congregation to which he is preaching, like the arrows which Donne speaks of in the first of his sermons on the Thirty-eighth Psalm. Given the scholarly and learned quality of his sermons, there is a rare immediacy as he calls upon his congregation to repent and to accept the joy of a godly life. He uses his dramatic talents well as he draws his listener or reader directly into his discourse.

And to accompany these characteristics—indeed, to make some of them possible—Donne possesses a most astounding control of language. There is no need to quote further from his sermons to suggest the greatness of his style. A master of diction and image, of rhythm and change of pace, of tone, and of the concrete drawing of a scene, Donne is always an exciting writer. There was probably little enough dozing in his seventeenth-century congregations. And it is a happy fact that his sermons remain compelling to one who reads them over three hundred years after they were preached.

Index

King, Dr. John, Bishop of London, 25
King James Bible, *see* Bible

La Corona, 17, 18
Lactantius, 97
"Lancelot Andrewes," 244-47
Last Day, *see* Last Judgment
Last Judgment, 48, 54, 58, 129, 131, 139, 194, 201, 202, 223, 224
Latimer, Bishop Hugh, 234
Laud, Archbishop William, 149
Law, The, 36, 57, 61-62, 77, 97, 111, 116, 120, 123, 138
Leviathan, 101n
Lewis, E. G., 157n
Life of Dr. John Donne, 30
Lincoln's Inn, 11, 12, 27, 28, 50, 90, 106, 116, 166, 220, 224-25, 226, 227, 228; Reader in Divinity (Divinity Reader), 26, 27, 28, 220
Litanie, A, 17, 18
London, 28, 31, 103
Lord's Prayer, 215
Loseley, 13
Lothian Manuscript, 225, 226
Lovejoy, Arthur O., 37n
Luther, Martin, 12, 36, 71, 97, 98, 150, 178, 179, 181, 183, 186, 192, 193
Lutheran, 163
Lycidas, 21
Lyly, John, 107, 114

Maccabees, 97
MacLure, Millar, 28n, 88n
McNeill, John T., 65n
Mammon, 220
Manichaean(s) (*Manichean(s)*), 154, 164, 179, 229
Martin Marprelate, 238
Martyr, Justin, 157
Martz, Louis L., 21-22, 111
Mayne, Jasper, 210
Medina, Michael, 155
Mediterranean Sea, 141
Melancthon, 98, 203
Mendoza, 143

Merton Manuscript, 225
Michael, 174
Milgate, W., 8n
Millenarian, 202
Milman, Dr. Henry Hart, 232-33
Milton, John, 21, 165, 229n, 240
Mitcham, 14, 15, 17, 23
Mitchell, W. Fraser, 89n, 103n
Montgomery, Susan, Countess of, 87
More, Anne, 13, 32
More, Sir George, 13, 17
More, Sir Robert, 23
More, Sir Thomas, 9, 85
Morton, Bishop Thomas, 14-15, 17, 18, 19, 25, 35
Musculus, 203

natural theology, 24, 59-60
Nestorians, 154
New Jerusalem (*new Ierusalem, new Jerusalem*), 65, 140, 223
New World, 220
Nichols, James, 80n
Nicolaitans, 229
Ninety-Six Sermons, 235, 255
Noah's ark, 51, 56, 58, 206

Oath of Allegiance (*Oath of Allegeance*), 9n, 10, 18
Of the Laws of Ecclesiastical Polity, 52-53, 53n, 149, 156, 213-14
On the Bound Will, 178
On the Free Will, 178
Origen, 95, 97, 172, 200
Oxford University, 10, 12, 20; Hart Hall, 10

Paddington, 26, 148
Paradise Lost, 165, 174-75, 229n
Parsons, Father Robert, 9
Paul's Cross, 28 and n, 29, 88, 211, 214, 215
Pelagian(s), 154, 179, 180, 186, 191
Pellicanus, 71
Peputians, 229
Perkins, William, 80n
Petrarchan, 11
Phalaris, 147

[262]